THE
HUMANITIES
HANDBOOK
PART II

THE HUMANITIES HANDBOOK

PART II

JOSEPH SATIN

Midwestern University

HOLT, RINEHART and WINSTON, INC.

*New York   Chicago   San Francisco   Atlanta   Dallas
Montreal   Toronto*

FOR MY WIFE
through whom random events acquire purpose and meaning

TO THE STUDENT

In *Science and the Modern World* philosopher Alfred North Whitehead discloses how all general outlooks became their opposites at the start of the seventeenth century. Philosophy and the arts turned subjective, where they had been objective before; and science became objective, bequeathing its earlier subjectivity to the arts. Where philosophy and the arts had been the means to truth from Greece through the Renaissance, and science mere conjecture, the seventeenth century reversed those roles and thus ushered in "the modern world." Alois Riegl corroborates this reversal from the vantage point of art alone: All art up to the seventeenth century, he explains, concerns itself with external objects; all art after that, with subjective consciousness. From observations such as these, two facts emerge: The humanities materials covered in Part II will be vastly different in subject and purpose from those in Part I; and, being modern, Part II will convey a new and sudden sense of immediacy.

Part I was able from the long-range perspective of the present to survey its periods as if from a mountain top, where each cluster of arts and events occupied a cleanly marked-off stretch of terrain. The Golden Age of Greece turned inward to perfect a seamless pattern. The Hellenistic Age exploded outward, its bits and pieces glowing here and there, each in the main preoccupied with its own light. Rome marched heavy-footed along the ground, covering immense horizontal distances. The Middle Ages stood almost still, gazing upward. The Renaissance fused the pattern of the Golden Age of Greece, the individual glow of Hellenism, the earth of Rome, and the heaven of the Middle Ages into a special synthesis that perfected and at the same time depleted all that had gone before.

Part II deals with the modern world, and to do so must leave its vantage point in time and confront materials across a leveled plain. It thus gains a more detailed and intimate knowledge of its subject, but at the threatened expense of perspective. For like more specialized studies, the humanities approach must deal now not with total periods but with aspects of them. Chapter 6 explores the seventeenth-century reversal of values. Chapter 7 dissects a unique seventeenth-century and eighteenth-century style of life and art. Chapter 8 applies a horizontal view to the tensions and emotionalism of the eighteenth and nineteenth centuries. Chapters 9 and 10 apply this same view to the twentieth century, with Chapter 10 offering a close-up scrutiny of the past twenty years.

But because it is broad-based, the humanities approach yields a special advantage even from ground level, for it permits us to see how seventeenth-century Reason and the baroque are really the opposite banks of a single stream that flows into the headwaters of Romanticism. The humanities approach further reveals the dramatic difference between Romanticism and the Age of Anxiety and the subtle shadings between Anxiety and what is happening in our own time. The five chapters of Part II, therefore, cover one complete period in subdivided aspects and then continue on with the beginning of a second period. And, as you will see, far from losing perspective, the humanities approach achieves an even sharper focus from its new angle of vision.

Wichita Falls, Texas
October 1968   J. S.

ACKNOWLEDGMENTS

I owe thanks to many people for help in the writing of this book: to my colleagues in humanities courses, Stephen F. Crocker and Frank Manning of West Virginia University, the late Edward Emley of Eastern Michigan University, and Delsie Holmquist and Gerald Ippolito of Moorhead State College; to Professors Ivy Boland and John Carson of Midwestern University, whose advice as specialists filled in several gaps; to Midwestern librarians Calvin Boyer and Louise Gregg, whose cooperation was unstinting; to the Piper Foundation of San Antonio, Texas, whose Piper Professorship award made possible a research trip to Europe; to Dean N. W. Quick of Midwestern, for his awareness and concern; and as climax, not resolution, my warmest gratitude to the editorial staff of Holt, Rinehart and Winston, Inc., most notably to Kenney Withers for his vision and to Jane Ross for her monumental tact and understanding.

J. S.

CONTENTS

LIST OF ILLUSTRATIONS

PART II

CHAPTER 6
THE AGE OF REASON

THE TIDES OF WAR

The century which ushered in the Age of Reason and saw the torch of European civilization carried to far-flung outposts throughout the globe was marked by almost continuous warfare. The major wars alone included the Spanish-Netherlands War (to 1609), the Thirty Years' War (1618–1648), the Franco-Spanish War (1635–1659), the English Civil War (1642–1649), the French Civil Wars (1648–1653), the English-Dutch Trade Wars (1652–1674), wars with the Ottoman Turks (1666–1696), the Wars of Devolution (1667–1678), the War of the League of Augsburg (1689–1697), the Northern War (1699–1721), and to round out this particular sequence, the War of the Spanish Succession (1702–1713). Though consistent, these wars were rarely intense, for poor roads, hard winters, and problems of troop deployment and logistics kept the fighting fitful and sporadic. Despite its pose of constant conflict, the main concern of this period was commerce.

With the death of Philip II in 1598 and Elizabeth I in 1603, who were both replaced by weak successors, the one major Renaissance king left was Henry IV of France, but he was struck down by an assassin in 1610. The lack of great kings left room for a new emphasis on industry and trade, particularly the latter. Thus it happened that the Netherlands, always more a federation than a kingdom, and always prone to exploration and enterprise, emerged as a power. By the end of the sixteenth century Dutch companies had invaded Portuguese trading territories in Africa and South America. Within ten years they were in a position to control tropical trade in both hemispheres. To implement this trade they launched the chartered company, the national bank, and the stock exchange. Under the leadership of Frederick Henry of Orange (1625–1647), they became the most prosperous and enlightened state in Europe. Descartes, Grotius, Rembrandt, Hals, and the University of Leyden added luster to their commercial glory. Their success in war added further glory.

In 1623 the Netherlands resumed its war of independence against Spain following the truce of 1609. After a sharp setback in 1625, when Catholic armies were everywhere victorious, Dutch pirates led by Piet Hein ravaged Spanish fleets in South America and by 1628 captured and held Pernambuco, the rich Brazilian coastline territory belonging to Spanish-dominated Portugal. As a countermeasure Spain launched an armada against the Dutch comprising eighty ships and 24,000 men. It was shattered by a Dutch fleet of one hundred ships in 1639, just fifty years after the defeat of the first armada by England. Holland emerged from this battle as a major naval power, while Spain was finished on the high seas. To hasten her collapse, Portugal revolted the following year and won its independence after three hours of fighting.

While commercial progress, especially that of Holland, formed the mainstream of European development in the first half of the seventeenth century, the Thirty Years' War (1618–1648)—actually four wars—occupied the center of the stage. It started in proper Medieval-Renaissance tradition as a war of religion. The Protestant Bohemians (Czechs) rebelled in 1618 against Hapsburg imperial rule, and Emperor Ferdinand II (1619–1637), intense and Jesuit-trained, overran Bohemia and by 1623 outlawed all creeds except Catholicism. Thus ended phase one of the war. Phase two (1624–1629) began with early Spanish victories over the Dutch and with a thrust toward Austria by the Protestant army of Danish King Christian IV; England and the Protestant North German city-states also entered the war. Catholic armies led by their finest general, the cynical adventurer Albert of Wallenstein, turned the tide and gained a complete Catholic victory. It resulted in the Edict of Restitution which returned to the church all German Catholic property secularized since 1552. Church and empire now seemed supreme in the German city-states, but there were stirrings of discontent. The Catholic League of Nobles demanded the dismissal of Wallenstein, lest Ferdinand become too powerful and assume complete imperial control; Ferdinand, who distrusted the growing power of Wallenstein, acquiesced. Religious motives had begun to give way to the secular concerns behind this conflict.

Phase three (1629–1635) began with Protestant Sweden advancing against Ferdinand and the league. The Swedish army was a new blend of swift-striking cavalry, open, more mobile infantry, and a prime emphasis upon artillery. The army was led by King Gustavus Adolphus, the greatest general of his age and an administrator whose methods and dedication recalled Augustus Caesar. He received support in money and troops from the new French chief minister, the Duke of Richelieu, a Catholic cardinal shrewd enough to see that the root cause of the conflict was not religious but dynastic conflicts. By 1631 the Swedish army swept into southern Germany laying waste to a countryside and population already decimated by two wars, and a desperate Ferdinand promised Wallenstein huge hereditary estates to return and lead the imperial armies. Wallenstein agreed, and during the bloody stalemate battle of Lützen in 1632, Gustavus, adrift in the fog, was accidentally shot and killed. Two years later at Ferdinand's behest Wallenstein, who had been negotiating secretly with Sweden, was murdered by one of his own captains. The Peace of Prague in 1635 seemingly ended the war, but Sweden and Richelieu remained dissatisfied, mainly because the emperor managed to maintain the same strong position with which he had started.

Phase four (1635–1648) saw France join the conflict openly. She attacked Catholic Spain and joined with Sweden in attacking Austria and its allies. It was now apparent that France's motive was a desire for power. The death of Ferdinand II brought to the throne a new emperor, Ferdinand III (1637–1657), who was anxious for peace, especially since the war was going badly. Negotiations dragged on amid sporadic battles until the elaborate Peace of Westphalia ended six years of diplomatic bickering. The peace made Sweden supreme in the north; it widened French frontiers by the acquisition of Metz, Verdun, Alsace, and Breisach; it insured the right of German states to carry on their own affairs and left the Hapsburg empire a mere geographical expression; it insured the independent status of Calvinists as well as Lutherans; it made room in Europe for popular governments by establishing the Netherlands and Switzerland as independent republics; and it marked the end of wars of religion—later wars would be commercial and national ones.

England had participated only slightly in the Thirty Years' War, for she was preoccupied at this time by civil disturbances at home. The kings who succeeded Elizabeth lacked her rapport with the people and with Parliament. James I (1603–1625), scholarly, petty, and superstitious—the Duke of Sully called him "the wisest fool in Christendom"—antagonized the Puritan middle class and after 1611 ruled virtually without Parliament. His son Charles I (1625–1649) was even more autocratic and intolerant. In 1629 he disbanded Parliament altogether and sought to enforce conformity to the Anglican Church. Scotland revolted and defeated the royal army, and Charles was forced to call a meeting of Parliament in 1640. This Parliament, instead of helping in the present crisis, denounced the king and sent his Anglican archbishop to the scaffold. In 1642 Charles declared war on Parliament. Aligned with him were the nobility, the Anglican clergy, and the Catholics; opposed were the middle class, the Puritans, the moderate Anglicans, and the nonconformists. Led by Oliver Cromwell, whose smartly drilled cavalry copied the tactics of Gustavus Adolphus, the Parliamentary forces defeated Charles and took him prisoner in 1645. A final Royalist effort launched in 1648 was crushed the following year by the Parliamentary army. That army was made up of two diverse groups, Presbyterians and the more numerous Independents, radicals in politics and religion. When the Independents learned that Charles was negotiating secretly with the Presbyterians, they purged the latter from Parliament. Then the remainder or Rump Parliament met and convicted Charles of high treason. He was executed on January 30, 1649.

COMMERCE AND COLONIZATION

This victory of middle class over king is a sharp reminder that might lay with commerce during this period. The Dutch still led the way, but all of the other European nations had begun to follow a similar course of exploitation in the East and West. Until 1600 Spain had held a monopoly in the Americas; her territories stretched from Florida to Argentina with the only sizable hiatus, Brazil, controlled by her vassal Portugal. About 200,000 Spaniards ruled 7 million Indians from 2000 urbane Spanish communities in the New World. After 1600 Spain established no new American colonies. In 1614 the United Netherlands Company built a fortress town on Manhattan Island and established New Netherlands along the Hudson and Mohawk rivers. The Dutch also captured Pernambuco. France planted settlements in Canada to trade for fur, timber, and fish. Under Samuel de Champlain, the "Father of New France," Quebec was fortified and a chain of trading posts established on the middle St. Lawrence. England concentrated on North America: the Virginia Company landed at Jamestown in 1607, and the Puritans landed at New Plymouth (Massachusetts) in 1620. In its early stages the Virginia colony nearly starved to death but was saved by an adventurer named John Smith. Within two generations it had set up a self-contained, slaveholding tobacco plantation economy, its 5000 settlers self-governed by a local governor and House of Burgesses. The colony of New Plymouth early established a democratic government by signing a covenant "To enact, constitute and frame just and equal laws for the general good of the colony." Other New England settlements during the next two generations included the Massachusetts Bay Company colony at Boston and the colony of Rhode Island founded by dissident Roger Williams. Unlike her rivals in America, England settled her colonies mainly with farmers and craftsmen who arrived intending to stay, to manage their own affairs, and to prosper. By 1650 they owned more ships and did more overseas trading than Ireland and Scotland together.

In the East the situation was quite different, for there the Europeans had ancient civilizations with which to contend. The American Indian had a Stone Age culture. The Eastern Indian emperor Shah Jahan (1627–1666), who had built the Taj Mahal, looked with raised eyebrow at these barbaric European traders. Canton, when the Portuguese discovered it, was cultivating art and scholarship under the Mings. Large-scale settlement here was out of the question; the only possible course was the establishment of trading posts. Portugal early entered into trade with the Spice Islands, Bengal, China, and Japan. France made tentative trading voyages to India. The English East India Company opened trade with India in Golconda and established a garrison on the Spice Islands. The Dutch, ambitious to dominate world commerce, succeeded for a time in the East. In 1623 they wiped out the English Spice Islands garrison and controlled its trade. They displaced the Portuguese in China and monopolized traffic in tea. They rediscovered Australia, renamed it New Holland, and monopolized trade with Java, Borneo, New Zealand, and Japan. They inaugurated slave trading from the Guinea coast and in 1619 delivered the first shipload of African slaves to Jamestown. And they introduced into Europe a new way of life known as mercantilism.

Mercantilism, a term first used by economist Adam Smith in his *Wealth of Nations* (1776), views trade as competition, or warfare if necessary, between states. A many-sided economic theory, it advocates state protection of commerce and industry for the increase of national wealth. Its tenets include the hoarding of precious metals, principally gold; maximum exports and minimum imports; and the use of colonies or overseas trading as a source of raw materials. Its effect on Europe was to make that continent the recipient of unprecedented luxury. Tobacco, snuff, tea, coffee, chocolate, the tulip, the gladiola, quinine, potatoes, whisky, gin, rum, champagne, and billiards all became commonplace by 1650. At this time, too, great forward strides in science—by Kepler and Galileo in astronomy; by Harvey in the circulation of the blood; by Glauber with nitric acid; by Torricelli with the barometer; by the development of reading glasses, microscopes, and watches—made Europe itself a new source of luxury and wonder.

In the second half of the seventeenth century France led all other European countries in lavish elegance and comfort. She also rose to eminence as a power, in part out of foundations laid during the Renaissance, in part because her two main challengers, England and Holland, had reached a stalemate. In England civil war had led to the formation of a Protectorate with Cromwell, as Protector, serving as a kind of benevolent tyrant from 1653 until his death in 1658. Despite the *Instrument of Government,* the first modern constitution, Cromwell's Parliament became a committee without authority. Cromwell established an aggressive commercial policy, and when this brought him into conflict with the Dutch in 1652, he declared war. When Charles II, son of the executed king, was restored to the throne in 1660, the English policy of commercial aggression against Holland continued and the Anglo-Dutch Wars went on intermittently until 1674, hampering the development of both nations. During this time France became *the* European power.

FRANCE AT ITS ZENITH

After the assassination of Henry IV, France floundered until 1624. Henry's widow, Marie de Médicis, convened the Estates General in 1614, but this measure only infuriated the nobles who discovered how wealthy the middle class had become in comparison to themselves. The political solution for France lay not in parliamentary procedure but in absolute rule, which was first supplied by Armand Jean du Plessis, the Duke of Richelieu. Frail, intellectual, and dedicated to the destiny of France, Richelieu dominated every facet of French life including its limp king, Louis XIII. He controlled state administration, court politics, foreign policy, the theater, and the newspaper, manipulating everything according to his own slogan of *raison d'état,* for reason(s) of state. His well-timed entry into the Thirty Years' War assured France of a position of supremacy in Europe. After his death in 1642 his carbon-copy successor, Jules Mazarin, continued Richelieu's policies under Louis XIII and then under the youthful Louis XIV. Less powerful than Richelieu, Mazarin had to weather a nobles' revolt known as the Wars of the Fronde (slingshot), a kind of civil war consisting of localized pitched battles, and the holdover war with Spain after the Treaty of Westphalia. When the latter finally ended with the Peace of the Pyrenees in 1659, Mazarin arranged with that exhausted nation for the marriage of Maria Theresa, eldest daughter of Philip IV, to Louis XIV. For Spain thus to allow a Bourbon within striking distance of a Hapsburg throne showed how high the star of France had risen since Richelieu.

With the death of Mazarin in 1661 Louis XIV, at twenty-three, took personal control of his kingdom. He had inherited a tradition of absolutism from France's two previous ministers, and no one in history would exploit that tradition more fully than he. Gifted with clearheaded Gallic logic and great dignity, he moved decisively at home and abroad. He appointed a draper's son, Jean Baptiste Colbert, minister of finance, and that cold, scrupulously honest official made mercantilism into a fine art. Colbert established the first modern tariff system, subsidized French industry, founded an Academy of Science, and lowered the public debt. He believed that the future of France lay in monopoly of commerce and colonies, but *Le Roi Soleil,* the Sun-King, as Louis liked to be called, decided otherwise. For Louis foreign policy meant the enlargement of French boundaries in Europe.

When Philip IV died, Louis as his son-in-law claimed the Spanish Netherlands and moved against them in 1667. Alarmed by his easy conquest of Flanders, England and the Netherlands ceased hostilities and joined with Sweden to form the Triple Alliance against France. This coalition checked Louis for a time and also provided the basic countermeasure that Europe would use henceforth to prevent dominance by any one of its members: a balance of power. From 1670 to 1684 Louis, allied with several German princes, garnered territories in the Dutch Netherlands, Strasburg, and Alsace. At this time he attained the height of his power, and his army, the largest since the Roman Empire, numbered 300,000 men. In 1682 he moved his court to Versailles, which he had been building for twenty-one years, and there he played the role of king with oriental magnificence. Ten thousand candles burned nightly in the mirrored halls and tapestried chambers of the palace, and courtiers in their brightest finery wandered through its vast salons and gardens and manicured woodlands awaiting the Sun-King's pleasure. Versailles was the most splendid spectacle of the seventeenth century, but it reduced the French nobility to impotence and it cut Louis off from contact with his people.

In 1685 he married Madame de Maintenon, an ardent Jesuit, and revoked the liberal Edict of Nantes. This led to fresh persecutions of the Huguenots, and some 200,000 of them, mostly skilled workers, fled France and settled in other European countries and colonies. This final religious purge by any western European nation came fifty years after religious causes had ceased to motivate national policy; it indicated how far removed Versailles was from the current of events. In 1689 the War of the League of Augsburg got under way when Louis decided to seize territories along the Rhine. For eight years France battled a Grand Alliance of German princes, England, the Netherlands, Savoy, and Sweden. Outnumbered, France suffered a decade of destruction, and in the Peace of Ryswick (1697) Louis was forced to return most of the territories he had captured in earlier wars. Versailles continued to glitter, but it cast its light upon scenes of desolation.

THE CLOSE OF THE SEVENTEENTH CENTURY

Vital as it was for France, the later seventeenth century also brought key changes to Holland, England, Sweden, Prussia, Turkey, and Russia. Holland, in a vulnerable middle ground between France and the northern powers, was overrun by France in 1672, while England buffeted her at sea. The Dutch were driven to reject their republican government—its leader Jan De Witt was murdered by a mob—and to turn to William, Prince of Orange, for protection. William made peace with England, joined the Triple Alliance, and then managed to stave off the French armies. He also married Mary, eldest daughter of Charles II of England.

Upon his restoration to the throne Charles II hoped for an absolute rule modeled on that of Louis XIV, but Parliament controlled the nation's wealth, leaving Charles only the right to veto laws and the outlet of living almost entirely for pleasure. During his reign the Whig and Tory parties arose, representing middle class and landed gentry respectively and marking the beginning of representative government. At Charles' death in 1685 his brother, James II, tried to restore absolutism and Catholic supremacy, whereupon the Whigs and Tories invited William of Orange, Charles' son-in-law, to be their king. When he invaded England in 1688, James fled at once, and the Glorious or Bloodless Revolution was over almost as soon as it had begun. Parliament passed the Bill of Rights, which guaranteed regular sessions of Parliament, personal liberty, trial by jury, habeas corpus, and freedom of speech.

Sweden, after her major role in the Triple Alliance, transferred control of her government from an aristocratic council to an absolute king, Charles XI. Charles elected to change sides and join with France against the Grand Alliance. Almost overnight his army was crushed by Brandenburg and his fleet destroyed by the Dutch.

Brandenburg, in northeast Germany, was typical of German principalities at this time, but with two exceptions. In the early seventeenth century it acquired Prussia (which, however, remained under Polish suzerainty until 1660) and Cleves-Mark; and its prince from 1640 to 1688 was Frederick-William of the family of Hohenzollern, "the Great Elector." Daring, and with a bent for power politics, Frederick-William could profit even in adversity. By the close of the Thirty Years' War his state, riddled by fighting and disease, had fewer than 600,000 citizens. Nevertheless he diverted all available manpower into a strong army so that when peace came he could demand favorable terms; he obtained East Prussia from the Poles. By 1688 Brandenburg-Prussia, or Prussia as it would soon be called, had a population of one and a half million and an admirable military reputation following its decisive defeat of Sweden. It also had an advantageous balance of parts: Brandenburg supplied administration and trade; the Junkers of Prussia furnished military skills and dedication; Cleves-Mark, on the lower Rhine, contributed only territory and population at this time— but it contained the Ruhr Valley. Frederick III, who succeeded the Great Elector, was a patient, manipulative organizer who built up the treasury and the population with a view to making Prussia an actual kingdom. This he succeeded in doing in 1701.

Turkey, crushed at Lepanto in 1571, retired from its normal occupation of threatening war until the severe and energetic Kiuprili dynasty took control in the later seventeenth century. The Turks advanced along the Danube in 1664, but were defeated by a coalition of Austrian, French, and Hungarian troops. They joined with Russia in an attack against Poland, captured Crete in 1669 after a bitter seige, and then built up the Ottoman Empire to a fresh peak. In 1687 their invasion of western Europe was repulsed by a coalition of Poland, Russia, Venice, Savoy, and Austria, and the Treaty of Karlowitz sliced up their territories and left them defenseless.

In Russia, Michael Romanoff became czar of Muscovy in 1613, and his dynasty continued to rule Russia into the twentieth century. Internal troubles preoccupied Russia through most of the seventeenth century, but in 1694 Peter the Great, a savage and remarkable man, became czar and brought Russia dramatically into the mainstream of European civilization. In 1696 he captured the Turkish fortress of Azov and thus gained an entrance to the Black Sea. Peter's great accomplishments, however, would come in the following century.

By 1700 France had begun to decline; Turkey was no longer a serious threat; Sweden still dominated northern Europe, but there its influence stopped; Holland, too small and vulnerable for her vast ambitions, was forced to become a second-class ally of England; and England, Prussia, and Russia emerged as the new major powers. These developments were in large part reflected in the commerce and colonization of the later seventeenth century. In the East, England and Holland took virtually all trade away from Spain and Portugal; Holland, however, lost control of Formosa to China in 1661. India was still forcibly united under the crafty Mogul Emperor Aurungzebe, which made the establishment of European garrisons there almost impossible. England did secure a foothold in Bombay by 1686, and its East India Company began to prosper.

In the Americas Dutch commerce and fortunes dwindled. In 1661 Holland lost Pernambuco to Portugal and three years later surrendered New Amsterdam to England as an outcome of the Anglo-Dutch wars. With the acquisition of this colony, renamed New York, England could confront the expanding French holdings to the north with a solid expanse of territory. Supported by Colbert, French explorations multiplied in the later seventeenth century. Robert de la Salle opened up the Ohio and Illinois rivers and claimed Louisiana in the name of Louis XIV. Louis Joliet explored the heartland of the continent, the Mississippi River valley. By 1700 France claimed an arc of territory stretching from the Gulf of St. Lawrence to the Gulf of Mexico within whose boundaries were 20,000 French settlers. English holdings in America at that time were smaller but contained 300,000 settlers. The English Hudson's Bay Company settled New York, and the Quaker William Penn founded the haven colony of Pennsylvania and concluded with the Indians the only treaty never broken.

In a wilderness so different from England and in a milieu designed for an artisan class, the colonists began to feel a sense of separation from their mother country. The appointment of a royal governor for Virginia, the revision of the patent of the Massachusetts Bay Company, and the attempt to regulate colonial shipping through the Navigation Acts touched off angry revolts in 1676 and again two decades later. For the most part the colonists remained loyal, however, and during the War of the League of Augsburg, which they called King William's War, they fought an indecisive border conflict against their homeland's enemies, the French. Both countries' colonies emerged from it unscathed and continued to prosper. The case was quite different for Spain. Although she owned territories that spanned a continent, her gains from them fell to almost nothing. The Dutch and English navies crippled her shipping, and buccaneer fleets under Henry Morgan administered the *coup de grâce*. They let so little bullion slip through from America that at the death of King Charles II of Spain in 1700 there was scarcely enough in the treasury to pay for his funeral.

SHIFTS IN POWER IN THE EIGHTEENTH CENTURY

While the world across the ocean was realigning and changing and an empire was coming to life in eastern Europe, western Europe still saw itself as the hub of the universe. The leading country inside Europe still seemed to be France, and in 1700 French was the language of war, diplomacy, and manners. French dress, French art, and French cooking still set the standards for others to imitate. French salons, where cultured ladies, artists, and noblemen mingled on an equal footing, became the models of civilized society everywhere. French precision and logic gave further sanction to science, which at this time produced the adding machine of Pascal and his studies leading to the invention of the barometer, the syringe, and the hydraulic press; the science-based philosophy of Leibnitz; the *Principia Mathematica* of Newton; and the steam engine.

The next European war, however, would make the decline of France visible for all to see. It began in the eighteenth century but belonged actually to the series of seventeenth-century wars set in motion by Louis XIV for territorial gain. Its immediate cause was the death of Charles II, the last of the Spanish Hapsburgs, who left a legacy of Spanish ships rotting in their harbors for want of trade. With no direct heir, Charles bequeathed his throne to his cousin Philip V, a Bourbon and the grandson of Louis XIV. To prevent Bourbon domination of Europe, a Grand Alliance was formed by England, the Netherlands, and Austria, and the War of the Spanish Succession (1702–1713) began. France had only Cologne, Bavaria, and Savoy—the buffer state between France and Italy—as allies, but her army now numbered 400,000 men. Savoy soon switched sides and Prince Eugène, its leading general, combined forces with the English under the Duke of Marlborough at the West Bavarian village of Blenheim along the Danube River. Marlborough, the war's finest general, could move troops with an efficiency amounting to genius. At the Battle of Blenheim in 1704, Marlborough and Eugène totally defeated the French army and fixed the outcome of the war, though it continued for another bloody decade and involved every western European nation except Spain. For the first time during the reign of Louis XIV France was invaded. The famine of 1708–1709 saw bread riots in the Paris streets, one tenth of the population reduced to begging, and Louis XIV forced to sell the gold plate and silver tables of Versailles to keep his army going. It was not the French army, however, but English politics that averted total French disaster. England was ruled at this time by the gullible Queen Anne (1702–1714) whose early favorite, Marlborough, was a prominent Whig. In 1710 she changed her support to the Tories, Marlborough was discredited and replaced, and the English war effort sagged. The French began winning battles in the Netherlands, and in the middle of this apparent reversal the Peace of Utrecht was arranged. The most elaborate treaty since the Peace of Westphalia, it by and large fixed the map of western Europe for more than a century. Spain lost her holdings in Italy as a result of this peace. She had dominated Italy all through the seventeenth century, and Spanish viceroys had ruled there like kings and bled the country dry. Now Austria obtained Naples, Sardinia, and Milan, while Savoy was awarded Sicily. (In 1720 Savoy exchanged Sicily for Sardinia, thus transforming the Duchy of Savoy into the Kingdom of Sardinia, an event which would prove of major importance in a century and a half.) By taking control of the Italian peninsula, Austria replaced a Bourbon ruler with a Hapsburg; and by acknowledging Philip V as king of Spain, the peace replaced a Hapsburg ruler with a Bourbon. England was awarded Newfoundland, Hudson's Bay, and Nova Scotia; the kingdom of Prussia obtained Neuchâtel; and France lost its final chance to master Europe. Louis XIV who had once proclaimed, *"L'état, c'est moi,"* (I am the state), now wrote to Philip V: "We grow old like ordinary men, and we shall die like them." After ruling seventy-two years he died at Versailles of gangrene of the leg; with him died the tradition of dynastic warfare.

The Northern War (1697–1721) began like the War of the Spanish Succession with nations closing in on what they believed to be a weakly held throne. Charles XII of Sweden was crowned king in 1697 at the age of fifteen, and Denmark, Poland, and Russia joined forces against the boy king so as to end Swedish domination of the north once and for all. With English help Charles invaded Denmark and subdued it almost immediately. He routed the Russians at Narva, although outnumbered six to one. He removed Saxon Augustus II as king of Poland and pursued him to Saxony where he badgered and humiliated him until 1707. Next he marched into the Russian interior with a Swedish-Saxon army of 45,000 men. Huge and energetic, with a madman's fearlessness, this stripling seemed likely to control all of eastern Europe, except that the Russian czar, Peter the Great, was an even more amazing ruler. His aims were to westernize Russia and to obtain "a window through which my people might look into Europe," meaning a section of Swedish-held territory on the Baltic Sea. The Battle of Narva destroyed all of his artillery, and for nine years while Charles burned cities in Poland, Saxony, and Russia, Peter studied Swedish military tactics and whipped unkempt Russian troops into disciplined order. Charles advanced into Russia destroying everything in his path until in 1709 his exhausted army arrived at Poltava in the Ukraine. There Peter wiped out the army, and the following year he seized the near defenseless territories of Estonia and Vidzeme on the Baltic. Sweden was finished as a first-rate power; Charles was killed in an assault on Norway in 1718; and in 1721 the Peace of Nystadt ended the fighting and ceded most Swedish territory to Russia.

In a tract of swampland along the Baltic, Peter built an imposing city of stone and brick, St. Petersburg, which soon had 75,000 inhabitants and was the most important city in northern Europe. Peter had a dark streak of savagery that made him enjoy killing servants with his bare hands and forcing his empress to keep her lover's head in a bottle of alcohol by her bedside. But he reformed the Russian alphabet, underwrote the first Russian newspaper, encouraged commerce, and organized his government into administrative bureaus the way Gustavus Adolphus had done. He civilized his boyars (noblemen) according to western European standards, made education compulsory for them, made them shave their beards, and forbade them to spit on the floor at mealtimes. He oppressed the peasants cruelly, however, and opened up a greater gap than ever before between them and the upper classes.

AN INTERLUDE OF PEACE

After the treaties of Utrecht and Nystadt Europe entered a period of peace. France, who had lost a million people in wars during the last thirty years, welcomed the tame reign of Louis XV, who heeded the pacifist counsels of his teacher, Cardinal Fleury. England, again without a ruler when Queen Anne died, turned to the House of Hanover, descendants of James I, and presented the throne to George I (1714–1727). Most happy when he could visit Hanover, this "honest blockhead" (Lady Mary Wortley Montagu's indelible phrase) turned over the reins of government to his prime minister, Sir Robert Walpole. Thus began a tradition of placing full control of, and responsibility for, the British kingdom in the hands of a prime minister, who would have to resign if his government failed. Under Walpole England thrived and became the leading sea power of the world, and George II (1727–1760) wisely continued his father's hands-off policy. The Netherlands, now subordinate allies of England, lapsed into a closed, hereditary oligarchy anxious only to maintain its present position. In Prussia King Frederick-William I (1713–1740) encouraged industry and manufacture and quietly prepared the best disciplined army in Europe. A cautious, practical diplomat, his most aggressive act was to discipline his nervous, flute-playing, sensitive son Frederick by beheading the boy's best friend in front of his eyes; it was a lesson in ruthlessness that Frederick the Great would learn well. After Czar Peter, Russia continued to look to civilized western Europe, although many a sadistic political murder took place in its subterranean dungeons.

The first half of the eighteenth century witnessed the full flowering of the scientific, social, and humanitarian developments of the seventeenth century—the Age of Reason reached its zenith. The "moral sentiment" of Lord Shaftesbury with its optimistic view of man's perfectibility sounded the keynote of this period. Crop rotation and new methods of cattle breeding promised to end the threat of famine once and for all. The classification system of botanist Carolus Linnaeus, the *Natural History* of zoologist Georges Buffon, and the experiments with electricity by Benjamin Franklin were all exercises in applied science to make the world better. The French encyclopedists led by Diderot criticized injustices, and Voltaire championed tolerance in every facet of life. The benevolent, impersonal

God of the Deists left man freer than ever before, and bejeweled ladies and beribboned men dancing the gavotte, the minuet, and the sarabande capped that freedom with unprecedented elegance. But Deism and the intellectual tolerance of Voltaire could appeal only to the few; the common people responded to the simpler Pietism of Quaker John Fox and the emotional appeals of John and Charles Wesley. A change in values was brewing that would bubble over by the end of the century.

THE AGE OF REASON CLOSES

Its prelude was a series of experimental skirmishes, calculated moves for quick gains in commerce or territory. The War of the Polish Succession saw France, Spain, and Sardinia balanced against Austria and Russia in a dispute over succession to the Polish throne. Five years of war and diplomacy, mostly the latter, confirmed Saxon Augustus III king of Poland in 1738 and redistributed sections of Italy to France, Spain, and Austria. In 1739 a sea captain named Jenkins appeared at the House of Commons claiming that Spanish coast guards in America had mutilated his ear. Though Walpole knew the story was false he was forced to sanction raids on Spanish holdings in the New World. This so-called War of Jenkins' Ear gave England a decade of profitable looting. The most typical and most earnest of the mid-century skirmishes was the War of the Austrian Succession (1740–1748), set off by the death of Hapsburg Emperor Charles VI. He had secured the consent of England, France, and Spain to accept his daughter Maria Theresa as his successor, but his death left her surrounded by enemies, including France, Spain, and Prussia. To counterbalance them Austria, England, Holland, Sardinia, Saxony, and Bavaria formed a coalition. The key figure in this intermittent conflict was Frederick of Prussia, who changed allegiance twice and ended by acquiring the productive lowlands of Silesia and the title of Frederick the Great. A wily opportunist, Frederick was also one of the most brilliant tacticians of all time. Eight years after the War of the Austrian Succession Maria Theresa felt strong enough to challenge him, with French and Russian help, and Frederick with his new ally, England, won some stunning victories in this Seven Years' War (1756–1763). The dynastic issues of this war had run their course, however, and were about to be superseded by significantly different ones involving the colonies.

In India Aurungzebe died in 1707, and within a generation England and France managed to penetrate his disintegrating kingdom. By 1751 English forces led by soldier of fortune Robert Clive defeated the French and took sole control of commerce with India. Nine years later Clive smashed a final French attempt to invade India and this "heaven-born general," as Prime Minister Pitt called him, became the unofficial ruler of Bengal.

By the late seventeenth century, wars in Europe had carried over into the American colonies. The War of the Spanish Succession found Frenchmen fighting Englishmen in Louisiana and Englishmen driving French and Spanish colonists out of Carolina. The War of the Austrian Succession marked a fresh outburst of fighting in America between the French and English. The Seven Years' War, known in America as the French and Indian War, brought that fighting to a decisive conclusion. In 1756 a frontier army led by General George Washington defeated France at Fort Duquesne. England overran French Acadia and deported its inhabitants. When the French army, pushed back to its strongholds of Montreal and Quebec, was wiped out in 1760 by an army led by General Wolfe, all Canada was in English hands. Meanwhile in the extreme north a Russian explorer, Vitus Bering, sailed through the straits that bear his name and claimed Alaska for Russia.

In 1733 a reformer named James Oglethorpe brought a group of imprisoned debtors to America and founded a humanitarian colony whose freedom of worship, within certain restrictions, attracted John and Charles Wesley. The colony, Georgia, was the thirteenth British colony established in the New World. Between 1700 and 1760 the population of the colonies quadrupled and their wealth and size grew in proportion. They produced an international figure, Benjamin Franklin, and created their own centers of learning: Harvard, William and Mary, Yale. They began to resist and resent, in Boston especially, attempts at overseas colonial government. "I understand them no more than Hebrew," wrote author-dilettante Horace Walpole, and yet their doctrines of equality and of human rights were the distilled heritage of the now departing Age of Reason. Its quintessential spokesman, Voltaire, sounded its knell and a prophecy of things to come in the epitaph on his tombstone. It reads: "He taught us to be free."

THE HUMANITIES APPROACH

TRAITS AND IDEAS

The Thirty Years' War marked the splintering of Christianity into unreconcilable sects and sent men searching for new means of universal stability. In government the solution seemed to be absolutism, at least through the seventeenth century; in private life it seemed to be REASON, at least for those thoughtful enough to seek out an absolute. And as the Thirty Years' War is the first "modern" war—concerned with commerce and balance of power at the expense, if need be, of religious alliances—so seventeenth-century reason is the harbinger of modern thought. Reason in this period meant common sense, the property of all and shared equally by everyone. "The power of forming a good judgment . . . reason, is by nature equal in all men," wrote the philosopher René Descartes. This power, he felt, could overcome bad judgment, by which he meant the passions, for he, like all seventeenth-century proponents of reason, saw it as something *restrained* and *impersonal.*

How sharp a break reason makes with the Renaissance and Medieval worlds is everywhere apparent. Pierre Bayle in his caustic *Dictionary* (1696) asserted that the bones of a dog would prove as effective as the relics of a martyr; his bitter common sense was a jolting contrast to the idealisms of the past. "A wise man has but one religion, but what it is a wise man never tells," wrote the Earl of Shaftesbury, thus blandly shrugging off what martyrs in past centuries had died for by the thousands. And the amiable Horace Walpole made a point of dying as befitted a man of reason: "My plan," he wrote, "is to pass away calmly as cheerfully as I can."

Like the Renaissance ideal it sought to supplant, this new brand of reason was attained only rarely, and then only for brief intervals. While Harvey was announcing his discoveries about the circulation of the blood and refuting the superstition of spontaneous generation, the mass of people were dosing themselves with medicines composed of vipers' flesh, crabs' eyes, wood lice, and sweat. Even the supremely rational philosopher David Hume admitted that reason put the mind under an unnatural strain, that such perfect containment was impossible to sustain. After a brief exercise of it, he wrote, "I converse, and am merry with my friends; and when, after three or four hours' amusement, I return to these [rationalistic] speculations, they appear so cold and strained and ridiculous that I cannot find in my heart to enter into them any farther." In sum, belief that any man—let alone all men—could live a life of utter common sense was an illusion which flickered intermittently. Nothing is more important than this fact to an understanding of the Age of Reason.

In philosophy Descartes rejected all authority except reason. Starting with *Cogito ergo sum*—I think (reason), therefore I exist—he erected a system that adapted Christianity to mechanistic science and viewed the body as a machine within which was "the reasonable soul" with "its principal seat in the brain." Baruch Spinoza, seeking to extend Descartes' system into moral philosophy, substituted reason for revelation. "It is," he wrote, "of the utmost service in life to perfect the understanding or reason as far as we can; and in this one thing consists man's highest felicity. . . . To perfect the understanding is only to comprehend God." Moreover, for Spinoza the passions, meaning all desires that are not rational, always reveal "our impotence and fragmentary knowledge."

Thomas Hobbes in his *Leviathan* (1651) set up a rational basis for government that made use of all the qualities of reason. For him men's minds were equal, since all possessed common sense in "equal distribution."

To curb their passions, to prevent a state of "continual fear and danger of violent death," menaced as all men were by their equals, they had to be restrained. Their best choice was to surrender their liberties to an impersonal force, an absolute ruler who would govern the leviathan body with unemotional indifference to their competitive struggles.

John Locke, who supplanted Descartes as spokesman for the later half of the Age of Reason, wrote his *Reasonableness of Christianity* to call men away from theological speculation and back to the simplicity and reasonableness of the New Testament. "If reason alone is competent to reach God, revelation is superfluous," he argued.

LITERATURE.   Reason affected the content first of French and then of British literature, thus passing from absolute monarchy to parliamentary government, from Catholic to Protestant nation with equal relevance. The great French critic Nicolas Boileau defined its status in his *Art Poétique* as follows: after Descartes reason superseded the passions and became for literature the means to truth and the only acceptable form of beauty. Blaise Pascal, a scientist turned mystic, rejected reason aloud, but his religious writings are models of rational thought. The provincial "author" of his *Provincial Letters* is shrewdly rational. And Pascal's famous appeal to libertines (in his *Pensées*) to bet, since they are gamblers, on the existence of God rather than against it, by which they have nothing to lose and everything to win, makes masterful common sense. Pierre Corneille, a lawyer turned playwright, fills his plays with courtroom debates between love and rational concerns. In an early play, *Le Cid*, the outcome is debatable, but then the French Academy intervened and passion never again equaled reason in Corneille's plays. In his *Cinna* Augustus Caesar pardons the treacherous Cinna solely to prove how he, the master of the world, is also the master of his passions. In *Polyeucte* the hero dies for a rational Christianity while his wife rejects a former lover with the explanation: "*Et sur mes passions ma raison souveraine*" (my reason rules my passions). The greatest French tragic playwright, Jean Racine, was less bound by reason than Corneille but nevertheless made seminal use of it in his masterpiece, *Phèdre.* By abandoning reason and giving herself over to her passions, Phèdre destroys herself and everyone around her. The coldly logical second heroine, Aricie, is the only person who profits in this play. The greatest French comic playwright, Molière, lauds common sense in each of his comedies. He uses it to puncture the pretensions of affected ladies, bourgeois "gentlemen," doctors, fanatics, and misanthropes. One of his favorite character types is the earthy servant who flattens all hypocrisy with the bludgeon of common sense. His Dorine in *Tartuffe*, for example, boldly challenges her betters whenever any of them deviates from common sense. Voltaire forges the rational gaiety of Molière into an instrument of satire in *Candide*, which takes a rational look at this best of all possible worlds.

Naïve Candide and his sweetheart experience the horrors of war, shipwreck, torture, mutilation, an earthquake, an *auto-da-fé*, and every social and political injustice imaginable. At the end Candide, old and broken but seasoned by the restraints of reason, settles down in a small corner of the world to cultivate his garden.

Although more baroque than rational, John Milton does make vital use of the power of reason. In *Samson Agonistes* Samson triumphs at last because his reason—notably the restraint it teaches—comes to dominate his passions. In *Paradise Regained* Christ refutes the exciting inducements of Satan with a calm logic reflecting Milton's view that reason is the divine principle in man. In *Paradise Lost* Adam represents reason while Eve represents passion, and the fall is shown as a dramatic conflict between those two forces. A generation later reason had left all competition behind. The critic Thomas Rymer approached poetry with the question: does the poet describe nature and life exactly as they appear to the reasonable man? Alexander Pope emphatically did. His "Essay on Man" advocates a rational, restrained acceptance of man's position in the universe and claims that reason outweighs all other human faculties. Jonathan Swift applied hard common sense to the world around him and the result, like *Candide*, was satire. Book IV of Swift's *Gulliver's Travels* contrasts rational horses with irrational men. Upon learning of the political state of things in Europe the horse who is Gulliver's master concludes "That our [European] institutions of government and law were plainly owing to our gross defects in Reason, and by consequence, in Virtue; because Reason alone is sufficient to govern a *rational* creature."

ARCHITECTURE.   In the nonverbal arts reason appears in clearest form as restraint and impersonalism, qualities that strike the senses as well as the mind. "Perfect reason avoids all extremes" said Molière in *The Misanthrope*, and this insight became dogma for the visual arts. In France the interiors of mansions built at that time often had a cold, impersonal dignity. Except for the grand salons, their rooms were paneled from floor to ceiling and painted ivory white; they conveyed an effect of blankness. Even the exterior of Versailles (Figure 6.10), despite its vast dimensions, uses ornament with spare restraint. Middle-class architecture in France and elsewhere carried exterior restraint still farther. Bare walls, simple moldings around windows, and the absence of columns or even pilasters characterized its exteriors. Only occasional ornate frames around the central doorway broke the monotony of these façades.

In England Inigo Jones alone introduced the restraints of Neoclassicism. Under the influence of the mannerist Palladio (see Chapter 7) he copied Roman functionalism with academic purity. He stressed a basic rectangular form, lightly ornamented in the Roman fashion (Figure 6.12), with interiors composed of wood-paneled walls and bare plaster ceilings—

models of impersonal restraint. His eighteenth-century successors made his basic form even simpler in constructing honest functional homes for a middle-class society. London streets were lined with rectangular red brick houses with chaste window frames and doorways and white marble steps. America, with its middle-class majority, made this style its model dwelling. The streets of Philadelphia took those of London as their example, and even a more pretentious manor like Westover (Figure 6.1) in Virginia is, apart from its elaborate doorway, blank and anonymous: the façade is a series of flat planes almost bare of ornament. The plan makes pervasive use of Jones' rectangular forms. Three rectangles comprise the basic structure, and the rooms within are generally rectangular and wood-paneled with plaster ceilings. All in all Westover is admirable, and its rationalist (restrained and impersonal) purity makes it so.

At the close of the Age of Reason a classical revival led to imitations of ancient buildings, cold mechanical copies whose impersonal restraint was in the truest sense rational. The *Panthéon* in Paris and St. Isaac's Cathedral in St. Petersburg with their nearly identical porticoes, round peristyles, and domes illustrate how rational characteristics could indeed, like common sense, be equally shared.

SCULPTURE.   The legacy of Michelangelo made subsequent sculpture overwhelmingly baroque, but aspects of the Age of Reason can be found in the sculpture of this time. Jean Antoine Houdon was the greatest sculptor of his century, and his best-known work, the seated *Voltaire* (Figure 6.2), captures the essence of reason. Broad-folded draperies draw full attention to the face, which is where all the meaning lies. The expression is restrained, impersonal, sardonic; one can almost see the brain behind the half-turned quizzical face. If Houdon captured the essence of reason, lesser men made use of its characteristics by making restrained, impersonal copies of the classics. *Girl with Bird* by Johann Heinrich Dannecker (Figure 6.3) typifies their achievement. The statue has a hard gracefulness that leaves the viewer cold. The Greeks could make a theme like this suggest universal beauty, but *Girl with Bird* remains world-bound like reason itself. It conforms to the painter Poussin's rational observation that "it is impossible with nature that one woman possess all of those collected elements of beauty which the image of Helen had," and instead connotes the mathematical precision of Descartes and the spiritual indifference of Locke. Similarly cold copies of the classics also appeared at this time on chinaware made by Sèvres in France and, shortly afterward, by Wedgwood in England.

PAINTING.   The painter who used reason supremely was Nicolas Poussin. With conscious care he subordinated emotions to intellect, color to line, and produced a series of delicate, subdued masterpieces like *The Holy Family* (Figure 6.4). "The idea of beauty," he wrote, "does not infuse

Figure 6.1 Westover. (c. 1730). Charles County, Virginia. [Library of Congress].

Figure 6.2 JEAN ANTOINE HOUDON. *Voltaire*. (1781). Comédie Française, Paris. [Belloz: Art Reference Bureau].

Figure 6.3 JOHANN HEINRICH DANNECKER. *Girl with Bird.* (c. 1800). [Stattsgalerie Stuttgart: Art Reference Bureau].

Figure 6.4 NICOLAS POUSSIN. *The Holy Family.* (1651). Courtesy of the Fogg Art Museum, Harvard University, Gift of Mrs. Samuel Sachs in memory of Mr. Samuel Sachs.

itself into matter which is not prepared to the utmost. This preparation consists of three things: order, mode, and form." So reasoned an approach does much to explain *The Holy Family*. The Virgin and the children form a two-dimensional plane; Joseph, in contrasting diagonal, joins with them to form a three-dimensional triangle. The nature background is pared down into a series of relevant forms as thoughtfully ordered as the buildings nestling in the hills. The buildings at the upper right repeat the form structure of the Virgin and the children—man and nature equally and impersonally ordered. The quiet calm of Joseph and Mary is matched by the calm lake behind them and solidified by the segment of wall framing Joseph's head. The curved figure off to the right counterbalances the diagonal of Joseph and keeps attention focused on the center of the canvas. In an age when painters used sweeping curves and jagged lines to lure the viewer's eye off the canvas, Poussin sought visual restraint. In a letter to Chantelou, his patron, he urged use of a bare, simple frame so that "the eye shall remain concentrated, and not dispersed beyond the limits of the picture."

Because he achieved such sublime effects by rational measures, the French Academy of Painting and Sculpture, founded in 1648, made Poussin its first president. It sought to repeat his achievements by establishing rules such as these: drawing must supersede color; only noble subjects are to be painted. The artistic results were generally unfortunate. Some artists, however, not shackled by the academy, made the same rich use of reason as Poussin did. Claude Lorrain in works like *Embarkation of St. Paul at Ostia* (Figure 6.14) achieved Poussin's sublime calm and restraint in radiant nature scenes. Jan Vermeer created similar effects in tiny rooms. *Girl with a Water Jug* (Figure 6.5) like *The Holy Family* reduces everything to order. We see only what is reasonable to see, what the eye would seize upon. The girl, her tranquil face half hidden behind her cowl, remains impersonal, a part of a total pattern engulfed by mellow light. The effect is a lofty yet rational objectivity. A similar effect ennobles the genre paintings of Jean Chardin, who unlike the Dutch genre painters who were his contemporaries replaced baroque sentiment with reasoned calm.

In England the engravings of William Hogarth made the same use of rational content as Voltaire's *Candide*. London was at this time the largest and greatest city in the Western world, but alongside its vaunted bookshops and coffeehouses lay stench, poverty, and corruption. Filth and dead animals littered the streets; 20,000 Londoners were homeless; and fashionable society took tea at Bedlam where they could watch the madmen being whipped. Hogarth portrayed this London with cold common sense in several series of engravings. His *Marriage à la Mode* series narrates the marriage of a young viscount who needs money to a tradesman's daughter who wants a title. Plate I, *The Contract* (Figure 6.6) shows the bourgeois father squinting over the contract, the gouty nobleman displaying his family tree,

Figure 6.5 JAN VERMEER. *Girl with a Water Jug.* (c. 1665). The Metropolitan Museum of Art, Gift of Henry G. Marquand, 1889.

the groom simpering at the wall, the already jaded bride-to-be receiving the attentions of a lawyer. The five other pictures of the series depict boredom, infidelity, and the death of both partners. Subsequent generations have endowed the work of Hogarth with moral sentiment, but like Swift and Voltaire, Hogarth was portraying life as he saw it with the rational objectivity of a prose Vermeer.

MUSIC.   Jean Philippe Rameau best illustrates the application of reason to music. As a theorist he laid down rules for tonal relationships that were valid and lasting (p. 257). He also theorized that melody should be determined by laws of harmonic progression, thus subordinating inspiration to rational form. As a composer he followed his own theories, producing music

Figure 6.6   WILLIAM HOGARTH.   *The Contract.*   (1774).   National Gallery, London.

of Gallic clarity and logic; but his melodies were often coldly restrained and predictable. His pieces for clavicin show the most marked effects of reason, but his concertos and such ballet suites as *Indes galantes* and *Paladins* display it as well.[1] At the close of his life when an Italian opera company presented Pergolesi's bubbling *La Serva Padrona* (the Servant Mistress) in Paris, Rameau felt a strong desire to imitate its style but, as he put it, "the mind refuses to obey."

Indicative too of rationalism was a new clarity and conciseness of melodic line which became fashionable toward the close of the seventeenth century. A pioneer in concise thematic writing was Antonio Vivaldi, whose melodies, in his concertos especially, are often models of restraint: his surging, overlapping variations make them seem much longer than they really are. Bach learned thematic concision from Vivaldi, and a comparison between Bach's early and late chorales—extended themes compared to restrained ones—shows how valuable a lesson it was. The later symphonies of Mozart and Haydn (particularly Haydn's finales) also turn to themes stripped of all ornament, like the façades of English and Dutch row houses.

---

[1] With a rich store of post-Renaissance music available, the illustrations used for this and subsequent periods will be more numerous and generalized than they were for the previous periods, with emphasis, however, on major works of major composers.

By the start of the eighteenth century Italian opera introduced *recitativo secco* (dry recitative), that is, dialogue intoned rapidly against a background of simple chords. Restrained and impersonal, it sounded the same in any context and served mainly to keep the plot moving. Mozart made use of it in such operas as *The Marriage of Figaro* and *Don Giovanni.*

The seventeenth century discovered that matter, for earlier ages a plastic substance shaped by the hands of God, conformed to clear and logical mathematical laws—in short, that man could manipulate matter. "I have," wrote Sir Isaac Newton, "subjected the phenomena of nature to the laws of mathematics to explain the universal order of the heavens." By this vast claim he dramatized the appeal of science to the intellectuals of the Age of Reason. Thus SCIENTISM, the belief that science and scientific method offer the true means to knowledge and well-being, joined as copartner with reason to dominate the intellectual life of the age. The roster of its champions is impressive: Kepler, Galileo, Torricelli, Harvey, Glauber, Pascal, Newton, Boyle, Priestley, Cavendish, Scheele, Lavoisier, Linnaeus, Buffon, and Benjamin Franklin. Its Renaissance origin has an equally impressive spokesman, Leonardo da Vinci, who expressed the scientific method in such statements as: "But first I shall test by experiment before I proceed further, because my intention is to consult experience first and then with reasoning show why such experience is bound to operate in such a way." But it was the propaganda of Francis Bacon that made the scientific method a vital part of European life.

Bacon believed that induction, testing by every possible experiment until one is "inducted" or led into the inevitable answer, was the means by which every man could share the fruits of genius. By induction one might "establish progressive stages of certainty." The English Royal Society, founded in 1660, set out to fix certainty once and for all, and the *Principia Mathematica* of Newton (1687) was its greatest product and in a sense its new absolute. England led in seventeenth-century science and was also the fastest rising nation; God seemed to favor scientism, and Shaftesbury's view of Him as a benevolent geometrician seemed just and apt. With science the avenue to truth, other areas of knowledge strove to become more scientific. Giovanni Battista Vico converted history into a scientifically predictable cycle of causes and effects with theocratic, heroic, and human phases marching in inevitable progression, declining into chaos, and then beginning over again. The arts too turned to science, as will be seen.

In philosophy Descartes explained the universe by means of the science of mathematics. God could be deduced from the geometric formula that "the three angles of a triangle equal two right angles." Descartes also formulated a series of rules for himself that smack more of science than philosophy: "never to receive anything as a truth which I did not clearly know to be such," for example, and "to divide every problem I examined into as many parts as possible." Spinoza too endeavored "to treat by a geometrical method the vices and follies of man." His *Ethics* is laid out in the form of a geometric proof, and like Descartes he sought the sure support of rules: "there must be one and the same method of understanding the essence of all things, that is to say, the universal laws and rules of nature."

Leibnitz went beyond the use of scientific method; he sought to integrate science itself with philosophy. He adopted the modern scientific concept of matter as energy, which he claimed was subdivided into centers of force called monads. Each monad possessed individuality and all were arranged into a "pre-established harmony" by God, the supreme monad. For Leibnitz the harmonic energy thus created was forever self-sustaining; it resembled two perfectly made clocks that correspond eternally in time, "a contrivance of the divine foreknowledge, which has from the beginning formed each of these substances in so perfect, regular and accurate a manner that by merely following its own laws, which were given to it when it came into being, each substance is yet in harmony with the other." Locke's concept of the mind as a blank white tablet upon which knowledge is etched by experience echoes this view of a universe left to run machinelike by itself.

By the close of the Age of Reason scientism had grown so powerful that it rose up to challenge the religion it used to serve. In his *System of Nature* (1770) Baron Paul Henri Holbach contended that God was an unscientific illusion and that "these supernatural ideas [religion] . . . have obscured morality, corrupted politics, hindered the advance of science, and extinguished happiness and peace in the heart of man."

LITERATURE.   In the arts scientism resulted in the unnatural following of rules calculated, like Baconian induction, to establish by progressive stages the uniform production of masterpieces. Since "rules" in art meant imitation of Greek and Roman classics, art by the eighteenth century came to be known as "Neoclassical." Rules for the epic included such Homeric devices as an opening invocation, a suitable epic hero, a plot that begins *in medias res*, and formal, high-flown speeches: Milton's *Paradise Lost* obeys such rules. Rules for tragic drama exercised the most importance in the Age of Reason, and these too derived from classical sources. Tragedy, like that of Sophocles and Aeschylus, had to be written in verse, divided into five parts or acts, make use of characters of noble blood, and have the catastrophe occur near the end of the play. It also had to follow the three so-called unities: (1) have only one principal action, (2) be completed in one place, (3) in one day's time (the first and third unities derived from Aristotle).

In France the unities influenced dramatic form by 1630, and in 1635 the French Academy of Letters was begun by Richelieu "to give rules to our language." Corneille's *Le Cid*, which deviated from those rules, was censured by the academy, and in subsequent plays he adhered to the rules, especially the unities. Their formal restrictions probably hampered his work. Racine managed to follow the rules without letting them affect the essence of his work, an achievement few Neoclassical artists would manage. His *Phèdre* conforms to the unities and his *Athalie* even adds a Greek chorus. Voltaire follows the rules in his epic *Henriade*, a treatment of the religious wars during the time of Henry IV, and the result is a cold and mechanical work.

England too used rules for the scientific production of masterpieces; some were contributed by home theorists like Hobbes who subdivided poetry into three genres (heroic, comic, pastoral) and decreed that an epic ought to have seven virtues. Milton in *Samson Agonistes* follows all of the rules for classical tragedy; in *Areopagitica* and in all of his other important prose he handles the Scriptures like scientific evidence and marshals it to lead toward vast, inductive conclusions. Ben Jonson followed the unities in most of his plays, *The Alchemist* and *Epicene* for example, and John Dryden in heroic tragedies like *The Conquest of Granada* adopted most of the rules of the French Academy. His *Essay of Dramatic Poetry* upholds those rules, as does Pope's "An Essay on Criticism" which declares that:

> Those rules of old discovered, not devised,
> Are Nature still, but Nature methodized.

While scientism had its strongest effect on the forms of literature it sometimes penetrated its content as well. *The New Atlantis* of Bacon describes a scientific Utopia; the *Sommium* of Kepler narrates a voyage to the moon; the *Vulgar Errors* of Sir Thomas Browne punctures superstition with the dart of scientific authority.

ARCHITECTURE.   In 1671 the Academy of Architecture was founded in France. In keeping with the absolutism of Louis XIV it decreed a central body of rules for building which, like the rules for literature, advocated classical forms, orders, and proportions. Scholars like Brisieux gave scientific sanction to these rules by illustrating them with graphs and tables. In England Roger Morris in his *Lectures on Architecture* laid down rules for the height, width, and length of every type of building and even for the window sizes to be used in each kind of room.

Until the eighteenth century architectural rules derived not only from classical sources but from Italian Renaissance adaptations of them as well. Then the new science of archeology led to the excavation of the Roman cities of Herculaneum (1738) and Pompeii (1763) and created fresh interest in precise copies of ancient architecture. This interest flourished during the mid and later eighteenth century and came to be known as Neoclassicism. Where earlier ages had viewed Greek and Roman civilization as a single totality, Neoclassicism disclosed their separate identities. Meticulous engravings of Greek and Roman monuments became the commonplace property of Europe, and rules for architecture now meant following the ancients with scientific exactitude. In Paris the portico of the *Panthéon* duplicated that of a Greek temple, as did that of the Cathedral of St. Isaac in St. Petersburg. The Brandenburg Gate in Berlin copied the Propylaea in Athens. Thomas Jefferson designed the Virginia State Capitol at Richmond in close imitation of the Roman *Maison Carrée* at Nîmes.

SCULPTURE.   In 1648 the French Academy of Painting and Sculpture was founded to place those arts under absolute, centralized control, in imitation of the Academy of Letters. Art and sculpture were made "scientific" by means of a series of finical rules. With the birth of archeology sculpture became Neoclassical, and its rules demanded imitation of Praxiteles or Polyclitus or just straight copy of Hellenistic art. The Greeks, early and late, represented "pure beauty," as the archeologist Johann Winckelmann asserted in his *Imitation of Greek Art in Painting and Sculpture* (1758). He called the *Canon* of Polyclitus "the perfect canon of all art" and reminded sculptors that the Greeks "began to form general concepts of beauty for the individual parts of the body as well as for its proportions." Such concepts, he wrote, included the rule that "With gods and goddesses the forehead and nose formed an almost straight line."

A late Neoclassical work is the *Pauline Borghese* of Canova (Figure 6.7). The head is that of the sister of Napoleon, the body an out-and-out copy of a Hellenistic statue of Venus. The profiled head with its near classical hair style and straight-line forehead and nose seems almost appropriate to the body, except that the body angle is not quite right for the pose of the head. The statue is a model of mechanical excellence but without the warmth of true beauty; it is a tribute to science if not to art.

PAINTING.   The first president of the Academy of Painters and Sculptors was Poussin, and his work, or at least the removable parts that could be held up to scientific scrutiny, became the basis for a tyranny of rules. The diagonals in his paintings often seemed to divide his canvas into a three-fifths to two-fifths proportion, as the figure of Joseph does in *The Holy Family,* and this proportion became a rule of composition. The lawgiver of the academy was Charles Le Brun, a favorite of Louis XIV, whose propounded rules took on official sanction. Those based on Poussin's work were moderate: copy the classics; stress drawing over color; paint only lofty subjects. Others were less moderate; for example, Le Brun's rule for depicting admiration:

> The face also changes little, and if there is any change it lies only in the raising of the eyebrows, but the elevation will be equal on both sides, and the eye may be a little more open than usual, the pupil centered between the lids and motionless, fixed on the object which will cause admiration. The mouth will also be partly open, but will show no more expression of suspense than the other parts of the face.

Figure 6.7 ANTONIO CANOVA. *Pauline Borghese.* (1808). Borghese Gallery, Rome. [Alinari: Art Reference Bureau].

A disciple of Le Brun, Roger de Piles, carried scientism to greater extremes by setting up a table of basic art elements—he found only four—which lists the quantity of each element possessed by various artists. Here are three examples from that table (the maximum score for each element is twenty):

	Composition	Drawing	Color	Expression
Le Brun	16	16	8	16
Leonardo da Vinci	15	16	4	14
Michelangelo	6	6	16	0

In 1665 an Academy of Art was founded in Antwerp to uphold rules laid down by a painters' guild; its dictates marked the end of the great age of Flemish painting. In England a Royal Academy of Art was chartered and the portrait painter Sir Joshua Reynolds was named its first president. Although less bound by rules than its French model, the Royal Academy did hold to some. An interesting answer to one of them, that warm colors (red, yellow, orange) should be dominant, and cool colors (blue, green, violet) recessive, was Thomas Gainsborough's famous *Blue Boy*, which defied the rules by using them in reverse, the blue-costumed boy being in the foreground of the painting.

With archeology, classical copies became the rule. In Germany, Neo-classicist Anton Raphael Mengs followed the dictates of Winckelmann in pallid Hellenistic imitations like *Parnassus*. In America, Benjamin West used both Reynolds and Mengs as his mentors.

Painting in the Age of Reason was also on occasion scientific in content. Seventeenth-century science probed into the physical properties of nature, and a number of landscape painters made similar examinations with color and brush. Important among them were Canaletto in Venice and Jacob van Ruysdael (in his early work), Meindert Hobbema, and Albert Cuyp in Holland. Rembrandt van Rijn in some sixty self-portraits experimented with inductive thoroughness with the texture, coloring, and alteration of the human face. His *Dr. Tulp's Anatomy Lesson* (Figure 6.8), whose subject would have been unthinkable in any previous period, makes science a jarring center of attention. The partly dissected corpse lies in a glare

Figure 6.8   REMBRANDT VAN RIJN.   *Dr. Tulp's Anatomy Lesson.*   (1632).   Maurit-shuis, The Hague.   [Alinari: Art Reference Bureau].

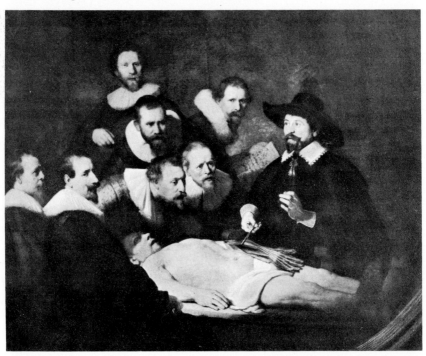

of light which sets it in dramatic focus. Everything else is secondary to the corpse and even that is secondary to the tendon held up by the forceps. Curiously, the dissected fingers remain flat despite the lifted tendon, possibly because the baroque Rembrandt, while deigning to use science for content, purposely refused to obey its rules.

MUSIC.   With no Greek or Roman music to refer to, music in the Age of Reason devised its own rules. As a result, where architecture, sculpture, and painting were called Neoclassical, eighteenth-century music, by furnishing its own past, was labeled Classical. Its fundamental rules were those governing tonality or key relationships as codified (they had been in practice earlier) by Jean Philippe Rameau. According to Rameau the key in which each composition begins is called the tonic key; its perfect contrast is the dominant key, which begins five notes higher than the keynote (first note) of the tonic key. The dominant tends to return to the tonic, and the tonic tends toward the subdominant, a key beginning five notes lower than the keynote of the tonic: for example, if the tonic key were C Major (that is, C D E F G A B C), the dominant key would begin on G, and the subdominant would begin on F. With both dominant and subdominant five notes away from keynote C, C serves as a central point between two opposing poles. This tonic-dominant-subdominant relationship became the form, and rule, for the Classical symphonies, sonatas, concertos, and string quartets of Mozart and Haydn and remained basal to music into the early twentieth century. The universe of Newton shaped scientific thinking for just about the same length of time, and the similarity does not end there. For Newton every action engenders an equal and opposite reaction; for Rameau the keynote, balanced between equal extremes, combines the extremes in a unified harmonic relationship.

A favorite form during the Age of Reason was the fugue, which also follows prescriptive rules: the opening melody, in the tonic key, must include the opening notes of the dominant and subdominant keys; the answering melody must be the same as the opening one but must begin in either the dominant or subdominant key; the next "answer" must begin with the opening melody in the tonic key; the next, if there are subsequent answers, must begin in the dominant or subdominant key; and so forth. Bach in his *Art of the Fugue* includes one fugue in six parts.

In his *Well-Tempered Clavier* Bach explores tonal relationships with inductive fullness in forty-eight preludes and fugues, divided into two sets or books of twenty-four; each prelude and fugue uses as the tonic key a different one of the twelve major and twelve minor keys. In *Art of the Fugue* Bach "inducts" a rather trite melody through eighteen fugues of increasing intricacy, providing a lesson in every possible kind of fugal composition. The last one, interrupted by death, includes a play on the notes B A C H (H in German, is B flat).

Rules for the classical symphony, sonata, concerto, and string quartet were formulated in this period and fixed the form of the music of Haydn and Mozart. These rules, models of balance and proportion, will be discussed in connection with the trait of balance, symmetry, and proportion that follows this one.

Joining reason and scientism to provide a trinity of clarity and order for the Age of Reason is a concern for BALANCE, SYMMETRY, AND PROPORTION. Like the balance of the Greek Golden Age, balance, symmetry, and proportion are techniques classifiable as trait; and since the Age of Reason tended to clothe itself in classical trappings, they probably owed their existence in part to Golden Age balance. They became, however, far more pervasive than their possible source, structuring not only the arts of the Age of Reason but its politics and society as well. The Thirty Years' War introduced balance of power as an antidote to the excessive strength of an individual state. The Triple Alliance and Grand Alliance were formed to establish an equilibrium of forces. This same equilibrium appeared in English politics with the rise of the Whig and Tory parties after 1660. L'Esprit des lois of the Baron de Montesquieu recommended an offsetting balance of functions in government among the executive, legislative, and judicial branches—a theory that would influence the American Constitution. The universe of Isaac Newton, the accepted view of the universe for the Age of Reason, was built out of his law of gravitation which stated: "Every particle of matter in the universe attracts every other particle with a force varying inversely as the square of the distance between them and directly proportional to the product of their masses."

In philosophy Descartes held that human beings possessed two souls, a "corporeal soul" which was mechanical, and an "incorporeal soul" defined as "a substance which thinks." The two were not in tension but were rather the balanced parts of a whole somehow reconciled by the pineal gland in the brain. For Descartes' pineal gland Leibnitz substituted a pre-established harmony of monads. "The soul follows its own laws and the body likewise follows its own laws," he wrote in echo of Descartes, "and they agree with each other in virtue of the pre-established harmony between all substances." For Leibnitz this pre-established harmony was established by God, who made balance and proportion His aims. For this world Hobbes asserted—and deplored—that all men had proportionately similar amounts of strength and intelligence: "For as to strength of the body, the weakest has strength enough to kill the strongest," and an "equal distribution" exists in natural gifts of the mind. It remained for John Locke to find equal proportion as useful to men as to God. "All men are created equal," he wrote, and from this basis preached tolerance, democracy, and the pursuit of knowledge.

LITERATURE.   Balance, symmetry, and proportion affected both form and content in literature. The dramas of Corneille and Racine show their effect on form. These dramas were written exclusively in pairs of closed couplets, each line of which was an alexandrine composed of twelve syllables. The following couplet written by Corneille on the death of Richelieu reflects the precise balance of this form:

> Il m'a fait trop de bien pour en dire du mal;
> Il m'a fait trop de mal pour en dire du bien.

(He has done me too much good to speak ill of him; he has done me too much harm to speak well of him.) In England also drama was written in balanced verse, and heroic tragedies such as Dryden's *The Conquest of Granada* and *Aureng-Zebe* were written in so-called heroic couplets. These used the same closed, rhymed couplets as did French dramatic verse but contained ten syllables per line instead of twelve and strove for still more perfect balance by casting each line in a basic iambic (unstressed-stressed) rhythm. The greatest practitioner of heroic couplets was not a dramatist but a didactic poet, Alexander Pope, famous for such neatly balanced couplets as this one from "An Essay on Criticism":

> True wit is Nature to advantage dressed;
> What oft was thought, but ne'er so well expressed.

Balance, proportion, and symmetry had their most marked effect on the content of Molière's comedies, some written in closed couplets, others in prose. In each comedy Molière held up a trait for scrutiny and urged a balanced approach to it, a kind of Aristotelian Golden Mean. In *Tartuffe* he advocated a "reasonable" Christianity; in *The Misanthrope*, a sensible tolerance of this world's evils; in *School for Husbands*, a proper share of trust in the opposite sex. Voltaire as critic urged balance and proportion in form and content—he modeled his tragedies on Racine, his comedies on Molière—and denounced "that clown" Shakespeare for his lack of proportion. Swift in *A Tale of a Tub* championed the Anglican Church as a mean between the extremes of Catholicism and Puritanism. Pope in "An Essay on Man" sees the universe as a work of perfect proportion, as Newton and Leibnitz had, and admonishes:

> All Chance, Direction, which thou canst not see;
> All Discord, Harmony not understood.

ARCHITECTURE.   The most striking seventeenth-century architectural production, Versailles, is a symmetrical tour de force. It is built around a central axis which divides building, gardens, and grounds into two vast symmetrical complexes then continues northward into the heart of Paris. An air view of Versailles (Figure 6.9) reveals how the central axis dominates the entire setting, how the side roads lead into it at equal angles, and how even the bosquets (woods) are clipped to form symmetrical shapes on either side of the axis. Overriding and compelling, the axis forces the spectator to stand in line with it in order to get a proper view of the spectacle as a whole. In the Spanish Escorial, a similar symmetrical complex, the chapel occupied the center of the axis; in Versailles the king's bedchamber occupied that center, and was a testimony to the absolute authority of Louis XIV. A front view of Versailles (Figure 6.10) reveals the overriding importance of the gardens of André Le Nôtre. Set up around the central axis in an area of unprecedented breadth they counterbalance lawns, pools, canals, fountains, and sculpted bosquets with quiet grace and absolute precision. Three is the controlling number at Versailles, and the building itself is an exercise in threes: the façade is composed of three sections; the windows of all three stories are predominantly grouped in threes; three axes lead into and away from the central structure; and the celebrated Gallery of Mirrors is flanked by the smallish salons of War and Peace. Such stupendous proportion and symmetry tends, it must be confessed, toward a monotony which is its own comment on the tyranny of science over art.

After the Greek studies of Winckelmann and the rise of Neoclassicism, another palace was built at Versailles, the *Petit Trianon* of Jacques-Ange Gabriel (Figure 6.11). Using a central axis, precise symmetry, and a three-part façade, the Trianon achieved a "pure beauty" rivaling the Greeks by virtue of its smaller size and its delicate, near perfect proportions. It bears comparison with the Temple of Athena Nike (Figure 2.6).[2]

The vastness of Versailles found congenial company in the spacious squares laid out in France during the Age of Reason. The *Place de la Concorde* with its matched pairs of buildings is perhaps the most beautiful. Other notable squares include the *Place Royale* in Nancy and the *Place Vendôme* in Paris. In Germany Frederick the Great used Versailles as the model for his palace at Potsdam.

In England Inigo Jones, following the contrived classicism of Andrea Palladio (see Chapter 7), developed a style notable for its restraint and proportion. His Banqueting House (Figure 6.12), designed for a proposed new palace at Whitehall, anticipated the graceful outlines of the *Petit Trianon*. Without its crowning balustrade the building would seem flat; with it the Banqueting House becomes a rectangle of harmonious proportion. The façade contains numerous examples of balance including the group of four emerging columns on the first and second stories, the single and then double pilasters on both sides of both stories, and the pattern of jutting supports on the balustrade. Like Versailles the Banqueting House has a tripartite façade, as indicated by the extended columns in the center, by the jutting capitals above those columns, and by the balustrade supports

[2] All figures from Chapters 2–5 can be found in Part I of *The Humanities Handbook*.

Figure 6.9   Louis Le Vau and Jules Hardouin-Mansart.   Palace of Versailles, aerial view.   (1669–1685).   [Bulloz: Art Reference Bureau].

Figure 6.10   Louis Le Vau and Jules Hardouin-Mansart.   Palace of Versailles, garden façade.   (1669–1685).   [Bulloz: Art Reference Bureau].

Figure 6.11   JACQUES-ANGE GABRIEL.   Petit Trianon, Versailles.   (1762–1768).
[Bulloz: Art Reference Bureau].

Figure 6.12   INIGO JONES.   Banqueting House.   (1619–1622).   London.   [Crown
Copyright: Art Reference Bureau].

above the capitals. Together they form a sort of axis with a perfectly sym-metrical façade on either side. Jones' style remained a dominant one throughout the Age of Reason and claimed a host of disciples. Eminent among them were a father and son, both named John Wood, whose Prior Park owes much in spirit and detail to the Banqueting House. In America almost all of the New England houses were symmetrical, with balanced pairs of windows on either side of the central doorway, geometrical roofs, paired chimneys, and paired dormers. Westover, though more elaborate, is by and large balanced and symmetrical, and other southern mansions like Washington's Mount Vernon are similarly symmetrical in keeping with the dictates of the Age of Reason.

SCULPTURE.   Examples of balance, symmetry, and proportion are rarer here than in the other arts, but enough exist to illustrate the vitality of the trait. Canova takes refuge in the proportions of Hellenism, and those sculp-tors who assisted masters like André Le Nôtre with garden decoration became especially sensitive to symmetry and balance. François Girardon who worked with Le Nôtre at Versailles underscores balance and proportion in reliefs like *Bathing Nymphs* (Figure 6.13). The rocks and draperies at each end balance one another, and the pair of figures at one end precisely counterbalances the pair at the other end; each outermost figure even has one foot thrust outside the framework. The figures themselves

Figure 6.13   FRANÇOIS GIRARDON.   *Bathing Nymphs*. (c. 1670).   Versailles. [Archives Photographiques].

seem curiously stylized, as do the expressions on their faces. That is because their poses and movements, as well as proportions, obey rules set down by the academy. Girardon, incidentally, was Le Brun's favorite sculptor.

PAINTING.   Formal balance is a guiding principle in the work of men like Vermeer and Poussin. In *Girl with a Water Jug*, Vermeer set up an all-inclusive coordination of forms. Casement, map, wall surfaces, chair back, water jug, tablecloth, and table top all start to form rectangles, all of

Figure 6.14 CLAUDE LORRAIN. *Embarkation of St. Paul at Ostia.* (c. 1650). Museo Del Prado.

them incomplete and all of them interlinked by this very incompleteness so as to form a harmonious unity. In *The Holy Family* Poussin arranges his figures, buildings, and nature elements in serene equilibrium. The perpendicular head of the Virgin bisects the canvas, and this axis is underscored by the vertical edge of the monument behind her. Balanced groups of figures on either side of her form balanced triangles. The bowl of water at her feet forms with the pools behind her a matching horizontal triangle. Offsetting towers rise above both edges of the landscape, and both geometrical clusters of buildings are similarly flanked with trees, one in broad compass, one in narrow—the whole forming a study in proportion.

Balance in Claude Lorrain is less calculated, but he makes more sweeping use of central axis. In the *Embarkation of St. Paul at Ostia* (Figure 6.14) a beam of light bisects his canvas and flows onward into infinity, a technique typical of almost all of his paintings. On either side of that axis of light stand classical buildings, counterbalanced, and ships with matching vertical masts. The trees on the right, shaped as deliberately as the bosquets of Le Nôtre, cradle and emphasize the axis.

MUSIC.   Based as it is on mathematics, music makes extensive use of balance, symmetry, and proportion. The bar of measure—patterns of strong and weak beats—was introduced early in the seventeenth century, and at that time melodies often were cast in two- or four-bar lengths. These tailored melodies, and their variations *in similar length,* account in large part for the balanced phrasing in the music of Haydn and Mozart. The *aria da capo,* a three-part A B A structure—first melody, second melody, first melody—also came into widespread use in the seventeenth century; its B part formed a kind of central axis between the symmetry of the A parts. Used by such early opera composers as Monteverdi and Alessandro Scarlatti, it became the basic design of the minuet and trio (third movement) of the Classical symphony, best exemplified in the symphonies of Haydn. An expanded variation of it was the third rondo form, ABACABA, used on occasion as the fourth movement of the Classical symphony and the finale (third movement) of the Classical concerto.

Balance or, better, counterbalance of speeds also shaped the music of the Age of Reason. The trio sonatas of Arcangelo Corelli often consisted of four movements running slow-fast-slow-fast; the *Concerti Grossi* of Handel made use of this same balance of speeds. Most of the 600 cantatas of Alessandro Scarlatti consisted of counterbalancing pairs of recitatives and arias running recitative-aria-recitative-aria.

A range of techniques using balance and symmetry came together in the Classical symphony, sonata, and string quartet. Made up of four movements, the general structure of each of these forms is as follows:

1. First movement, in sonata allegro form:
   A. Exposition:
      a. vigorous first theme in the tonic key.
      b. lyric second theme.
      c. occasionally a third or closing theme.
   B. Development: free treatment (variation) of themes a, b, (c).
   C. Recapitulation: restatement of exposition in the tonic key.
2. Second movement: an *adagio,* slow movement, generally in ABA form.
3. Third movement: a minuet and trio in ABA form. (This movement is omitted in the Classical concerto, the only structural difference between it and the other Classical forms.)
4. Fourth movement: a repetition of the sonata allegro form, or in some cases a rondo, in either case again beginning in the tonic key.

This structure has a symmetry as intricate and intellectual as Versailles or a canvas by Poussin. It became the framework for the symphonies, sonatas, quartets, and concertos of Haydn and Mozart, although those composers altered or embellished it in nearly every case. (The ideal vehicle for studying the structure of the classical symphony is, ironically, the *Classical Symphony* of the twentieth-century composer Serge Prokofiev.)

> The Age of Reason gave rise to an impressive number of ideas, and many of them extended well into the future. They did not, however, penetrate far into the arts of their own age. Restraint, rules, and symmetry made for surface shapes but not for depth, allowing little room for the infusion of ideas. The baroque style, too, set up a special obstacle to rational ideas, as will be evident in Chapter 7.

The shifting alignments of the Thirty Years' War seemed to confirm that the Christian unity of the Middle Ages, and still an ambition of the Renaissance, was no longer possible. The popular sects that grew up in the Age of Reason—Pietists, Quakers, Methodists—turned their backs on it. The intellectuals devised their own concept of man's relationship to God in keeping with the science and reason of the time—DEISM. Deism sought to remove the irrational and mysterious elements from Christianity, to remove God from the everyday life of men, and to define religion as obedience to moral laws. It based its belief in God on universal mechanical laws like those laid down by Newton and transformed Him into an efficient scientist who no longer had any need to be triune: "I do not believe in God the Father, God the Son, or God the Holy Ghost," explained the Deistic founder of the French *Encyclopedia*, Denis Diderot.

Bacon anticipated the Deist belief that God had removed Himself from this world when he stated: "If any man shall think by view and inquiry into sensible and material things to attain to any light for the revelation of the nature and will of God, he shall dangerously abuse himself." Shaftesbury stated the positive aspect of Deism, its belief in man's innate moral sense, as follows: "A common honest man whilst left to himself and undisturbed by philosophy and subtle reasonings about his interest, gives no other answer to the thought of villainy than that he cannot possibly find in his heart to set about it, or conquer the natural aversion he has to it." Voltaire advocated this "natural religion" of the moral sense in his *Le Philosophe Ignorant* and defined God in proper Deistic fashion as the architect of the universe, the cosmic clock-maker. Pope addresses his "Essay on Man" to the Deist Lord Bolingbroke, and includes basic concepts of Deism in this work.

The Age of Reason adapted nature to the service of man far more than any previous age had done. Chemists dissected it and physicists probed its laws, stripping away its mysteries and revealing it to be an accessible target for study. The French Encyclopedists called it "the facts of experience," and they along with the scientists and Deists championed the revolutionary idea of NATURE AS MATTER. Bacon summarized man's new-found relationship to nature as follows: "Man, as the minister and interpreter of nature, does and understands as much as his observations on the order of nature, either with regard to things or the mind, permit him, and neither knows nor is capable of more." For Descartes this idea was a vital part of God's plan: "the reality of matter [nature] must be admitted; else God would be responsible for making us believe a lie," he wrote in philosophic echo of Bacon. Holbach believed that the physical laws of nature were the rightful successors of universal law. "Nature bids man consult his reason and take it for his guide . . . let him study that nature, let him learn her laws, let him apply his discoveries to his own felicity, let him undergo without a murmur the decrees of universal force."

In literature Charles Sorel's satiric novel, *Le Berger Extravagant* (the silly shepherd), ridicules the notion that nature might be anything other than matter. The light that burns the shepherd's head is not a glance symbolic of the divine eyes of his lady, but the sun's reflection from a mirror held by a servant. The tree trunk he falls into is not a mysterious protector, as in Ovid, but a damp and uncomfortable crevice. Sir Thomas Browne, a devout physician turned scientist, investigated the eyes of moles and the legs of badgers and described them on the basis of pure mechanics in *Vulgar Errors*. At the same moment that his counterpart, Blaise Pascal, a scientist turned mystic, was dying in a glow of ecstasy Browne was busy examining birds' eggs in Norwich. Samuel Johnson countered Berkeley's assertion that nature was merely an extension of the mind by "striking his foot with mighty force against a large stone, till he rebounded from it, 'I refute it [Berkeley's thesis] *thus.*' "

In architecture Le Nôtre treated nature like modeling clay in designing his gardens. In painting, Hobbema, Cuyp, and Canaletto produced representational landscapes dedicated to the proposition that nature was matter, although Canaletto shrouded his Venetian scenes in a blanket of atmosphere. Poussin and Claude molded nature with the same controlling hand as Le Nôtre.

In Holland and England the middle class rose to new eminence in the seventeenth century and as a result both countries prospered; this fact plus the democratic bases of seventeenth-century science and reason gave fuel to the growing concept of the equality of all men. This concept led to the predicament best expressed by Hobbes: men being equal are dangerously capable of mutual destruction. His solution was a contract, "convenient articles of peace upon which men may be drawn to agreement," whereby the general body of men permanently surrendered their rights to an absolute ruler who would hold this dangerous equality in check. A more congenial and lasting solution was the idea of SOCIAL CONTRACT, whereby men surrendered their rights to a group of men chosen from among themselves and for a limited time. An early expression of this idea was the *Grand Dessein* (great plan) of the Duke of Sully, minister of Henri IV, who proposed a contract dividing Europe into fifteen equal powers. Another anticipation of the idea was the covenant signed by the Pilgrim fathers who journeyed to America on the *Mayflower*. Social contract proper began with the English Commonwealth, whose *Instrument of Government* formulated the first constitution of modern times. The philosopher who set down the idea in most effective form was John Locke. Here are a few of his more influential tenets:

> And thus every man, by consenting with others to make one body politic under one government, puts himself under an obligation to every one of that society to submit to the determination of the majority, and to be concluded by it; or else this original compact, whereby he with others incorporates into one society, would signify nothing, and be no compact if he be left free and under no other ties than he was in before in the state of Nature.
> And thus, that which begins and actually constitutes any political society is nothing but the consent of any number of freemen capable of majority, to unite and incorporate into such a society.

Social contract would have great consequences in the period to come, but apart from a few polemics it had little impact upon the arts of the Age of Reason. The Academies of Literature, Painting, Sculpture, and Architecture did bind men to a form of social contract, but this contract owed more to Hobbes than to Locke.

Man in the seventeenth century seemed on the verge of overcoming nature. His new-found sciences, in Bacon's words, "grow and perfect themselves daily as if enjoying a certain vital air." Faith in science grew along with achievement, and Newton's *Principia Mathematica* with its scheme of the universe appeared to have crowned that faith with everlasting victory. Man also seemed about to master his intolerance and to achieve at last a vital Christian brotherhood. Calvinist recognition after the Thirty Years' War and the English Toleration Act of 1689 led the Abbé de Saint Pierre and scores like him to preach the perfectibility of man. That perfectibility also seemed to have liberated mankind from the economic restraints that had ground down peasantry and middle class alike for so many centuries; the doctrine of *laissez faire*, governmental noninterference in enterprise, developed by François Quesnay, sanctioned a new and unlimited opportunity for anyone. This trend toward betterment seemed

documented by the facts of the early eighteenth century, the most prosperous era to date, and THE IDEA OF PROGRESS infected kings and merchants,
scientists and clerics alike. "We are but men," wrote Anglican Bishop
Gilbert Burnet, "and ought not to be ashamed that we grow in knowledge."

Descartes envisioned that growth as boundless, provided man relied
upon scientific methods: "We apply them . . . and thus make ourselves the
lords and possessors of nature." Leibnitz envisioned this as the best of all
possible worlds (eliciting Voltaire's sardonic response in *Candide*), his
optimism a natural outgrowth of the idea of progress. The Deist Lord
Shaftesbury, poles apart from the Abbé de Saint Pierre, insisted too on the
perfectibility of mankind. The idea of progress penetrated into every
corner.

It showed up in literature as defiance of the ancients and as assertion
that the Age of Reason had surpassed them. Charles Perrault, who was,
perhaps appropriately, a distinguished author of fairy tales, defended
modern superiority in his *Parallèle des anciens et des modernes* (1688), thus
touching off the so-called Quarrel of the Ancients and Moderns that swept
across Europe. Even Swift had some words of praise for the moderns in his
Battle of the Books, and Pope, icy and bitter by nature, was constrained by
the optimism of the age to conclude that "Whatever is, is right." Both
sides showed a willingness to compromise while claiming victory, and even
though eighteenth-century archeology ushered in a fresh wave of admiration for the Greeks, the moderns had struck a blow for progress that would
complicate that Neoclassical revival almost from the start.

Like the Hellenistic period the Age of Reason admired and imitated a
classical past; and the new age shared with the old one an extremist view
of the idea of TWO PUBLICS. The chief example of this in the Age of Reason
was the yawning gap between peasants and nobles, in France, Germany,
and Russia especially. In France, for instance, all peasants had to pay a
heavy direct tax, the *taille*, while the nobility, clergy, and most of the
middle class were exempt. And the French criminal code administered two
distinct sets of justice, as Diderot's *Encyclopedia* made plain.

Other aspects of the idea were no less influential. Two publics bred
two types of religion, Deism for the intellectual few, and the more fervid
Pietism, Methodism, and Quakerism for the majority. Even "God-intoxi-
cated" Spinoza, as the novelist Novalis called him, restricted his religious
philosophy to the few: "If salvation were easily attained, and could be
found without great labor, how could it be neglected by nearly everyone?
But all excellent things are as difficult as they are rare." The literature
steeped in the traits of the Age of Reason was written for the upper layer
of society. Corneille constrained his art to please an intellectual public.
Pope's "Essay on Man" was snobbish if not cohesive or profound. Ver-

sailles functioned as a dividing wedge, separating court architecture from town architecture and the court itself from the nation as a whole. In his *Discourses* to the Royal Academy, Sir Joshua Reynolds presented this view of the artist's public: "It must be remembered, that as this great style itself is artificial in the highest degree, it presupposes in the spectator a cultivated and prepared artificial state of mind. It is an absurdity therefore to suppose that we are born with this taste . . . ." He was speaking for music as well as for art, for Classical music appealed only to the few who were willing to cultivate a taste for it. The exquisite art songs of Purcell and Mozart failed to reach out and touch the majority, the way the Medieval motet or the Renaissance chanson which made everyone a participant had done. The fugues of Bach and the symphonies of Mozart and Haydn are among our most treasured musical legacies, but in keeping with the idea of two publics they were suited for the listening elite instead of participating masses.

FORMS AND TECHNIQUES

Form, then, was the guiding principle in the Age of Reason. Even its traits turned out to be applications of form or technique: reason emerged as restraint; scientism gave rise to formal rules; balance, symmetry, and proportion were inherent in each aspect of the age. Any horizontal humanities view of the Age of Reason ends up as formal comparison; for example, it is a form (balance) that relates the heroic couplet of Pope, Versailles, the *Bathing Nymphs* of Girardon, *The Holy Family* of Poussin, and music measured by bar lengths. One can best study the physical stance of this period, therefore, through its traits, and any additional forms and techniques are really offshoots of those traits. The following are a few of the more notable ones:

CLARITY: Little concerned with symbolism or with personal interpretations of the universe, the arts of this period achieved a diamond clarity, as in the style of Corneille and Racine; the epigrams of La Rochefoucauld and Pope; the functional architecture of Westover; the straightforward intention of *Girl with Bird;* the visual emphasis of Poussin; the themes and phrasing of Mozart and Haydn.

"PURE BEAUTY": We mean by this Neoclassical imitation of Greek originals, as in the Brandenburg Gate, the Bank of England, *Pauline Borghese,* and Mengs' *Parnassus.*

SATIRE: Examples are the poetic satire of Boileau and Pope; the prose satire of Sorel, *The Silly Shepherd;* that of Montesquieu, *Persian Letters;* of Voltaire, *Candide;* of Swift, *Gulliver's Travels;* the mock epic of Tassoni, *La Secchia rapita* (the stolen bucket); of Boileau, *Le Lutrin* (the choir desk);

of Pope, *The Rape of the Lock;* the painting of Hogarth, *The Contract,* and the entire *Marriage à la Mode* series; the opera of Mozart, *Cosí Fan Tutte* (they all behave thus) for satire on women, and *Le Nozze di Figaro* (the marriage of Figaro) for social satire.

The Age of Reason with its segregated publics, its cold reason, and its scientism presents an unnatural and constrained appearance. After all, a tradition dominated by forms and mechanics can achieve no more than partial life and partial validity. All men do not share the same amount of common sense, as the smallest sampling of history or society makes clear. All despots were not enlightened, as England learned in 1688 and France learned when Louis XIV grew old. Mankind resented the cold progress of the mind and turned from it to the warmer comforts of salvation or gin or the battlefield. Hume who was the quintessence of rational man admitted that its comforts were at best momentary ones. The Age of Reason waned with the eighteenth century, but even at its height something else overflowed its boundaries from all directions. That something else we call the baroque, and the following chapter will trace its course alongside the Age of Reason. Why and how the two coexisted will become apparent as you study the humanities approach to the baroque.

SELECTED BIBLIOGRAPHY

History

Beloff, Max. *The Age of Absolutism.* New York: Harper Torchbooks, 1962.
Bruun, Geoffrey, *Europe in Evolution, 1415–1815.* Boston: Houghton Mifflin, 1945.
Durant, Will, and Ariel Durant. *The Age of Louis XIV.* New York: Simon and Schuster, 1961.
———. *The Age of Reason Begins.* New York: Simon and Schuster, 1961.
Ergang, Robert. *Europe from the Renaissance to Waterloo.* New York: Heath, 1939.
Hyma, Albert. *Europe from the Renaissance to 1815.* New York: Appleton, 1931.
Trevelyan, G. M. *England Under the Stuarts.* London: Methuen, 1947.

Social and Intellectual Background

Becker, Carl L. *The Heavenly City of the Eighteenth Century Philosophers.* New Haven, Conn.: Yale University Press, 1932.
Berlin, Isaiah. (Ed.) *The Age of Enlightenment.* New York: Mentor, 1956.

Bury, John B. *The Idea of Progress.* New York: Macmillan, 1924.
Cassirer, Ernst. *Philosophy of the Enlightenment.* Boston: Beacon, 1955.
Friedrich, Carl J. *The Age of the Baroque, 1610–1660.* New York: Harper & Row, 1952.
Hampshire, Stuart. (Ed.) *The Age of Reason.* New York: Mentor, 1956.
Hazard, Paul. *European Thought in the 18th Century.* New York: Meridian, 1954.
Lecky, W. E. H. *History of the Rise and Influence of the Spirit of Rationalism in Europe.* 2 vols. New York: Appleton, 1914.
Lewis, Warren H. *The Splendid Century.* Garden City, N.Y.: Anchor, 1953.
Lovejoy, Arthur O. *The Great Chain of Being.* New York: Harper Torchbooks, 1962.
Manuel, Frank E. *The Age of Reason.* Ithaca, N.Y.: Cornell University Press, 1951.
Martin, Kingsley. *The Rise of French Liberal Thought.* Boston: Little, Brown, 1929.
Miller, Perry. *The New England Mind.* Cambridge, Mass.: Harvard University Press, 1953.
Mowat, R. B. *The Age of Reason.* Boston: Houghton Mifflin, 1934.
Ogg, David. *Europe in the 17th Century.* New York: Collier, 1965.
Stephen, Leslie. *History of English Thought in the Eighteenth Century.* 2 vols. New York: Peter Smith, 1949.
Tawney, R. H. *Religion and the Rise of Capitalism.* New York: Mentor, 1947.
Willey, Basil. *The Eighteenth Century Background.* Boston: Beacon, 1961.
———. *The Seventeenth Century Background.* Garden City, N.Y.: Anchor, 1953.

Literature

Bagley, C. R. *An Introduction to French Literature of the 17th Century.* New York: Appleton, 1937.
Caudwell, Hugo. *Introduction to French Classicism.* New York: Macmillan, 1951.
Grierson, Herbert J. C. *Cross Currents in English Literature of the Seventeenth Century.* New York: Peter Smith, 1929.
Jones, R. F. *Ancients and Moderns.* St. Louis, Mo.: Washington University Press, 1936.
Nicolson, Marjorie. *Newton Demands the Muse.* Princeton, N.J.: Princeton University Press, 1946.
Stephen, Leslie. *English Literature and Society in the Eighteenth Century.* London: Duckworth, 1920.
Turnell, Martin. *The Classical Moment.* New York: New Directions, 1946.
Wright, C. H. C. *French Classicism.* Cambridge, Mass.: Harvard University Press, 1920.

Architecture, Sculpture, Painting

Blunt, Anthony. *Art and Architecture in France—1500 to 1700.* Baltimore: Penguin, 1953.
Hamlin, Talbot F. *Greek Revival Architecture in America.* New York: Oxford University Press, 1944.

Reynolds, Sir Joshua. *Discourses on Art.* New York: Dutton, 1906.
Summerson, John N. *Architecture in Britain, 1530–1830.* Baltimore: Penguin, 1953.

Music

Carse, Adam. *The Orchestra in the 18th Century.* Cambridge: Heffer, 1940.
Einstein, Alfred. *Mozart, His Character, His Work.* New York: Oxford University
   Press, 1945.
Geiringer, Karl. *Haydn, A Creative Life in Music.* New York: Norton, 1946.
Kirkpatrick, Ralph. *Domenico Scarlatti.* Princeton, N.J.: Princeton University Press,
   1953.

CHAPTER 7
THE BAROQUE

THE BAROQUE AS STYLE

A musical form current in the seventeenth century was the passacaglia, whose harmony was a precise four- or eight-bar pattern above which soared the voices of melody. And as reason, scientism, and balance supplied the Age of Reason with a harmonic grid, so the baroque rose up melodically around them. The baroque is not a separate period; it is, rather, a separate style that speaks for the unleashed aspects of the Age of Reason. It is so compelling a style, however, that it always receives a separate chapter in art surveys, and historians sometimes label this period the Age of the Baroque. The purpose of the present chapter is twofold: to sketch the style of the baroque in a humanities profile; and by so doing to show how that style is not a separate entity but a part of a considerably larger unit.

Baroque style emerged a shade earlier than the Age of Reason, about the mid-sixteenth century, but its golden period was the seventeenth century, and with its transformation into rococo it accompanied the Age of Reason to its close. It dominated the arts of the age much as Hume's "three or four hours' amusement" canceled out his cold cerebrations, and it moved like that amusement as far away as possible from the bedrock of rationalism. For the "reason" of the Age of Reason it substituted emotion; for scientism, subjectivity; for balance, movement. It courted complexity by affixing space, size, sensualism, contrast, and heaped up ornament to its dynamic core. Sources for the word "baroque" include the Portuguese *barroco*, meaning an irregular pearl, *baroko*, a term in logic which defines a complex form of syllogism, Giacomo *Barozzi* da Vignola, the first baroque architect, and the Arabic word *buraq*, meaning uneven, pebbly ground. Baroque is a merger of all these derivations.

THE NATURE OF BAROQUE

Baroque reflects the paradoxes that play across the Age of Reason: the increasing absolutism in government alongside revolutionary concepts in social thought; the idea of progress alongside the disillusion typified by Voltaire and Swift; the ideals of good sense, taste, and moderation in an age of continual warfare; the belief in innate moral sense by skeptics; the belief in man's depravity by mystics; the new materialism of capitalism stimulated by the revived asceticism of the Counter Reformation. Thus the historian Willi Hausenstein could say, "Baroque means the unthinkable, the river with two mouths," while the philosopher Hegel assessed the baroqueness of Spinoza by comparing his view of the absolute to a lion's den to which all tracks lead and from which none return.

From a more positive standpoint, baroque reflects a challenge to rational complacency. In religion the cool reason of Deism was undermined by all of the orthodoxies, including some new ones. The Counter Reformation brought a fresh zeal and new religious excitement to Catholic countries. Its seventeenth-century champions, the Jesuits, made the church a sumptuous, ecstatic, dynamic experience. Their chief rivals in France, the Jansenists, were equally opposed to rationalism although along different lines. They taught that man was by nature weak and depraved, that reason was helpless to aid him, that only divine grace, inscrutably predestined by God, could save him. Their ascetic moral code and deep-seated emotional orthodoxy found a Protestant parallel among the Methodists, who under John Wesley split off from the Church of England and preached an emotionally charged doctrine of personal salvation. Other sects which sought refuge from reason in subjectivity were the Society of Friends, or Quakers—so named because they trembled with emotion during meetings —who relied for guidance upon "inward light," and the Moravians of Pennsylvania, Lutheran refugees who found all necessary truth in simplistic ritual.

In society, baroque idosyncrasy clashed with good sense among those very upper classes to whom the Age of Reason addressed itself. Nothing spotlights this clash so brightly as the style of dress, described by the seventeenth-century biographer, Anthony à Wood as follows: "A strange effeminate age when men strive to imitate women in their apparel, viz., long periwigs, patches in their faces, painting, short wide breeches like petticoats, muffs and their clothes highly scented, bedecked with ribbons of all colours." Exhibitionism swept across Europe and moved men everywhere to cast off restraints. Extremes of sensuality, asceticism, and gluttony broke the bounds of reason. The gardens of Versailles (Figure 6.10) bear witness to the dazzling court life of Louis XIV. The stark black costumes of the English Puritans were in their own way equally dramatic. The sensational success of Honoré D'Urfé's pastoral novel, L'Astrée, led forty-eight staid German princes and princesses to form an Academy of True Lovers and play at being D'Urfé's characters. Social groups like the affected précieuses in France and whole urban populations threw off the traces of reason and luxuriated in emotion, subjectivity, and a spacious, colorful life of action.

No city matched the extremes or captured so much of the essence of baroque as Venice at the start of the seventeenth century. Though her power was almost gone, her wealth and sophistication were unrivaled, and Venice basked in an aura of glory. Public festivals and ceremonies filled the Grand Canal with gold and silver gondolas. Private entertainments included six-hour banquets consisting of ninety courses. Venetian prostitutes—there were 20,000 in a city of less than 200,000 people—often lived in palaces and daily sifted gold dust into their hair to make it the reddish-gold color celebrated by Titian. Matrons as well as *filles de joie* wore topless dresses. When wigs became the fashion the ladies wore wigs three feet high; when raised heels grew modish they reached a height of half a yard and ladies had to be helped to walk. Men as well as women bathed in perfumes and decked themselves in ermine, rubies, pearls, emeralds, and diamonds; their every event, from births to funerals, from a cup of chocolate at bedside to an evening at the opera, became a drama filled with pomp and magnificence.

PHILOSOPHY AND BAROQUE CHARACTERISTICS

The baroque catered to the emotional side of man, the side sustained longer, as Hume understood, but not the side congenial to a discipline as rational as philosophy. The philosophers of this period cast their lot by and large with reason and scientism, but the steady pressure of the baroque affected all of them upon occasion and touched philosophical thought while sweeping society before it. We can find philosophical articulations of all the baroque characteristics except the last one—ornamentation—a technique really and outside the scope of philosophy.

Baroque *emotion* colors Hobbes' view of man as the potential victim of his passions. Hobbes called the emotions "active powers" which make "the life of man solitary, poor, nasty, brutish and short." Spinoza labeled all nonintellectual desires passions, and on that basis offered this supremely baroque definition of emotion: "An emotion, which is called a passion of the soul, is a confused idea through which the mind affirms the energy of existence possessed by its body." Pascal, with Berkeley the most baroque of philosophers, saw reason as a mere chip on the ocean of God's love: "Our intellect holds the same position in the world of thought as our body occupies in the expanse of Nature."

Despite their mathematical trappings Descartes, Spinoza, and Leibnitz were all deductive, as opposed to inductive, philosophers; that is, their cornerstone premises were *subjective*. Descartes posited the existence of God and matter, and so did Spinoza; Leibnitz' monads were his subjective starting point, attained without proof. Descartes' *Cogito ergo sum* is arrived at by a drawn out process of subjective analysis. The *petites perceptions* of Leibnitz were his pioneer, and subjective, suggestion of a stream of consciousness: "For a better understanding of *petites perceptions* let me give as illustration the moaning of the sea, which we dimly notice when we are on the shore," (and which, of course, gives us a sense of mental continuity). For Berkeley every object was the subjective projection of the mind, and nothing really existed outside of it: "Neither our thoughts, nor passions, nor ideas formed by the imagination exist without the mind . . . . their *esse* is *percipi* [their being is to be perceived]; nor is it possible they should have any existence out of the minds of thinking things which perceive them."

Berkeley turned to subjective idealism as a refuge from the scientism of the Age of Reason. Locke, in exploiting that scientism, upheld at least obliquely *sensualism*, another baroque characteristic. For Locke, as for Bacon earlier, the only reality was nature, and it could only be perceived through the senses. For Locke all that we could know came from the physical, that is, the sensual world around us. From sensations came facts; from evaluation of those sensations came ideas.

First, our senses, conversant about particular sensible objects, do convey into the mind several distinct perceptions of things, according to those various ways wherein those objects do affect them; and thus we come by those ideas we have, of yellow, white, heat, cold, soft, hard, bitter, sweet, and all those which we call sensible qualities; which when I say the senses convey into the mind, I mean they from external object convey into the mind what produces there those perceptions. This great source of most of the ideas we have, depending wholly upon our senses, and derived by them to the understanding, I call "sensation."

The dynamic energy monads of Leibnitz give an impression of constant *movement*, the baroque characteristic which offsets rational balance and symmetry. Pascal in his *Pensées* writes at length of *Disproportion de l'homme*, thus contradicting symmetry, and later speaks of "Infinite movement, the point which fills everything." Pascal also sets *size and space* in proper baroque perspective, as a yearning for infinity, in a passage fraught with baroque emotion:

I see those frightful spaces of the universe which surround me, and I find myself tied to one corner of this vast expanse, without knowing why I am put in this place rather than in another, nor why the short time which is given me to live is assigned to me at this point rather than at another of the whole eternity which was before me or which shall come after me. I see nothing but infinites on all sides, which surround me as an atom and as a shadow which endures only for an instant and returns no more.

Finally, baroque *contrast* may be found in Descartes' dichotomy between mind and matter, in Leibnitz' *petites perceptions* set against the pre-established harmony of the universe, and fullest of all in Pascal's juxtaposition of infinite and finite, light and darkness, certainty and uncertainty, ecstasy and fear, heaven and hell. For Pascal men were puny beings in a vast universe, and their greatness lay in knowledge of their own insufficiency. Suspended between the two infinites of the all and the nothing, mankind lived, according to Pascal, in a purgatory of contrasts: "It is incomprehensible that God should exist, and it is incomprehensible that He should not exist; that the soul should be joined to the body, and that we should have no soul; that the world should be created, and that it should not be created; that original sin should be, and that it should not be."

The baroque, then, offers a picture of its own society and is touched with thought, like a well-made play, and as such it also falls into three parts, a beginning, a middle, and an end, which we may subtitle mannerism, the baroque proper, and rococo, and which we shall examine one at a time in order to build up as detailed a picture as possible of the baroque style.

MANNERISM

Mannerism is a recent term, introduced in this century, which has been variously defined to the point of confusion. The following items are certain: mannerism flourished around the mid and later sixteenth century; it evolved because the Renaissance fusion of worldly and sublime brought art to a still point of perfection which could go no farther along those lines without leading to pallid imitation; and its purpose was to break away from Renaissance style. Its method, *the one demonstrable one*, was to imitate earlier classical and/or Renaissance styles, and thus achieve originality by starting with a prefabricated manner and by moving on from there. Mannerist art therefore stressed form over content, and by so doing cleared the way for new content and for new experiments with form.[1]

LITERATURE.   In Italy Giangiorgio Trissino set out to write an epic using the style of the *Iliad* and Aristotle's rule that an epic deal with violent action and impressive spectacle. His *L'Italia liberata dai Goti* (Italy liberated from the Goths), 1547, makes the Emperor Justinian a latter day Achilles and tells the story of his triumph in blank verse, although Italian, unlike Greek, lends itself to rhyme. The result is a turgid twenty years' effort alien to Renaissance style and spirit. François de Malherbe (1555–1628) wrote poetry modeled on the prosaic style of Horace. His concern for Horatian simplicity of language and diction led to the foundation of the Academy of Letters and almost singlehandedly checked the continuance of the French Renaissance. In Germany Martin Opitz (1597–1639) followed Malherbe in urging "verbal correctness" and proposed a mannered imitation of Renaissance authors. In Spain Luis de Léon (1527–1591) wrote poetry in the style of Horace remarkable for its spare simplicity. In England Ben Jonson blended mannerist ingredients—characters and situations from Plautus and Terence, the unities of Aristotle—with his own sardonic savagery to produce the best literature in this style. *Every Man in His Humor* and *Epicene* are among his finest mannerist plays.

---

[1] This explanation of mannerism can be confirmed by the humanities approach, as will be shown. The many additional interpretations blend mannerism with the baroque, as their proponents come to admit. The most challenging interpretation is one by Arnold Hauser (*The Social History of Art*) which demonstrates, through painting only, that mannerism contains the germ of intellectual surrealism.

ARCHITECTURE.   For a brief period in the later sixteenth century architecture witnessed a revival of the forms of ancient Roman building. Its champion was Andrea Palladio (1518–1580) who wrote four books of architecture modeled on the rules laid down by Vitruvius. In his preface (to his architectural canon) Palladio states:

> I ever was of opinion that the ancient Romans did far exceed all that have come after them . . . I betook myself to the search and examination of such ruins of ancient structures as, in spite of time and the rude hands of barbarians, are still remaining; and finding that they deserved a much more diligent observation than I thought at first sight, I began with the utmost accuracy to measure even the minutest part by itself.

Guided by these principles he produced a series of distinctive mannered works that broke away from accepted Renaissance practice. His *Villa Rotonda* (Figure 7.1) exemplifies the detached purity of his Roman imitation. Its four identical entrances copy the raised front of a Roman temple façade. Its dome surmounting the square body of the building itself resembles the exterior of the Pantheon, and the total effect is chilly in contrast to the harmonious warmth of a true Renaissance structure like the *Tempietto* of Bramante (Figure 5.20). The Roman Palace of Caprarola by Vignola

Figure 7.1   ANDREA PALLADIO.   Villa Rotonda, Vicenza. (Begun in 1550).   [Alinari: Art Reference Bureau].

adheres to Palladio's mannerist style, but it is one of the few buildings to do so. For the most part later so-called Palladians, from Inigo Jones to Thomas Jefferson, combine his mannerism with special adaptations. Palladio himself introduced an adaptation known as the Palladian Motive, an arched opening bracketed by two shorter rectangular ones, in such works as his Basilica at Vicenza.

SCULPTURE.   Mannerism at its earliest and worst form in sculpture appeared in the statues of Baccio Bandinelli (1493–1560), inflated doughy imitations of the style of Michelangelo. The finest of the mannerists was Giovanni da Bologna (c. 1524–1608), and his *Rape of the Sabine Women* (Figure 7.2) is his best work in that style. It takes three different figures—female, youthful male, and mature male—through a range of contortions. Like the Hellenistic sculptor of *Venus of Milo* (Figure 2.18), Giovanni captures in stone the soft texture of female flesh, in contrast to the firmer musculature of the men. The bodies of the girl and older man are twisted in the *contrapposto* style of Michelangelo; the youth's left shoulder is hunched upward like Michelangelo's *David* (Figure 5.8); his body, like the *David*, hints at the Praxitelian S-curve; and the work as a whole, like the *David*, is more than thirteen feet tall. The head of the older man is copied directly from *Laocoön* (Figure 2.24). The contortions lead the viewer around the work and make it effective from every angle. This impulse to movement foreshadows the baroque, and Giovanni's famous bronze *Flying Mercury*, where movement overshadows classical style, is a baroque rather than a mannerist work. A number of contemporary sculptors, notably Hubert Gerhard—best known for his *Fountain of Augustus* in Augsburg which is reminiscent of *Augustus Addressing His Troops* (Figure 3.7)—imitated the mannerism of Giovanni by copying his style, thereby limiting themselves to a reality three times removed. These sculptors spread the mannerist protest across western Europe.

PAINTING.   By the mid-sixteenth century painters like Pontormo, Bronzino, and Parmigianino had broken loose from the Renaissance by means of mannerism. In 1583 three cousins, Ludovico, Agostino, and Annibale Carracci founded the Bolognese Academy, a mannerist school, which held that by starting with the power of Michelangelo, the color of Titian, and the sweetness of Raphael the artist could go on to excel his sources. The *Galatea* (Figure 7.3) typifies the work of this academy. A wall decoration for the palace of a Roman cardinal, it depicts the love of Acis and the nymph Galatea, but with no hint of the tragedy to come. Galatea has the wide-eyed face of a Raphael Madonna and the ripe body of Titian's *Sacred Love* (Figure 5.24); the suave coloring too belongs to Titian. Acis is copied from a Hellenistic statue of Hercules. The seated figures on either side of him derive their power and *contrapposto* poses from Michelangelo. The winged

Figure 7.2 Giovanni da Bologna. *Rape of the Sabine Women.* (1583). Loggia dei Lanzi, Florence. [Alinari: Art Reference Bureau].

Figure 7.3   ANNIBALE AND AGOSTINO CARRACCI.   *Galatea* (ceiling fresco).   (c. 1600). Farnese Palace, Rome.   [Alinari: Art Reference Bureau].

putti resemble those of Raphael. A whimsical mannerist touch is the frame painted around three sides of this mural and underneath its lower edge, giving it the look of a framed canvas.

Painting was influenced by mannerism more than any other art form, probably because the largest number of great creative Renaissance artists were painters; they offered a greater range of manners to imitate. Mannerist painters did work of some significance in almost every country of Europe. In France François Clouet combined the elegance of Raphael and the psychological insight of Holbein in his portraiture. Flemish Jan van Sorel combined Michelangelo's power with German somberness of color and background. In Spain Luis de Morales based his style on the *contrapposto* of Michelangelo and on da Vinci's handling of darkness and light.

MUSIC.   The dynamism of Orlando di Lasso, succeeding the serene balance between sonority and structure in the music of Josquin and Palestrina, heralds the coming of mannerism in music. But di Lasso remains at core a Renaissance composer, and it was somewhat later that a composer broke away from Renaissance perfection. Carlo Gesualdo, Prince of Venosa (c. 1560–1613), did so by turning toward chromaticism. Chromaticism makes use of tones not in the regular diatonic (eight-note) scale of a composition, and in general favors half steps instead of whole steps—in a sense it reverts to the smaller intervals favored by the ancients. Gesualdo used it to achieve unique emotional impact, and his madrigals mark a novel change in sound from the music of the Renaissance. His madrigal *Io pur respiro* (in Davison-Apel, *Historical Anthology of Music*, Volume I) illustrates not only his chromaticism in melody but also his chordal use of it to achieve special and different harmonic effects. The Florentine Camerata, a late sixteenth-century group dedicated to reviving Greek and Roman music, might also be classified as mannerist. Without actual classical models, however, their output had the rarified quality of speculation. Their most ambitious production, the *Dafne* of Ottavio Rinuccini (1594), now lost, apparently was a tame forerunner of the burst of baroque operas that followed soon after.

Gesualdo and Rinuccini fall short of being major composers, a penalty that they like all purely mannerist artists would have to pay for novelty and for emphasizing form over content. Once mannerism had paved the way for a new form of art, however, content too could be developed and the resultant art could be brought to a pitch of greatness. That greatness arrived with the baroque.

BAROQUE

Baroque art pulsates with vivid characteristics, commingled and further complicated by the state of seventeenth-century Europe. Individual and distinctive nation-states emerged at this time; thus the baroque had to accommodate Catholic courtiers, Anglican gentry, Lutheran middle classes, and Slavic near-barbarians. With variants like these to contend with, plus the natural tendency of baroque emotion, subjectivity, movement, space, sensualism, contrast, and ornament to jumble together, isolating individual characteristics will be at best arbitrary. We will use the scalpel of classification in order to build a composite picture of the baroque, but overlapping will be fluid and national colorings diversionary, as may be expected.

Emotion

In baroque art, emotion is expressed by an intensity of feelings which mounts on occasion to dramatic or melodramatic heights.

LITERATURE.   Emotion buffeted early baroque literature with an explosion of feeling, almost as though the dikes of Renaissance serenity had burst. The *Adone* of Marino (1623), tells the story of Venus' mad passion for a jittery Adonis melted to tears or ardor as the situation warrants. His reactions are like those of a chaste and fearful maiden, adding a perverse sensual fillip to the emotional excitement of the situation. In *L'Astrée* (1627), Honoré D'Urfé uses a similar timorous chastity to achieve a pathos bordering on the absurd. Celadon, in love with the shepherdess Astrée, vows to separate from her for three years. He hides in the forest where she resides, weeps incessantly, and lives on a diet of watercress. In *La Princesse de Clèves* (1678) Mme. de Lafayette uses a self-imposed emotional strain as motivation for the first modern psychological novel. Although she is in love with another man, the Princess remains true to her husband and then to his memory, while her passion ebbs with the slow passing of time. Corneille in *Le Cid* let Chimène's passion for Rodrigue overcome her sense of duty, and the rationalistic Academy of Letters made the author pay for it. Racine's *Phèdre* suffers a passion so intense that it batters against the stiff academic structure of his drama. Molière in *George Dandin* prods the emotions to a painful peak. Dandin, like Molière a member of the middle class, marries a noblewoman who betrays him, because it is the fashionable thing to do, while he waits outside in an agony of shame. Donne in his *Meditations* broods on the ecstasy of union with God and on the torment of man's responsibility to man. The metaphysical poetry of Richard Crashaw throbs with an almost embarrassing intensity of passion; an excellent example is "The Flaming Heart," with its grand apostrophe to St. Theresa beginning, "O thou undaunted daughter of desires." Milton's *Paradise Lost* is a succession of melodramatic episodes: the fall of Satan; his renewed defiance of God; the devils' transformation into hissing snakes; the temptation of Eve; the fall of Adam. His *Samson Agonistes* heightens drama with subjective feeling in the scene where the blinded Samson confronts his father (much as Milton imagined he and his own beloved father might have done). *Paradise Regained* closes with one of the most dramatic scenes in all literature, where Satan, toppled from the minaret, realizes that the man he has been tempting and taunting is actually the Son of God.

In Germany the bitter lyrics of Andreas Gryphius are uncontrolled outcries against the worthlessness of life. In Spain the plays of Lope de Vega combine Spanish intensity with baroque emotion; in *Fuente Ovejuna* the rape of Laurencia, the torture of the villagers of Fuente Ovejuna, and their gallant courage form a dramatic crescendo not found in the work of any previous Spanish writer.

ARCHITECTURE.   Baroque buildings tended to become an integrated and dramatic whole whose size, ornament, color, and imbalance strike the senses with dramatic impact. Sacred or secular, baroque buildings alternate open, lighted spaces with closed, dark ones; ornate naves or salons lead into cramped vaults or to square rooms that alternate with circular ones. Pediments are broken, columns twisted, cornices projected, and scrolls, *putti*, and leafy ornaments sprout everywhere. Bare walls clash with rich wood panelings and straight lines alternate with restless, curving ones.

Bernini's colonnade (Figure 5.14) which serves as prologue to St. Peter's illustrates the dramatic impact of a baroque exterior. Its size alone is overwhelming and its austere Doric columns form provoking contrast with the cluttered façade and scalloped dome. The interior of the *Gesù* (Figure 7.4), the first church built by the Jesuits, points up the dramatic quality of baroque interiors. Built by Vignola with additions by his pupil

Giacomo della Porta, the *Gesù* ushers in the full tide of the baroque. The *Spiritual Exercises* of Ignatius Loyola, founder of the Jesuit order, aimed to lead the novice to a mystic ecstasy engulfing the senses as well as the intellect, and the *Gesù* realized that aim in stone. The nave, long and wider than usual, focuses attention upon the altar where the drama of the Mass is enacted. Instead of side aisles to distract from the central thrust of attention, chapels are recessed into the walls, their arched openings alternating with rectangles in abrupt contrast. Above the arches and rectangles patterns of ornament contribute a heavy, sensual effect. The nave is dark (difficult to tell in a photograph) and the light pouring through the central dome sets off the altar in theatrical contrast. Dramatic focus, contrast, and sensuous ornament combine to form an integrated whole; the entire effect is at once lush and compelling. So successful was this plan that it became the model for baroque Jesuit churches everywhere, and soon reappeared as far away as Mexico.

Figure 7.4   Giacomo Barozzi da Vignola and Giacomo della Porta.   Il Gesù, Rome.   (c. 1568–1584).   [Alinari: Art Reference Bureau].

In Venice the high-domed *Santa Maria della Salute* by Baldassare Longhena made vaulting space the basis for dramatic effect. In Paris Jules Mansart's *Dome des Invalides,* a triple dome, achieves a similar effect. In Spain the church of *Santiago de Compostela* by Fernando Casas y Novoa achieved a telling impact by means of its lavish, light-sprayed façade. The Viennese Belvedere Palace of Lukas von Hildebrandt translates the sensuous drama of the *Gesù* into secular terms.

SCULPTURE.   Toward the close of the Renaissance, Michelangelo and Cellini provided transition to the baroque by encompassing both styles within their work. The hushed feeling in Michelangelo's *Pietà Rondanini* (Figure 5.16), the dramatic power of his *Moses,* and the melodrama of Cellini's *Perseus,* where blood spurts from the severed neck and gory head of Medusa, all introduce the coming style. Gian Lorenzo Bernini raised the style to its apex. His early *David* shows a youth with lips disfigured by emotion, who is about to launch a rock from his sling. *The Ecstasy of St. Theresa* (Figure 7.5), intensifies emotion into wonder. In her autobiography St. Theresa of Avila describes how an angel appeared to her in a dream and pierced her body with an arrow; the ecstasy of this wound caused her to faint. It is this dramatic moment that Bernini portrays. The saint, her head thrown back, has given way *physically* to her ecstasy while the angel, sculpted in cream white marble, smiles like a coquette. Flowing robes cast a shimmer of movement over the entire work and draw attention to the dreamer's naked foot, its fleshy texture a firm contrast to the vaporous clouds on which she reclines. Light from a gold-tinted window hidden in the ceiling bathes the figures in golden rays and contrasts with the darker recess behind them. Set in a niche of colored marble the work resembles a scene from the theater; or, better, the *Gesù* in another art form.

Like Michelangelo, Bernini had no comparable successors. Those who came after him mastered parts but not the whole of baroque complexity. Alessandro Algardi conveyed excitement and bustling movement in his relief altarpiece of *St. Leo and Attila.* Guillaume Costou achieved these same qualities in his prancing *Horse* (Figure 7.11). Pierre Puget, one of the most original of baroque sculptors, conveys a special sense of agony in his *Milo of Crotona* (Figure 7.16). The works of Gregorio Hernández are bathed in sentimentality; one example is his wooden statue of *The Dead Christ* in the Valladolid Museum, with its painted staring eyes and its lips parted as if about to speak in pain. Andreas Schlüter went to comparable extremes in his giant masks of dying soldiers.

PAINTING.   Matching the rampant emotionalism of Marino and D'Urfé are Caravaggio's canvases, which are forerunners of several new developments. His *Entombment of Christ* (Figure 7.6) contains them all. For one thing it is more representational, more concerned with straight photographic repro-

Figure 7.5 GIAN LORENZO BERNINI. *The Ecstasy of St. Theresa.* (1645–1652).
Santa Maria della Vittoria, Rome. [Alinari: Art Reference Bureau].

duction than any previous painter's work. Like Bernini's *Ecstasy,* the *Entombment* might well be a scene from the theater, but from a realistic drama. Caravaggio went into the streets for his models, and the careworn face of the Virgin and the wrinkled brow and sturdy feet of Nicodemus have a street-scene quality that heightens the physical impact of this work. Caravaggio also handles light in a special way, setting up extreme contrasts between light and dark for dramatic effect; the starkly lighted body of Christ is shocking against its brown-black background. And Caravaggio pioneered in the exploration of emotion; here it is muted in the expression of the Virgin, affecting in the expression on the dead Christ, unstoppered in the rolling eyes, open mouth, and flailing arms of the Magdalene. With all that he added to seventeenth-century painting, Caravaggio remained an explorer. How far he fell short of achievement may be seen in the work of the following artist who profited from his innovations.

In *Supper at Emmaus* (Figure 7.7) Rembrandt van Rijn channels emotion into undercurrents of piety and mystery. The face of the risen Christ, which has looked through death and beyond, glows with unspeakable knowledge, and the soft brown and grey background enhances the mystery. A mild light hovers around him, contrasting with the background but at the same time commenting by its own mysterious illumination upon the meaning of the scene. Like Caravaggio, Rembrandt took his models from everyday life, in this case from the Amsterdam ghetto, but he manages to transform realism into a deep-felt *essential* authenticity.

Baroque emotion found widespread favor among painters of this period. Tintoretto expresses it through gesture in his *Last Supper.* The "Little Dutch Masters" express it through genre: Brower through rollicking tavern scenes; Ostade through somber scenes of peasant life; Steen through sentimental middle-class episodes. In Spain Jusepe Ribera imitates Caravaggio, while El Greco (Figures 7.9, 7.17) uses fervor as part of a rich complex of moods and meanings. Light and distance cover the work of Claude Lorrain (Figure 6.14) with a soft veil of sentiment.

MUSIC.   In one of the most ingenious studies of any of the arts, Heinrich Wölfflin (*Principles of Art History*) conceives of a dividing wall between Renaissance and baroque painting. According to him Renaissance painting is enclosed within the borders of its canvas, set in a series of recessive planes, with its figures encased in linear outlines; baroque painting leads the eye beyond the borders of the canvas, makes depth a unified space, and blurs the outlines of its figures. These dichotomies are often, though not always, apt. A sharper and perhaps more universal distinction might be drawn between Renaissance and baroque music, the former self-contained, the latter charged with feeling. There is a wide contrast between a Josquin motet and a Vivaldi concerto, the most obvious and essential cause of which is the baroque characteristic of emotion. Technically the overriding emotionalism of baroque music means dissonance, shifts in rhythm, larger intervals,

Figure 7.6   CARAVAGGIO (Michelangelo Merisi).   *Entombment of Christ.*   (c. 1603).
Vatican Gallery, Rome.   [Alinari: Art Reference Bureau].

Figure 7.7 Rembrandt van Rijn. *Supper at Emmaus.* (1648). Louvre, Paris. [Photographie Giraudon].

shorter notes. Essentially it derives from Italian preoccupation with melody plus German concern for intensity of expression. In Italian opera Claudio Monteverdi, the first major opera composer, set the style by stressing vivid portrayal of feelings. The famous lament salvaged from his lost opera *Arianna* is a milestone in vocal expressiveness, and his passionate and moving *Coronation of Poppea* is still performed. The Neopolitan opera style that succeeded Monteverdi stressed vocal gymnastics and affecting, sentimental arias, appealing to ears and emotions alike, as in the early operas of Alessandro Scarlatti. In England Henry Purcell combined the features of both sources in his opera *Dido and Aeneas.* Dido's aria, "When I Am Laid in Earth," rivals Monteverdi's lament for purity of feeling. The operatic reforms of the Bohemian Christoph Willibald Gluck sheared away useless ornament and returned opera to the dramatic purity of Monteverdi; *Orfeo* and *Alceste* contain undercurrents of feeling akin to those in *Supper at Emmaus.* Mozart superadded classicism and rococo courtliness to his operas but retained and brought to fresh perfection Italian concern for melody. *Voi che sapete* (you who know) and *Dove sono* (where am I) from *The Marriage of Figaro* and *Non mi dir* (tell me not) from *Don Giovanni* are a few masterful examples from among many.

Among other forms of vocal music, the cantata—a scene or scenes for chorus, soloist, and instrumental accompaniment—was developed in Italy and brought to dramatically expressive perfection by Johann Sebastian Bach. An expanded form of cantata narrating the Passion, the so-called Passion Oratorio, received powerful emotional treatment by Bach in his *St. John* and *St. Matthew Passions*. George Frederic Handel blended opera, cantata, and the English choral style of writing to create oratorios, operas presented in concert form, on biblical themes for the most part, where the chorus serves as a powerful and dramatic organ of expression: his *Messiah* has become one of the best known works in all music.

In instrumental music the concertos of Vivaldi first stressed the importance of slow movements, which in these works became singing and expressive. Bach in his concertos, chorale preludes, suites, *partitas,* toccatas, and fugues mingled every current of baroque musical feeling together with his own high seriousness to create a special atmosphere of musical expressiveness. Haydn and Mozart in their instrumental works stayed within the general confines of Classical form, but like Racine in *Phèdre* rattled against that form with bursts of emotion. Haydn characteristically stirs up feeling through his crispness and drive, as in the final movements of his London symphonies; Mozart does so through an undercurrent of sorrow, almost pain, that plucks at the surface gaiety of his music, as in his last piano concerto and final symphonies.

Music in America at this time also tended toward baroque emotionalism, in the deep-felt chorales of Johann Conrad Beissel, for example, sung by his Seventh Day Adventists in Ephrata, Pennsylvania, and in the taste for Italianate opera first nurtured in Charleston, South Carolina.

Subjectivity

Baroque subjectivity meant a drive toward self-expression at the expense of existing standards and styles. Subjectivity had influenced earlier art to some degree through the individualism of the Renaissance, and in cases where isolated geniuses like Euripides and Michelangelo, in the *Bacchae* and the *Pietà Rondanini* (Figure 5.16), broke through into private worlds. With the baroque such subjectivity became the property of many, and a need to push beyond boundaries in order to achieve a special voice became a way of art, showing up in all areas as experiments in style. In literature, music, and some painting, it also appeared as probing introspection.

LITERATURE.   The controlled tension of Racine, working within the fixed couplet form that he makes his own special instrument, achieves stylistic effects like those of no other writer, as in the third scene of *Phèdre* where his heroine confesses her passion to Oenone. The poetic style of Donne, a blend of earthy images and writhing emotion, is also special. The allusive and sonorous "Miltonic line" of *Paradise Lost* was never heard before, nor was the amazing, contrived style of Sir Thomas Browne, who said of sleep and dreams:

> But the quincunx of heaven runs low, and 'tis time to close the five ports of knowledge; we are unwilling to spin out our awaking thoughts into the phantasms of sleep, which often continueth precogitations, making cables of cobwebs and wildernesses of handsome groves. Besides Hippocrates hath spoke so little and the oneirocritical masters have left such frigid interpretations from plants that there is little encouragement to dream of paradise itself. Nor will the sweetest delight of gardens afford much comfort in sleep; wherein the dullness of that sense shakes hands with delectable odors, and though in the bed of Cleopatra, can hardly with any delight raise up the ghost of a rose.

The savage style of Gryphius and the distinctive blend of ornament and thoughtfulness of Spanish dramatist Calderón de la Barca have their own inimitable qualities. Here is Calderón punning profoundly on dreams:

> *Que es la vida?—Una ilusión,*
> *Una sombra, una ficción,*
> *Y el mayor bien es pequeño;*
> *Que toda la vida es sueño,*
> *Y los sueños sueño son.*

(What is life?—an illusion, a shadow, a fiction, and the greatest good is but little; all life is a dream, and dreams themselves a dream.)

Subjective introspection in literature enriches *The Princess of Cleves* of Mme. de Lafayette, whose heroine indulges in long analytical monologues on why she wished to, but cannot in all conscience, marry the Duke of Nemours. Milton's analyses of Samson in *Samson Agonistes* are mainly subjective analyses of himself. Racine probes the unconscious with a depth possible only in an age concerned with the subjective workings of the mind. Phèdre's speech to Hippolyte on how she would have accompanied him into the labyrinth so they might face the Cretan bull together is a remarkable anticipation of Freudian symbolism. In *Life Is a Dream* by Calderón, Segismundo, shuttled between his dungeon and the outside world, learns in the dark dream of his dungeon to understand his deepest self.

Architecture.   All of the baroque visual arts displayed the new concern for subjective expression. Architecture deserted such collective styles as Gothic, Romanesque, and blunt imitation of classical forms in favor of individual styles and ornamentation; sculpture followed Michelangelo away from Renaissance composure into a realm of speculative tension; painting cut itself adrift from rigid classical and Christian symbolisms and ventured far afield. Subjective expression not only evolved a new way of art but also a whole new theory of creativity. Federigo Zuccaro offers this typical presentation of it in his *Idea of Sculptors, Painters and Architects:* "By Inward Design is meant the concept in our minds which allows us to imagine the shape of any object and to work from that image. Thus we artists who wish to paint or sketch some object suitably, for example the Annunciation, first form in our minds as clear an image as possible." In other words, a work of art is endowed with form not by divine inspiration nor by infallible rules but by the subjective working of the artist's mind.

Michelangelo gave impetus to subjectivity in architecture in works like the vestibule of the Laurentian Library in Florence, where, at the architect's whim, blind windows set in interior walls let in no light and recessed columns support nothing. Though the *Gesù* of Vignola lost most of its distinctiveness by being copied everywhere, its original creation marked a breakthrough for self-expression. Borromini played with curve, contrast, and distortion as it pleased him, thereby achieving the unique style of the Church of San Carlo (Figure 7.10). Wren mingled tradition and his own fancy to create the spiny church steeples he erected all over London

Figure 7.8   REMBRANDT VAN RIJN.   *Rembrandt Laughing Before the Bust of a Roman Emperor.*   (c. 1668).   Museum, Cologne.   [Marburg: Art Reference Bureau].

Figure 7.9 EL GRECO (Domenico Theotokopoulos). *View of Toledo.* (c. 1610). The Metropolitan Museum of Art, Bequest of Mrs. H. O. Havemeyer, 1929. The H. O. Havemeyer Collection.

(Figure 7.19). Hildebrandt gave vent to sheer fantasy in producing interiors like Pommersfelden Castle (Figure 7.18). And the *Petit Trianon* of Gabriel (Figure 6.11) glows with an inimitable sense of harmony that transcends scientific rules.

SCULPTURE. The one major baroque sculptor was Bernini, and he achieved subjective self-expression in a variety of modes. In dramatic genre work, *The Ecstasy of St. Theresa* has a flamboyant intensity all its own. In ornamental sculpture, the twisting columns and overladen *Baldacchino* (canopy) above the High Altar in St. Peter's Cathedral (Figure 7.20) are as elaborate and original as any work of supreme quality has ever been. His fountain of Triton at Rome vies with the movement of the water to achieve a rare fluidity. His free-standing *David* is alive with a momentary tension that creates its own school. The only other sculptor of the period who achieved a high degree of subjective originality was Pierre Puget, whose *Milo of Crotona* (Figure 7.16) contrasts violent movement with rigid form to fabricate a scream encased in stone.

PAINTING.   Baroque painting went beyond sculpture or even architecture, its use of subjective distortion. Caravaggio makes light and dark the products of a special vision and emotionalism break through the barriers of taste. Rembrandt entered a world so private that he sealed himself off from the very age that produced him. In one of his final self-portraits, *Rembrandt Laughing Before the Bust of a Roman Emperor* (Figure 7.8), parts of the face dissolve in the mystery of darkness, and only uncanny attitudes remain exposed to light: a wrinkled eye that has seen what the shadows conceal; a still defiant nose; a suggestion of a mouth implying a mocking knowledge. To the left is the Roman emperor in dissected profile, gazing at Rembrandt like a ravaged alter ego. The lumpy surface of this painting matches its subjective thrusts, and is high or low according to degrees of light and darkness.

El Greco also achieved a unique subjectivity in works like *View of Toledo* (Figure 7.9), where nature and man's handiwork are restated in terms of an artist's astounding vision. The first painted landscape devoid of human figures, *View of Toledo* is infused throughout with the presence of its creator. A sky that never was presses down in puffs of blue and white upon a green landscape whose curves and clustered buildings bend to the maker's will.

Brueghel made peasant energy, with its closeness to nature, evoke a rugged world all his own, as in his *Wedding Dance* (Figure 7.12). Velásquez toyed with the appearance of reality in pictorial illusions whose true reality was space, as in *The Maids of Honor* (Figure 7.14). The fleshy dynamism of Rubens (Figure 7.15) was special to him alone. Even those masters who found the Age of Reason congenial partook of baroque subjectivity. The serene backdrops of Poussin (Figure 6.4), the ardent vistas of Claude (Figure 6.14), and the luminous geometry of Vermeer (Figure 6.5) made for styles as inimitable as those of Rembrandt and El Greco.

MUSIC.   Vivaldi, Bach, Handel, Haydn, and Mozart achieved unique sounds, as a hearing of their music makes apparent at once. In addition, baroque music, like literature, probed subjectivity through content as well as style. The organ preludes and fugues, the *St. Matthew Passion,* and the *Mass in B Minor* of Bach brood and ponder as no previous music had. Mozart's somber, contrapuntal *Adagio and Fugue in C Minor,* K. 546, and his final, unfinished *Requiem,* like Rembrandt's portrait, examine ultimate questions and hint at answers to them.

Movement

For the baroque artists, movement was the device by which they shook loose from Renaissance stability. Baroque movement tends toward imbalance, also in defiance of Renaissance poise, but not in every case; movement in baroque music, for example, stems from rhythmic as well as arhythmic effects.

new findings in astronomy and the voyages of discovery
̱e development of movement as an important element in
̱ture. The *Somnium* of Kepler narrates a voyage to the moon,
̱peare in such later plays as *Antony and Cleopatra*, *Pericles*, and
̱pest conveys a sense of movement whose essential impression is
̱ue. Movement penetrates baroque literature more deeply, though, in
̱ area of style. The elaborate style of John Lyly's *Euphues* ushered in a
̱aroque manner known as Euphuism matched by *Marinismo* (after Marino)
in Italy and *Gongorismo* (after Luis de Argote y Gongora) in Spain. Using
an assortment of devices including alliteration, contrast, allusion, and
figurative language, Lyly's manner inflates sentences to enormous length.
Broken into subordinate clauses, phrases, and single-word appositives they
take on a driving rhythm, now regular, now irregular, akin to the rhythms
of baroque music. As baroque style developed, this manner merged with
subjectivity to form the prose styles of Donne, Browne, Milton, and
Robert Burton, to cite only a few English examples. The following sentence
about air from Burton's *Anatomy of Melancholy* illustrates how movement,
in this case rising and falling, penetrates a seminal baroque style:

> As a long-winged Hawk when he is first whistled off the fist, mounts aloft, and for
> his pleasure fetcheth many a circuit in the air, still soaring higher and higher, till
> he but come to his full pitch, and in the end, when the game is sprung, comes down
> amain, and stoops upon a sudden, so will I, having now come at last into these ample
> fields of Air wherein I may freely expatiate and exercise myself for my recreation, a
> while rove, wander round about the world, mount aloft to those ethereal orbs and
> celestial spheres, and so descend to my former elements again.

ARCHITECTURE.   Michelangelo introduced movement as a major factor
into baroque architecture with the three not quite parallel, not quite
perpendicular, not quite level buildings he used to border the Capitoline
Hill in Rome. The sweeping oval of Bernini's colonnade (Figure 5.14) evokes
a sense of movement through size, curving shape, and rhythmic regularity.
The vaulted arches, circular dome, and jutting, broken cornices of the
Gesù give the effect of motion flowing in all directions. Curved or expanding diagonal staircases became a baroque specialty, as in Pommersfelden
(Figure 7.18) and in the Piazza di Spagna in Rome. The façade of the
Church of San Carlo by Francesco Borromini (Figure 7.10) is a whirlpool of
curves, ovals, broken lines, curling leaves, and figures in motion. Horizontal lines undulate in courses which are reversed from the first landing to the
second. The balustrades are similarly curved and reversed, and waving
curves around the upper oval keep the movement going right up to the
very top. The four pairs of columns provide a vertical thrust that clashes
with, and complicates, the horizontal movement, and the pair of towers
above with their curved faces and sharp-angled cornices cap the façade
with a fresh burst of movement. San Carlo is a small church, and all its
movement is cramped together, giving off a restless and disjointed energy
that speaks more properly for the architect than for its size.

SCULPTURE.   The *contrapposto* of Michelangelo charged baroque sculpture with a sense of movement—urgent in *Bound Slave* and *Moses,* muted in the *Pietà Rondanini* (Figure 5.16). In Bernini's *The Ecstasy of St. Theresa* rippling draperies, the angel's broad gestures, the *contrapposto* of the saint, and the floating cloud create a jumble of movements akin to Borromini's San Carlo. The spiraling columns supporting his canopy in St. Peter's (Figure 7.20) make ceaseless and irregular upward thrusts. Fountains received dramatic treatment in the baroque period, their flow of water matched by the flow of sculptural design, as in the Triton and Four Rivers fountains of Bernini and the fountains of Versailles. Movement is the salient characteristic of the *Horse* of Guillaume Costou (Figure 7.11), where forelegs, mane, tail, rearing stance, and trainer's tensed body contribute to the unit gesture of the work. In the statue of *Voltaire* by Houdon (Figure 6.2) the hunched shoulder and the play of the hands in part belie the body's repose.

PAINTING.   In painting, form was the basic cause of baroque urgency of movement. In place of the stable squares, circles, isosceles triangles, and straight lines of the Renaissance, baroque art tended toward trapeziums, ovals, diagonals, and curves whose irregularity and incompleteness made for a sense of motion. The *Wedding Dance* by Pieter Brueghel the Elder (Figure 7.12) quivers with baroque irregularity. Tree trunks and huts form skewed triangles, dancing groups form ovals, and spectators form a serpentine line that wanders off beyond the canvas. Each dancer bends in a way that clashes with his neighbors, and the earth beneath the dancers' feet creates a similar network of flowing curves. The surface activity of dancing is thus mirrored in the essential forms of nature. An early baroque master, Brueghel made his subjective world a place in which mankind and nature become one.

In the *Entombment* of Caravaggio movement as well as emotion is made obvious by the waving of arms. In the *Rape of the Daughters of Leucippus* by Rubens (Figure 7.15) movement stems from *contrapposto* and from the subtle pattern of interlinking ovals in the composition. In *View of Toledo* El Greco achieves movement through streaks of color and curving lines; in *Resurrection* (Figure 7.17) elongated bodies, an upward thrust, and a tangle of curves at the bottom of the canvas produce a dualism of movement central to meaning. The Dutch genre painters—Ostade, Steen, Terborch, de Hooch—make movement through gesture an important feature of their work. Vermeer (Figure 6.5) uses imbalance of design—rectangles, for the most part incomplete and arranged in an asymmetrical pattern—to suggest movement within the immovable boundaries of a room. Claude (Figure 6.14) makes his axis of light also serve as a shaft of motion.

MUSIC.   As was the case with emotion, the driving energy of baroque music is plainly apparent, as a Josquin motet and Vivaldi concerto will

Figure 7.10 FRANCESCO BORROMINI. Church of San Carlo, Rome. (1662–1667). [Alinari: Art Reference Bureau].

Figure 7.11 GUILLAUME COSTOU. *Horse.* (c. 1725). Paris. [Bulloz: Art Reference Bureau].

Figure 7.12 PIETER BRUEGHEL THE ELDER. *Wedding Dance.* (1566). Courtesy of the Detroit Institute of Arts.

again make clear. The bar length introduced in the seventeenth century made for a driving beat that, to trace one line of its development, became a part of Lutheran congregational singing and then of the style of Bach. His orchestral *Suite No. 3 in D Major,* for example, adds this driving beat to a stately melody by Lully to create a vigorous effect.

The technique of diminution, which broke up one long note into several shorter ones, added speed and energy to melody, as the concertos of Vivaldi (also strongly rhythmic) exemplify. The finales of Haydn's symphonies, the London symphonies particularly, make similar use of diminution and driving rhythms, and their greater economy of thematic materials gives them an even greater force of movement. Many of Mozart's arias, rapid and rhythmic, are marvels of energy; for example, *Non so più cosa son* (I no longer know what I am) and *Non più andrai* (you will go no more) from *The Marriage of Figaro,* Don Giovanni's drinking song, and the Queen of the Night aria from *The Magic Flute.*

A new ornament, the ballet, was joined with baroque music to add visual movement to the aural effect. Jean-Baptiste Lully first combined the two media in works like *Xerxes* and *The Triumph of Love.* An English variant was the masque—courtly drama, dance, and spectacle—such as the masque of *Comus* with music by Henry Lawes and a text by Milton.

Size and Space

The new astronomy and the voyages of discovery opened up a more spacious universe and a larger world, which affected the surface of baroque art somewhat. But a more central, more *baroque,* cause was the yearning for infinity that went hand in hand with the dramatic, the need for movement, and the subjective breaking of boundaries to make for vaster enterprises than were common to the Renaissance or Middle Ages.

LITERATURE.   The surgeon Sir William Osler once stated that Shakespeare lived in a world of time, while Milton lived in a universe of space. Shakespeare's earlier plays were time-bound, but his later ones often tend toward a baroque spaciousness. *Antony and Cleopatra* ranges back and forth across half the world; *The Tempest* sets an island microcosm adrift in infinity. Milton in *Paradise Lost* luxuriates in the boundlessness of space: the rebel angels, hurled from heaven to deepest chaos, wander about a "vast and boundless deep," and Satan, whose shield is like a moon, journeys across a darkness visible up to the infinite reaches of heaven. Donne's two *Anniversary Poems* are plays on space, the dwindling littleness of the first in contrast to the infinitude of the second. The metaphysical poetry of Henry Vaughan looks upon eternity and finds it "a great ring of pure and endless light."

Like the voyages of exploration, baroque impulse also made this world more spacious. Where an early picaresque novel (concerned with a wandering rogue or dolt) like *Lazarillo de Tormes* confines itself to parts of Spain, the baroque *Simplicissimus* by Hans Jakob von Grimmelshausen permits its picaresque hero to range across Europe; and Voltaire's *Candide,* also in the picaresque tradition, takes Candide from Westphalia across Europe to South America and finally to Constantinople, even stopping off at El Dorado along the way.

ARCHITECTURE.   Baroque architects often thought in terms of groups of buildings. The triad of buildings by Michelangelo on the Capitoline Hill are an early example of this thinking, their concern with spatial relationships making them almost as much a work of sculpture as of architecture. St. Peter's Square (Figure 5.14), although the work of several hands, also aims at baroque massive wholeness. Its facade, designed by Carlo Maderna, illustrates another aspect of baroque size, the giant order, columns spanning more than one story of a building, as do the ones below the central pediment. The Capitoline buildings and the *Palazzo Valmarano* of Palladio also make early use of the giant order.

In Paris city squares such as the *Place des Vosges,* the *Place Vendôme,* and the *Place des Victoires* were also designed as interrelated wholes. On occasion entire cities were even conceived as unit entities: the Austrian city of Salzburg was rebuilt as a baroque whole by three successive bishops.

Palaces were naturally suited to the baroque yearning for size and space; the seat of kings, they had to be overwhelming. The garden of Versailles (Figure 6.10) is a quarter of a mile in width and the parks designed by Le Nôtre extend for several miles. The group of palaces built in Potsdam by Frederick the Great rivals Versailles for size and scale. Baroque churches, palaces for God, often rival their secular counterparts. St. Peter's, when completed by Maderna and Bernini, became the largest church in existence, its nave stretching some 600 feet. St. Paul's, as rebuilt by Christopher Wren (Figure 7.13), is 480 feet in length and the summit of its dome, 360 feet above the ground, still towers over the city of London. The inner shell of the dome reaches a height of 216 feet, producing an interior effect of massive spaciousness. Other domed churches that make equally impressive use of interior space are the *Santa Maria della Salute* by Longhena and the *Dôme des Invalides* of Mansart.

SCULPTURE.   The more than thirteen-foot-high statue of *David* by Michelangelo (Figure 5.8) gave rise to a so-called colossal order of baroque sculpture whose chief practioners, Baccio Bandinelli and Giovanni dell Opera, achieved the bulk but not the masterful tension of Michelangelo's work. Bernini in his Fountain of the River Gods uses size with impressive power, and his bronze *Shrine for St. Peter's Chair,* in St. Peter's, makes teeming ornament climb aloft as though it were space. *The Ecstasy of St. Theresa* uses spatial depth for dramatic realism.

PAINTING.   In a typical work like *Wedding Dance* Brueghel crowds his canvas with men in a state of nature to convey the fullness of the world around us. El Greco in *View of Toledo* paints the city from a far-off perspective and, with city and sky divided by a rim of space, the terminus of that per-

Figure 7.13 CHRISTOPHER WREN. St. Paul's Cathedral, London. (1675–1710). [Crown Copyright: Art Reference Bureau].

spective is lost in the distance. In his self-portrait Rembrandt uses *chiaroscuro*, light and dark, for spatial as well as philosophical effect. The darkness that shrouds most of the canvas opens it to boundless imagination, so that what serves as a wall to the sensual eye becomes a gateway to infinity for the mind's eye. Diego de Silva y Velásquez made space a salient feature of his special world. His *Equestrian Portrait of Philip IV* outlines the monarch against an endless sky. His *Surrender of Breda* sets a courtly gesture of courtesy against a similar sky. But it is his handling of interior space that sets him apart. *The Maids of Honor* (Figure 7.14) depicts Velásquez working in his studio in the company of the Infanta Margarita, her maids, nuns, dwarf, playmate, and dog. A visit from the king and queen interrupts their activity, and this is the moment Velásquez captures on canvas. He and most of the others stare out at the visitors, establishing a focal point somewhere in front of the canvas. The central group, spotlighted by sunshine streaming through the side window, marks off another point in space. The blurred king and queen reflected in the rear mirror, reality twice removed, suggest anterior space and also establish a plane of space behind the central group. In the rear doorway a courtier, greeting the king and queen, is outlined against a void of space apparently without end. The apparent representationalism of this painting is in its own way as subjective as the work of El Greco. We see, not a literal scene, but those objects that the eye would catch by roaming back and forth across space. The intensity of light and color dims toward the rear, and the courtier's face, the pictures on the wall, and the upper corner of the ceiling all become blurred. The Infanta's dress, highlighted though she is, is not drawn in detail but rather with splotches of color to suggest what the quick-roving eye would see. For this same reason the standing maid of honor has half her face dis-

Figure 7.14   Diego de Silva y Velásquez.   *The Maids of Honor.*   (1656).   Museo del Prado.

solved in shadow, the faces of the nuns are blurred, and even the dwarf, pathetic in her finery, makes less of an impression and is seen more dimly than the more important personages.

Vermeer (Figure 6.5) like Velasquez called attention to interior space, but he did so by means of light rather than perspective. Claude (Figure 6.14) makes his axis of light illuminate space as well as motion. And the deep set landscapes of Poussin (Figure 6.4) gain tranquillity by their broad spaciousness.

MUSIC.   The "colossal baroque" style with its birthplace in luxurious Venice made sacred as well as secular music overpowering by sheer virtue of size. Giovanni Gabrieli opposed huge choirs and orchestras in the enormous and resonant Cathedral of St. Mark. Forty-eight part Masses were written for multiple choruses, and even these were topped by the fifty-three part Mass for eight-part choruses written for the consecration of the baroque Cathedral of Salzburg by Orazio Benevoli. Opera became sumptuous spectacle, its stage settings never surpassed for complexity and size. *Il pomo d'oro* (the golden apple) of Marc' Antonio Cesti outdid them all. First presented in Vienna, it cost a king's ransom to produce, used multiple choruses and an arena-sized stage containing machinery for presenting naval battles, shipwrecks, military scenes, and flying gods and goddesses. The operas of Lully and Rameau and the masques produced in England continued this tradition of elaborate hugeness. In addition, the orchestra, amplified by Gabrieli, continued to expand.

Heinrich Schütz combined colossal baroque resources to produce Oratorio Passions of outstanding power. A student of Gabrieli, his *Seven Last Words* uses all four Gospels instead of a single one. Bach transmutes the size of the colossal baroque into spaciousness in towering works like his *St. Matthew Passion* for double chorus and orchestra, and his mammoth *B Minor Mass* which fuses Catholic and Protestant elements into an overwhelming testament of faith. The oratorios of Handel and Haydn's *The Creation* and *The Seasons* also use size to convey a sense of spacious grandeur.

Sensualism

Greek art had veiled sensualism with universal purpose (Figures 2.7, 2.18) and Renaissance art had draped it with metaphysics (Figures 5.10, 5.24), but in baroque art sensualism became its own excuse for being. Moreover, with the psychological insight gained from subjectivity, baroque art found sensual appeal not only in fleshly allurement but also in color, sound, movement, size, contrast, and even pain.

LITERATURE.   In *Adone* Marino introduced the full range of eroticism into baroque literature. The physical love of Venus and Adonis is detailed at length several times. Subtler aspects of the same sensuality appear throughout: for example, the terrified Adonis pleads to Venus when Mars threatens him; he is forced to witness their love-making; an ugly sorceress attempts to make love to him; and Venus spanks Cupid with the brambles of a rose bush.

Donne rejoices in sensuality in his early punning lyrics; in his later Christian poems he finds a similar physical ecstasy in pain, for example in the holy sonnet beginning, "Batter my heart, three-personed God." Crashaw, for whom the trances and visions of St. Theresa of Avila became erotic torture, revels in flaming fountains of tears and the wounds of Christ like "bloodshot eyes." In *Comus* Milton counters the lady's cold praise of chastity with a passionate defense of sensual bliss, a theme restated during the temptation of Adam in *Paradise Lost.* Racine conceives a Phèdre so seized by sexual passion that it directs even the straying of her thoughts. In *Fuente Ovejuna* Lope de Vega makes sensuality the stepping-stone to shock and mass torture. Sensualism even affected baroque style: that of Browne rolls off the tongue, and the interwoven sound patterns of *Marinismo* and *Gongorismo* give physical pleasure.

ARCHITECTURE.   In keeping with Jesuit intention, the heaped up ornamentation and luscious play of colored marble on the walls of the *Gesù* overwhelm the senses. The serpentine undulations of San Carlo often succeed in making a beholder giddy. The patient tracery of Churrigueresque ornament (named after the architect José Churriguera) on Spanish façades has a tactile appeal enhanced by the play of light and shadow across its surface: its most painstaking example, the church of *Santiago de Compostela,* also conveys a sense of motion as complex as that of San Carlo. The wedding-cake interior of Pommersfelden (Figure 7.18) has a sensual prettiness akin to the *Adone* of Marino.

SCULPTURE.   Bernini presents several aspects of sensuality in *The Ecstasy of St. Theresa;* erotic in the soft texture of bare flesh; masochistic in the passionate expression of the saint about to be pierced by the golden dart; physical in the interplay of light, color, and space surrounding the figures. His early *Apollo and Daphne* matches in intention the *Adone* of Marino. The guardian of Costou's *Horse* adds sensual overtones to the work by his nudity and, equally important, by the rhythm of his movements. Puget (Figure 7.16) clamps a lion's claw on bare flesh to exploit the sensuality of pain. Although the poses of the *Bathing Nymphs* of Girardon (Figure 6.13) are academic, their charms are more baroque than rational.

PAINTING.   Most major painters of this period made sensuality an offshoot of more salient characteristics. The dark tones of Rembrandt hint at soft oblivion. Space takes on caressing qualities in *The Maids of Honor* of Velásquez. For Brueghel the world of nature seeps into the life of men, and that world can at times be sensuous, as in his famous *Harvest Scene.* Peter Paul Rubens made sensuality a central feature of his subjective world —fleshy women became a hallmark of his style. In *Rape of the Daughters*

Figure 7.15 PETER PAUL RUBENS. *Rape of the Daughters of Leucippus.* (c. 1617).
[Marburg: Art Reference Bureau].

of Leucippus (Figure 7.15), the daughters' bounteous heaviness contributes
as much as does their nudity to sensual impact. Contrast in hue and texture between male and female flesh makes the daughters more enticing,
and thick layers of glaze, one of Rubens' favorite techniques, makes their
bodies glisten. The composition is skillful and intricate, consisting of
curves—most of them would be ovals if completed—flowing in all directions, not only planar but three dimensional, some touching, some collid-
ing, some joined to form a figure eight, together providing a sense of rapid
motion that adds its own sensual overtone.

MUSIC.   The size, power, and resonance of the church music of the colossal
baroque had sensual overtones in keeping with Jesuit philosophy. Gabrieli's
Music for Organ and Brass glows like the gold mosaics inside St. Mark's
Cathedral and led to the sumptuous choruses in the oratorios of Handel
and Haydn.

A more pointedly sensual kind of music can be found in those operas of Mozart whose librettos were written by the vehemently baroque Lorenzo da Ponte. In *Cosí Fan Tutte* the theme that sex overrides all other considerations is brilliantly matched by the music, except for an occasional melancholy aside. In *Don Giovanni* Leporello's "Catalogue Aria" with its sidling, insinuating conclusion recounts in words and music a sexual tour de force; *Vedrai carino* (you will see, my dear), sung by Zerlina to her grumpy fiance, unites the most sensual of lyrics to a suave and seductive musical counterpart.

Contrast

Although essentially a technique, the intense effects of contrast made it a seminal characteristic of baroque art.

LITERATURE.   In the *Adone* of Marino the delicate Adonis is pursued by Venus and by the ugly witch Falerina; the bluff manliness of Mars contrasts with the timidity of Adonis—all this for sensual and emotional effect. Donne and the metaphysical poets use contrast for richer purpose, yoking homely, earthy images to metaphysical meanings. Donne's "devout fits come and go away like a fantastic ague," and on Judgment Day he finds trumpet-blowing angels "At the round earth's imagined corners"; for George Herbert man was drawn to God by a pulley; for Crashaw the ascetic St. Theresa became an "undaunted daughter of desires." In *Paradise Lost* Milton achieves titanic effects by opposing the light of heaven to the "darkness visible" of hell. In *Life Is a Dream* Calderón contrasts a dark cave with the glittering world and by so doing comments profoundly on dream and reality.

ARCHITECTURE.   The layout of baroque palaces became an exercise in contrasts wherein large rooms led to small ones, lighted rooms to gloomy ones, ornate rooms to stark ones. In Versailles the lavish Hall of Mirrors contradicts the spare decor of its façade (Figure 6.10). The dark nave of the *Gesù* contrasts with the brightness of the apse for sensual and dramatic effect. The horizontal curves of the San Carlo façade clash with stiff verticality to underscore the movement and subjectivity of the design. The bare floors of Pommersfelden (Figure 7.18) dramatically contradict its ornate walls and ceilings.

SCULPTURE.   In *The Ecstasy of St. Theresa* Bernini contrasts light and shadow, bare and covered flesh, joy and pain for dramatic and sensual effect. His *Baldacchino* (Figure 7.20) with its downward curves and pressing heaviness of ornament clashes excitingly with its spiral supporting columns. The *Milo of Crotona* of Pierre Puget (Figure 7.16) explores the fullest possibilities of contrast. According to legend, Milo, a man of superhuman strength, was caught and held fast by the trunk of a tree and devoured by wolves. Puget exchanges wolves for a lion and locks his scene of violent

Figure 7.16 PIERRE PUGET. *Milo of Crotona.* (1672–1682). Louvre, Paris. [Alinari: Art Reference Bureau].

action within the fixed form of a trapezoid. Further contrasts between strength and helplessness, physical beauty and imminent disfigurement, and a vivid scream locked in silent stone make this a work of stark dramatic power.

PAINTING.   Caravaggio manages contrast between light and dark with eye-catching effect; in this work he also sets up a significant psychological contrast between the maternal sorrow of the Virgin and the sentimental abandon of Mary Magdalene. Rembrandt uses *chiaroscuro* for deeper purpose, evoking emotion, a sense of infinite space, and a whole subjective world thereby. Velásquez opposes the irregular, curved grouping of his central figures with a precise, linear doorway and window and picture frames. The *Resurrection* of El Greco (Figure 7.17) is steeped in baroque characteristics. The subjectively elongated figures have a strange, dramatic force; their very length gives them a bizarre sensuality and connotes a thrust of upward movement through a space as angular as they. Contrast also plays its part: the rising Christ moves counter to the toppling devil; his serene vertical figure contrasts with the horizontal circle of writhing figures below; and the unearthly white so typical of El Greco clashes in this canvas with warm reds and yellows. In *View of Toledo* El Greco opposes white against black, light against darkness, frozen buildings against explosive sky.

MUSIC.   In Venice the colossal baroque as used by Giovanni Gabrieli pitted different sized choral-instrumental groups against one another for dramatic and echo effects. This practice led to the two types of baroque concerto: *concerto grosso,* which set a small group of instruments against a large group to provide tonal contrast, as in the early *concerti grossi* of Corelli and four of the Brandenburg concertos of Bach; and the *solo concerto,* a single instrument in opposition to a group, as in Locatelli's *L'Arte del Violino* and the innumerable concertos of Vivaldi.

A number of other musical forms and techniques were also structured upon contrast. In opera dry recitative as prelude to melodic aria became a practice of Roman comic operas and passed into the work of Mozart. The French Overture established by Lully to introduce his operas consisted of a slow, homophonic first part and a fast, polyphonic second part. The toccata and fugue (free-flowing rhapsody and restrictive form) offered polar effects that Bach handled with dramatic mastery. The so-called Mannheim crescendo, popularized if not invented by the orchestra at Mannheim, exploited dynamic contrasts between *piano* (soft) and *forte* (loud) tentatively in the symphonies of its founder, Johann Stamitz, notoriously in the *Surprise Symphony* of Haydn, and with supreme effect in the later piano concertos of Mozart. Mannheim also popularized the use of a lyric second theme to counter a vigorous first theme in the sonata allegro form (p. 265): the two are often referred to as feminine and masculine themes. They appear early in the symphonies of Stamitz and throughout the symphonies, concertos, sonatas, and string quartets of Haydn and Mozart, so that baroque contrast even infuses the supreme musical example of rational balance.

Ornamentation

Like contrast a seminal technique, ornamentation marks off the baroque from the rational more overtly than any other characteristic.

Figure 7.17   EL GRECO (Domenico Theotokopoulos).   *Resurrection.*   (c. 1600).   Museo del Prado.

LITERATURE. In England, as mentioned earlier, Euphuism turned a patchwork of stylistic ornaments into an audacious fad. Toned down, it passed into the style of Burton and Browne where it became serious though no less ornate. In Italy Marino evolved a style made up of puns, antitheses, and high-flown images that fitted the cosmetic quality of his *Adone*. Known as *Marinismo* it described a sweetheart as *dorata ed adorata dea* (golden and adored goddess) and Dante Alighieri as *Ben sull ali liggier* (*sic*) *tre mondi canta* [he sings well of three worlds on light wings (of poetry)]. The poet Hofmann von Hofmannswaldau introduced *Marinismo* into Germany where it found some adherents and after a time some Neoclassical opposition. In Spain the poet Luis de Góngora fabricated a style composed of classical allusions, Latin inversions, puns, and hyperbole that outdid *Marinismo*. Known as *Gongorismo*, in its pure state it lost itself in ornament, but as toned down by Calderón (p. 294) it had impressive moments. The puns and bizarre imagery in Donne's poetry echo these ornamented styles. The classical and biblical allusions of Milton add cerebral ornament as well as sonorous sound to his poetic lines.

ARCHITECTURE. Michelangelo added provocatively nonfunctional ornament for visual effect in the vestibule of the Laurentian Library, with its scrolls affixed to lower walls like paintings, its blind windows, and the recessed columns supporting nothing at all. The *Gesù* covered almost every inch of its interior walls with leaves, scrolls, pilasters, broken cornices, colored marble, reliefs, and inlaid designs. Borromini further congested his narrow curved planes with niches, ovals, and spheres. The Hall of Mirrors at Versailles was coated symmetrically with ornament. Churrigueresque decoration covered fronts and interiors of Spanish buildings with screens of tracery. The interior of St. Isaac's Cathedral in St. Petersburg mingles Churrigueresque decor with that of the *Gesù*. Lukas von Hildebrandt carried ornamental tendencies to airy and fantastic heights. His interior of Pommersfelden Castle (Figure 7.18) folds fretwork, foliage, erratic capitals, and overdelicate reliefs into a whipped cream extravaganza.

With the rebuilding of London after the Great Fire of 1666, Wren erected a large number of churches on narrow sites and compensated for their tight and limited façades with free-rising ornamental towers. That of St. Mary-le-Bow (Figure 7.19) follows the formula Wren used for most of them—a square base supporting graceful circular sections capped by a slender spire. These attractive skyline ornaments found many imitators: James Gibbs for his St. Martin's-in-the-Fields in London, The Old State House in Boston, and Independence Hall in Philadelphia, designed by Alexander Hamilton.

SCULPTURE. Sculpture added its share of ornament to baroque architecture. Reliefs, winged cherubs, and statues tucked in niches everywhere added further adornment to columns, capitals, arches, pediments, cornices, and

Figure 7.18 (left) LUKAS VON HILDEBRANDT. Pommersfelden Castle (interior), Germany. (1713–1714). [Marburg: Art Reference Bureau].

Figure 7.19 (right) CHRISTOPHER WREN. St. Mary-le-Bow, London. (c. 1680). Destroyed in World War II. [Crown Copyright: Art Reference Bureau].

varied colors and textures of stone. The *Gesù* mounted statues at the base of its ceiling vault and in its central dome; Borromini placed a row of them in the first story of San Carlo and flanked his upper oval with them. Hildebrandt set them in niches bordered by other statues.

Bernini's *Baldacchino* (canopy) above the High Altar of St. Peter's (Figure 7.20) is a deliberately mysterious compound of ornament upheld by ornamental columns resting on ornamented bases. His *Shrine for St. Peter's Chair,* less graceful than the canopy, is heaped even higher with ornamentation. Ornament was one purpose of the fountains (many by Bernini) that appeared all over Rome during this period. Ornament was *the* purpose of the *Horse* of Costou.

PAINTING.   Ornament as the piling up of detail found little favor among the great baroque painters. Lesser artists who turned to it included the Little Dutch Masters in their genre paintings, and the Le Nain brothers in similar paintings in France—works for a middle-class public interested in literal representation of material possessions. But if the masters excluded ornament and any other irrelevancies from their subjective worlds, the special style of each one in a sense became his characteristic ornament. *Style as ornament* might well define the *chiaroscuro* of Rembrandt, the elongated bodies and color contrasts of El Greco, the absorptive nature of Brueghel, the spatial probing of Velásquez, the fleshiness of Rubens, the design of Poussin, and the golden light of Vermeer.

MUSIC.   Here as in painting the style of each master became his special ornament, and the sound of Vivaldi, Bach, Handel, Haydn, and Mozart served as inimitable adornment. Operatic music made lavish use of physical ornament, in Venetian operas, for example, and in the legendary Viennese production of Cesti's *The Golden Apple.* English masques like *Comus* with their ballets, choruses, jeweled costumes, and stage settings by Inigo Jones rivaled the sumptuousness of Venetian spectacle. Operatic and instrumental music also superadded technical embellishments. Venetian opera in the later seventeenth century abandoned itself to vocal pyrotechnics that had no relation at all to text or story line. The advent of the violin brought with it a technical display that garnished the solo concertos of Corelli and Locatelli. This display led in turn to the cadenzas of Classical concertos, dazzling solos inserted just before the last few bars of the finale. Mozart, one of the earliest to use cadenzas, wrote them for all sorts of solo instruments.

ROCOCO

The rococo style which succeeded the baroque echoed it in kind if not in size and intensity. Its characteristics included emotion, subjectivity, movement, sensualism, contrast, and ornamentation. They also included a

Figure 7.20   Gian Lorenzo Bernini.   *Baldacchino* (canopy), St. Peter's Cathedral,
Rome.   (1624–1633).   [Anderson: Art Reference Bureau].

concern for size and space, but where baroque size and space explored magnitude, the rococo delighted in smallness. Rococo smallness made for an attractive list of surface assets: delicacy, charm, frivolity, intimacy, preciousness, playfulness, capriciousness, and gaiety. Its trappings included fluttery silk coats for men, painted snuffboxes, mincing courtly dances. It gave rise to superelegant salons where gifted women like Mlle. de Scudéry and Mme. de Maintenon collected gatherings of aristocrats and artists who met weekly to uphold the niceties of civilization. Its heart was France during the first half of the eighteenth century under Louis XIV grown old and tired and then under a foppish Louis XV controlled by his mistress, Mme. de Pompadour. Essentially it was an offshoot of the baroque style fitted into the aristocratic world of eighteenth-century France. Rococo even sounds—and is meant to sound—like a French diminutive of *barocco*, and it derives from the French words *rocaille* (pebble) and *coquille* (shell), small dainty objects that connote its style.

LITERATURE.   The rhymed fables of Jean de la Fontaine either make little statements, such as men think more than animals, or else simply serve as ornaments. Some, like the fable of the milk girl or of the lovely maiden who waited too long for love, touch the emotions. A few are prettily sensual. All are cast in the unique form and style, the subjective world, of their creator. The first to pronounce La Fontaine's fables "charming" was Mme. de Sévigné, one of the great letter writers of all time. Within the compass of the personal letter—hers were to her absent daughter—she achieved an intensity of feeling unmatched by any other letter writer. The letters of Mme. de Maintenon are less subjective, more filled with the bustle and movement of court life, but nonetheless carefully wrought ornaments in a limited and limiting frame.

Spain produced volumes of rococo lyric poetry of little value. In England John Wilmot wrote rococo lyrics of minor merit. And Alexander Pope in "The Rape of the Lock" surveyed the whole rococo world through a lorgnette of reason. The work is an epic, in miniature, complete with invocation, clashing armies, and high-flown heroic speeches. There are emotional crises, such as those before and after the rape; there is a rush of movement, of thousands of sprites flocking about Belinda's dressing table; there is sensualism, a rape accomplished—of a lock of hair; there is contrast, between the nature of this drama and its machinery, between Umbriel's voyage to hell and the final scene in heaven; and there is ornamentation—the poem itself. Moreover, Sir Plume, Belinda's champion, armed with clouded cane, amber snuffbox, and round unthinking face is the essence of the rococo man.

ARCHITECTURE.   Rococo appeared in architecture in the form of small rooms heaped with dainty details, asymmetrical design, oval shapes, *Chinoise-*

ries (Chinese decor), and *Singeries* (humanoid monkeys). The Salon of the *Hôtel de Soubise* decorated by Germain Boffrand (Figure 7.21) is an archetypal example of the style. A small room, some twenty-six by thirty-three feet—the Hall of Mirrors in Versailles is 240 feet long—it is alive with movement. Free flowing curves interlink panels, mirrors, and the shell-shaped ceiling design, and the oval shape of the room itself is repeated in the outlines of the wall panels and mirrors. Plaster ornaments above the oval arches lead to a climactic ornamental flower on the ceiling. A ring of paintings by Natoire narrating the Cupid and Psyche myth adds a sweet sensuality to the total effect, and the white painted panels with their gilded moldings—white, gold, and pastels were typical rococo colors—further titillate the emotions.

Rococo architecture found a congenial home in Germany where Frederick the Great dreamed of an absolutism akin to that of Louis XIV. The *Kaisersaal* in Würzburg by Balthasar Neumann was a swooning symphony of pink marble and white-and-gold paneling; the Zwinger Palace in Dresden by Daniel Pöppelmann boasted a rococo exterior as well as interior. In England rococo touches brushed parts of buildings, the balustrade of Burlington House, for example, and accounted for the shell patterns, ribbon backs, and occasional Chinese effects of Chippendale furniture. No furniture, of course, was as rococo as that of Louis XV with its carved woodwork, curved legs, and tapestried upholstery. Rococo touches also appear early in the façade of San Carlo and in the Pommersfelden interior, added evidence, as if more were needed, that rococo and baroque were aspects of a single style.

SCULPTURE.   The intimate boudoir quality of rococo architecture and its feminine elegance affected sculpture as well. The finest of rococo sculptors, Claude Michel, called Clodion, shows these qualities to best advantage in terra cotta figures like his *Nymph and Satyr* (Figure 7.22). The figures are softly sensual, with the body of the satyr almost as smooth and rounded as that of the nymph. The curves of the bodies endow them with a grace of movement, and their faces, aglow with the emotions of the moment, are also graceful, mobile, and superficial. The height of the statue is one foot, eleven inches. Etienne Falconet echoed the grace of Clodion in works of greater size, but comparable triviality; Jean Jacques Caffieri brought rococo prettiness to portrait busts of men wearing ecstatic expressions and swirling curls. Joseph Wilton sculpted a frilly rococo monument in Westminster Abbey for General Wolfe, hero of the French and Indian War.

PAINTING.   Like La Fontaine, Antoine Watteau converted rococo daintiness into art of real importance. His *Journey to Cythera* (Figure 7.23) depicts a throng of courtly lovers who have visited and are about to depart from Cythera, the purple island of classical tradition where Venus was

Figure 7.21 GERMAIN BOFFRAND. The Oval Room, Hôtel de Soubise, Paris. (1730–1740). [Marburg: Art Reference Bureau].

worshiped. Her statue stands to the right amid the trees, ornamented with roses as befits a rococo Venus. Ornamental too are the velvet and satin costumes of the visitors, reds and blues and pinks that flare up above the brown terrain. The foreground where they stand suggests a courtly park, some corner of Fontainebleau or Versailles, in contrast to the misty blue-green background that no mortal eye has ever seen. On the knoll three pairs of lovers pause for a final word or gesture. Their attitudes are graceful, yet artificial like those of actors. Theatrical as is their tableau, however, it conveys an undercurrent of sorrow, because lovers must always leave their island and because life is at heart a game of poses. *Journey to Cythera*, incidentally, measures some four by six feet, and its figures are a hand's breadth high. While Watteau transcended rococo furbelows, his more favored contemporaries, Jean-Honoré Fragonard and François Boucher, did not. Their pastel Venuses and garden scenes come closer to Clodion than to Watteau.

MUSIC. Rococo music meant the *style galant* that flourished under Louis XV. Distinguished by its courtly, elegant melodies, its short phrases repeated over and over, and its harmonic insignificance, *style galant* was mainly music for ornament, trifling, buoyant with movement, often cloying, as in the pastoral operas performed by Louis XV and his courtiers. The

Figure 7.22   CLODION (Claude Michel).   *Nymph and Satyr.*   (c. 1775).   The Metropolitan Museum of Art, Bequest of Benjamin Altman, 1913.

Figure 7.23 ANTOINE WATTEAU. *Journey to Cythera.* (1717). Louvre, Paris.
[Alinari: Art Reference Bureau].

composer who raised this style to a perfection rivaling the art of Watteau was François Couperin, whose *pièces* for clavicin and harpsichord are exquisitely enameled porcelain miniatures.

Style galant penetrated into Classical music, giving it a courtly tone. The symphonies and orchestral trios of Mannheimer Johann Stamitz made important use of it. So did the early serenades and symphonies (numbers 1–13) of Mozart, with their short-phrased repetitions. *Style galant* tinged most of Mozart's music and was a root characteristic of the works of Haydn, especially those written while in the service of the royal house of Esterhazy.

Our dissection of the baroque style enables us to fit several pieces of a complex period into place. For one thing we can see how the baroque, exuberant in contrast to the sober Age of Reason, has nevertheless absorbed rational elements into its every part: the emotionalism of Racine, Claude, Rembrandt, and Mozart is braced by rational form and subject matter; the subjectivity of Milton, Vermeer, and Bach has its ground in reason; the movement, size, sensualism, contrast, and ornamentation to be found in Donne, Calderón, Marino, Bernini, Puget, Wren, the Versailles architects, Boffrand, Velasquez, Rubens, Vivaldi, Haydn, and Couperin are in no cases devoid of rational balance, proportion, or symmetry. *In sum, the Age of Reason and the baroque style interpenetrate and form parts of a whole.*

Their nominal division is simply a matter of perspective. Being close to us in time, the seventeenth and eighteenth centuries lend themselves to a separation into parts which is basic to specialist investigations of the immediate past. On the other hand the humanities approach, concerned with the broader view, makes clear how those separate parts fit together. Like the scientism of the Hellenistic age which has merged (in perspective) with its worldliness, emotionalism, specialization, and individualism, the rationalism of this period when viewed from farther off adds a complicating touch to, and settles in as part of, the sum total of its traits and ideas.

Besides clarifying the long-range relationship between the baroque and the Age of Reason, our compartmented survey of the baroque will also help to fit the Romantic period into long-range perspective. As will be seen, *Romantic traits are combinations or else offshoots of baroque characteristics.* Moreover, the ideas introduced into the Age of Reason begin to penetrate the arts of the nineteenth century. And philosophers—Kant, Schopenhauer, Hegel—begin to appear who articulate what baroque art had been striving to say. Chapter 8 will discuss the core of Romanticism, and its joint role, *in perspective,* with the Age of Reason.

SELECTED BIBLIOGRAPHY

Literature

Cope, Jackson I. *The Metaphoric Structure of Paradise Lost.* Baltimore: Johns Hopkins Press, 1964.
Flores, Angel. *Lope de Vega, Monster of Nature.* New York: Brentano's, 1930.
Tuve, Rosamond. *Elizabethan and Metaphysical Imagery.* Chicago: University of Chicago Press, 1961.
White, Helen C. *The Metaphysical Poets.* New York: Macmillan, 1936.
Williamson, George. *The Donne Tradition.* New York: Noonday, 1963.

Architecture, Sculpture, Painting

Fokker, T. H. *Roman Baroque Art: The History of a Style.* New York: Oxford University Press, 1938.
Friedlaender, Walter F. *Mannerism and Anti-Mannerism in Italian Painting.* New York: Columbia University Press, 1957.
Fromentin, Eugène. *The Masters of Past Time: Dutch and Flemish Painting from Van Eyck to Rembrandt.* London: Phaidon, 1948.
Holt, Elizabeth G. (Ed.) *A Documentary History of Art.* Vol. II. *Michelangelo and the Mannerists: the Baroque and the Eighteenth Century.* Garden City, N.Y.: Anchor, 1958.

Kimball, Fiske. *The Creation of the Rococo.* Philadelphia: Philadelphia Museum of Art, 1943.

McComb, Arthur. *The Baroque Painters of Italy.* Cambridge, Mass.: Harvard University Press, 1934.

Powell, Nicolas. *From Baroque to Rococo: An Introduction to Austrian and German Architecture from 1580 to 1790.* New York: Praeger, 1959.

Schonberger, Arno, and Halldor Soehner. *The Rococo Age.* New York: McGraw-Hill, 1960.

Wittkower, Rudolf. *Art and Architecture in Italy, 1600–1750.* Baltimore: Penguin, 1958.

———. *Gian Lorenzo Bernini, the Sculptor of the Roman Baroque.* London: Phaidon, 1955.

Wölfflin, Heinrich. *Principles of Art History.* New York: Dover, 1956.

Music

Bukofzer, Manfred. *Music in the Baroque Era.* New York: Norton, 1947.

Davison, Archibald T. *Bach and Handel: The Consummation of the Baroque in Music.* Cambridge, Mass.: Harvard University Press, 1951.

Fuller-Maitland, John A. *The Age of Bach and Handel.* New York: Oxford University Press, 1938.

Grunfeld, Frederic V. *The Story of Great Music: The Baroque Era.* New York: Time, Inc., 1965.

Harman, Alec, and Anthony Milner. *Late Renaissance and Baroque Music.* Fair Lawn, N.J.: Essential Books, 1959.

Newman, William S. *The Sonata in the Baroque Era.* Chapel Hill: University of North Carolina Press, 1959.

Worsthorne, Simon T. *Venetian Opera in the Seventeenth Century.* New York: Oxford University Press, 1954.

CHAPTER 8

THE ROMANTIC
PERIOD

SEEDS OF REVOLUTION

"Everything I see," wrote Voltaire near the close of his life, "is scattering the seeds of an inevitable Revolution. Light has so spread from neighbor to neighbor that at the first opportunity it will kindle and burst forth." In the years following the Seven Years' War the light of reform spread across Europe, affecting even enlightened despots. Frederick the Great liberalized the laws of Prussia and made it possible for peasants pinched by lack of land to settle in Silesia. Catherine the Great of Russia (1762–1796) introduced legal reforms and opened Russia to refugees from everywhere in Europe. Widely read and indomitable, she placed her faith in science, introduced factories and hospitals into Russia, and set an example for medical reform by being one of the first in her empire to be vaccinated against smallpox. In England Lord Mansfield proposed an antislavery law in 1772, John Howard inaugurated prison reforms a year later, and within another few years torture was abolished as a means of extracting confessions. The *Sturm und Drang* (storm and stress) movement, which flourished in Germany for about two decades after 1767, had social and political reform as well as a German literary renaissance as its goals.

The immediate cause of much of this reform was one man, Jean Jacques Rousseau (1712–1778), whose writings became gospel for people as dissimilar as Catherine the Great, Thomas Jefferson, and Maximilien Robespierre. Sentimental, morbidly sensitive, often foolish, and perhaps insane, Rousseau advocated progressive education, the simple life away from civilization, and revolution. Yet this father of modern education deposited the five children born to his common-law wife in orphanages at birth; this passionate shepherd reveled in creature comforts; this revolutionary sought out wealthy patrons and groveled before them. His impact, hardly personal, stemmed from two sources: that his protests came at a turning point in history and that he wrote with an eloquence and passion rarely equaled. Nothing in Voltaire rings like Rousseau's famous "Man is born free, but everywhere he is in chains," from his *Social Contract*, the bible of the French Revolution. It stirred all of Europe, which a decade later viewed the partition of Poland with a new critical eye.

Poland was at that time one of the largest European kingdoms—and the most backward. Its serfs were oppressed; its nobles were so self-indulgent that the country was reduced to a state of anarchy. In 1772, with Austria and Russia on the brink of territorial war, Frederick the Great intervened and suggested they each take sections of Poland instead so as to maintain a balance of power. Their excuse for invading Poland was a threatened civil war because of differences between the Eastern and Roman Catholic churches. The threat ended, Austria sliced off Galicia for its "services," Russia took Lithuania, and Prussia annexed all of East Prussia. It must be remembered that Frederick, who instigated this partition, was an enlightened despot.

England, too, was governed by an enlightened despot, George III (1760–1820), who in contrast to his Hanoverian predecessors was English born, moral, thrifty, and obstinately determined to rule in place of Parliament. He overcame Whig supremacy in Parliament by splitting the party into factions and by placing his own choices at the head of each faction. He also appointed new colonial officials whom he could control. In 1763, Mir Cossim, the nabob of Bengal, led a revolt against the East India Company, and British troops were sent in and put down the rebellion. In that same year the Algonquin chief Pontiac laid siege to Detroit; British troops came in and drove him further west. In order to pay for these wars, and to assert his authority, George decided to tax the American colonists, who now numbered one and a half million, plus half a million slaves. Earlier attempts at taxation had resulted in evasion and smuggling. Nevertheless, in 1765 Parliament passed a Stamp Act requiring colonists to buy and affix stamps to all publications and legal documents. The act roused a storm of protest spearheaded by men in New York and Boston whom Colonel Barré described to a hostile Parliament as "Sons of Liberty." The phrase caught on in America, where Sons of Liberty clubs sprang up all over the country, and in 1766 the Stamp Act was repealed. A few years later England laid customs duties on a number of commodities including tea, and in 1773 some fifty men dressed as Indians boarded three British ships in Boston harbor and dumped the tea into the water.

These troubles, plus fresh revolts in India, forced George to appoint a strong and competent prime minister, Lord North. North relieved the tension in India by placing the East India Company under the partial control of Parliament and by appointing Warren Hastings, an able administrator, as governor general of India. There was no Hastings for the American colonies, nor could one have quelled the rising rebellion. The colonies had drifted far away from their mother country; forty percent of their population was not even English, and colonial standards of living were now improved enough to create a separate aristocracy and a different way of life. Underlying colonial discontent was the desire of American merchants and plantation owners, men like John Hancock and Thomas Jefferson, to cast off English economic restraints.

REVOLUTION IN AMERICA

In 1774 the First Continental Congress met in Philadelphia to demand self-government and freedom from all taxes. As North observed: "We are no longer to dispute between legislation and taxation but to consider only whether or not we have any authority in the colonies." In April 1775 English troops from Lexington, Massachusetts, on the way to Concord Bridge to seize local military supplies, were attacked by American militia; the American Revolution began. A sizable American army collected around Boston and fortified Bunker Hill, commanding the city. British troops under General Gage captured the hill (the battle was actually fought on nearby Breed's Hill) but suffered a thousand casualties. England, occupied with India, sent Hessian (German mercenary) reinforcements and enlisted American Indians to fight the colonists. She did not anticipate a lengthy war, especially since one third of the colonists were pro-British, one third were neutral, and only the remaining one third were in favor of revolution. The commander of the American troops was George Washington, a distinguished gentleman whose presence gave stature to the revolutionary cause. His ill-equipped, ill-trained troops were no match for professionals, however, and in 1776 General Howe with 30,000 troops swept down from the north and occupied New York, driving Washington's army out of the city. Howe could have beaten Washington then and there but chose instead to tarry in civilized New York.

On July 4, 1776, a harried Continental Congress adopted a Declaration of Independence drafted by Thomas Jefferson. The declaration, a mixture of the democratic theories of Locke and the ringing sentiments of Rousseau, proclaimed "that all men are created equal, that they are endowed by their Creator with certain unalienable Rights, that among these are Life, Liberty, and the pursuit of Happiness." It rallied support to Washington in Philadelphia and helped to inspire France, still smarting from her commercial defeats and her loss of Canada, to send supplies and volunteers led by the Marquis de Lafayette.

In 1777 the British planned a triple thrust to end the war: Howe was to occupy Philadelphia, the American capital, as well as New York, thus opening a broad barrier between north and south; British and Hessian troops under General Burgoyne were to move down from Canada and pin the New England army between Burgoyne and Howe; and English and Indian soldiers under General St. Leger were to advance from the west and hem in the American troops against the sea. Howe easily routed Washington's army from Philadelphia, but dallied there while Washington retreated west to Valley Forge. Burgoyne stalemated an American army at

Saratoga, in upper New York State. No reinforcements came from New York to help him, however, and St. Leger's Indian allies soon withdrew. The Americans, reinforced by an aroused New England countryside, compelled Burgoyne to surrender his entire army of 6000 men. This marked the turning point of the war. After a winter of hardship at Valley Forge, Washington emerged with seasoned, determined troops, more volunteers, and more French aid. The English generals, unable to defeat a ragged American militia, grew even more incompetent in the face of widespread resistance. A quip attributed to Lord North ran: "I do not know whether my generals will frighten the Americans, but they certainly frighten me."

The remainder of the war was a mopping up operation: French troops drove the British from New England; American troops under George Rogers Clark captured the British strongholds in the west; and in 1781 an army led by Washington and Lafayette encircled a British army led by General Cornwallis at Yorktown, Virginia, and forced him to surrender. The defeated British marched out to the popular tune "The World Turned Upside Down," and in 1783 England recognized American independence at the Peace of Versailles. Thus was launched the first experiment in self-government in history.

Although she lost America, England remained the world's leading colonial power. Some 50,000 American colonists had fought in support of the British troops, and a majority of these now migrated to Canada where they combined with the French settlers to form a British colony. Hastings had restored full British control over India, and in 1770 Captain James Cook rediscovered Australia, which England first used as a humanitarian penal colony, at Botany Bay, and then as ranch land for cattle and sheep.

REVOLUTION IN INDUSTRY

England's coal and iron deposits and gifted inventors put her on the winning side in another kind of revolution, the industrial revolution, a force that caused more basic changes than the more dramatic revolutionary wars. Vast improvements in crop production and cattle breeding in the later eighteenth century made farming a lucrative enterprise for large landowners. The raising of turnips and other root crops made it easier to feed cattle during winter, so that starvation became less of a menace. And the problem of employing dispossessed small farmers was solved by the rise of factories. Industrial Birmingham increased in population from 15,000 to 73,000 during the eighteenth century, thanks to the flying shuttle of Kay, the spinning jenny of Hargraves and Arkwright, Crompton's mule, which could twist threads suitable to the weaving of muslin, and Watt's steam engine which provided power to run these machines. English manufactured goods brought an increased flow of luxury and wealth to all of Europe, and these benefits, plus European forward strides in science—the discovery of the planet Uranus by Herschel, of geological laws by Werner, of the values of vaccination by Jenner, and of the properties of electricity by Volta and Galvani—made the world seem a more significant and desirable place in which to live and the gap between wealth and poverty seem more and more unbridgeable. "Man's inhumanity to man makes countless thousands mourn," wrote the Scottish poet Robert Burns.

The Hapsburg emperor, Joseph II, responded to the changing times by decreeing religious tolerance, more equal taxes, and a common national language, but succeeded only in alienating the church, the nobility, and the lower classes of Belgium and Hungary. He was the only enlightened despot to try to adapt to these new forces of revolution. The attitude of the others was best summed up by Catherine the Great: "Equality is a monster who wishes to be king," she said, and to repress it she joined forces with Frederick the Great.

America, which had fought for equality, now seemed content to ignore it. Covered wagons rolled westward into Indiana, Ohio, Kentucky, and Illinois carrying families intent on carving out a new life and indifferent to the problems of government that now were theirs. The original thirteen colonies were all unwilling to surrender any privileges to federal control. The Articles of Confederation, passed by the Continental Congress in 1781, gave them sole right to regulate their own affairs, which they did while the national debt of $56,000,000 remained unpaid and national unity slackened. Then, in 1787, delegates from the states met at Independence Hall in Philadelphia and framed a new Constitution. A canny compromise between states' rights and federal powers, it combined the principles of Montesquieu with English parliamentary practice, and some brilliantly prudent phrasing. To make it more acceptable, ten amendments were added, the so-called Bill of Rights, which included such guarantees as trial by jury, freedom of speech, and freedom of religion. The Constitution was ratified by the states and George Washington became the first president of the United States on April 30, 1789. A week later the French king summoned the Estates General for the first time since 1614, and French aristocracy faced the challenge of the rights of man.

THE FRENCH REVOLUTION AND NAPOLEON

The American Revolution had dealt the French treasury a crushing blow, and court intrigues encouraged by Marie Antoinette had replaced a competent finance minister with a pliable one who fawned on the nobility and taxed the peasantry very heavily. The French peasant was better off than his counterparts in Germany, Italy, Poland, Russia, or Spain, but such comparison tells little of his actual condition. State and church taxes took sixty percent of his income, and starvation always hovered nearby. In the words of one Brittany priest, "In my parish there are 2200 souls of whom at least 1800 beg for bread, which they cannot find, and most of them live on the boiled stalks of cabbage, or, lacking those, on grass." Louis XVI was a well-intentioned, gentle king who wished to help his subjects but who vacillated at every crisis. His wife, the lively and willful Marie Antoinette, dominated him, and France. In 1789 the country was bankrupt.

Louis summoned the Estates General to Versailles to explore ways of raising money, but the Third Estate, the commons, came there to explore ways of reforming the government. The Third Estate meant the middle class, the most substantial contributors to the national economy and culture, who were virtually voiceless in politics. Required to meet separately, as was traditional in meetings of the Estates General, and ejected from their chamber, which was being prepared for the arrival of the king, they met in a nearby tennis court and swore an oath to frame a constitution. Calling themselves a National Assembly, they wrung reforms from the king and organized a National Guard in Paris, which was trained by the Marquis de Lafayette. On July 14, 1789, the Guard attacked the Bastille, symbol of despotism, murdered the governor and his men—who had surrendered peaceably—and released the seven prisoners it contained: four counterfeiters, two madmen, and a debauchee. The French Revolution had begun. Revolutionary societies, such as the Jacobins, sprang up mainly in Paris, and their agitation plus widespread unemployment led to a bread march upon Versailles. A mob, assisted by the National Guard under Lafayette, brought the royal family back to Paris to reside in the Tuilleries. "We have the baker and the baker's wife," chanted the mob on the march back, "and the baker's little boy. Now we shall have bread." The National Assembly issued a Declaration of the Rights of Man whose rousing phrases bore the imprint of Rousseau: "Men are born and remain free and equal in rights." "Liberty consists in being allowed to do whatever does not injure others." "Property being an inviolable and sacred right, no one can be deprived of it, except when . . . necessary."

Charles Maurice de Talleyrand, Bishop of Autun, proposed to the Assembly that church wealth and property be surrendered to the state. Thousands of nobles, appalled by these changing attitudes, emigrated to other countries, and in 1791 the king tried to escape from the Tuilleries disguised as a servant. He and his family reached Varennes, 232 kilometers from Paris, where he was recognized and brought back. In that same year the Assembly completed its constitution, which Louis accepted—the revolution had apparently reached a successful conclusion.

The National Assembly now consisted of three factions: the conservatives, led by Lafayette; the Girondists (many from the region of Gironde), the moderate middle-class party led by General Charles Dumouriez; and the Jacobins, Paris radicals, who first met at a Jacobin (Dominican) monastery. The Jacobins were led by a violent unsuccessful scientist, Jean Paul Marat, a dramatic orator, Georges Danton, and an idealistic disciple of the theories of Rousseau, Maximilien Robespierre. The Assembly adopted the blue, white, and red tricolor as the national flag, voted to enforce the death penalty for treason (despite the pleadings of Robespierre), but agreed to use the guillotine on all classes (formerly nobles were guillotined and peasants were hanged).

At this juncture Austria and Prussia, disturbed by the revolution, declared war, and their armies advanced into France meeting little resistance. The Duke of Brunswick, speaking for both invading armies, issued a manifesto threatening any Frenchmen who harmed their king. In reply a mob broke into the Tuilleries, and Louis was relieved of all authority. The balance of power thus swung toward the Jacobins, and Danton was made minister of justice. Lafayette fled France to join the *emigrés*. In 1792 Danton initiated trials of "enemies of the revolution," and those found guilty were executed. To add to the frenzy, troops arrived from Marseilles singing a song that soon became the rallying cry of the revolution, the *Marseillaise*. The monarchy was abolished and on January 21, 1793, Louis XVI was guillotined; a roll of drums drowned out his last attempt to address the mob. England, Holland, Sardinia, and Spain joined Prussia and Austria in declaring war on France; Dumouriez deserted to Austria; a peasant revolt broke out in the southern district of La Vendée; and a Girondist dupe, Charlotte Corday, stabbed Marat to death while he was taking a bath. Jacobin had turned on Girondist, and the fall of France seemed assured—but then Prussia and Austria pulled back and joined with Russia in the second partition of Poland.

Poland, ruled at last by an enlightened despot, Stanislaus II, had inaugurated constitutional and economic reforms. An improved Poland would be a threat to Russia, Prussia, and Austria, however, and they moved against her in 1792, forced Stanislaus to rescind all reforms, and took still more Polish territories for themselves. Meanwhile the Jacobins gained full control of the French Revolution, and Marie Antoinette soon followed her husband to the guillotine. The Reign of Terror had begun; within a year some 2700 persons in Paris and another 17,000 throughout France were executed. Oddly, life in Paris was gayer than it had ever been: café life sparkled; men adopted a striking new fashion, long trousers (*sans culottes*, without breeches) to make all legs seem equal; women removed their wigs and wore their hair long and deliberately unkempt; churches gave way to Temples of Reason, where the female nude was idealized; and the calendar was altered to make this bright new year of revolution Year One. But the violence continued without a stop. Danton, sickened by bloodshed, exclaimed: "I shall break that damned guillotine before long or fall under it." He fell under it in 1794 and Robespierre, who succeeded him, decreed a fresh surge of executions; the ideals of Rousseau were erased by the concerns of power politics. Four months later Robespierre too fell under the guillotine and the Reign of Terror ended.

A five-man Directory assumed control of the government in 1795. At this time Prussia, left out of a third partition of Poland, made peace with France. Holland, Sardinia, and Spain also withdrew from the war; only England and Austria remained belligerent. The Directory granted freedom of worship, and the reopening of the churches eased tension somewhat. But bread riots occurred often, and in the fall of 1795 a mob attacked the Directory's National Convention building. The situation looked threatening until a young officer ordered his soldiers to fire grapeshot into the mob, which turned and fled. In 1796 a grateful Directory gave him command of the army bound for Austria-held Italy, and he married a general's widow, Josephine de Beauharnais, who was seven years older than himself. At twenty-seven General Napoleon Bonaparte already had a genius for recognizing what was risky but possible, which brought him success in brilliantly engineered enterprises. "If I seem always ready to meet any difficulty," he later confessed, "to face any emergency, it is because before undertaking any enterprise I have spent a long time thinking it out and foreseeing what might happen." Although slight and pale, he had infinite energy and an appetite for power which he foresaw would come from military conquests, the only distractions possible to a France wracked by bloodshed and poverty. The most audacious general in history, he set out to dazzle his nation with victories.

Outnumbered in Italy, he drove a wedge between the Piedmontese and Austrian armies, defeated both and advanced on Vienna, forcing Austria to sue for peace. To keep this dynamo occupied and out of the way, the Directory then sent Napoleon on another campaign, this time to Egypt. Control of Egypt would bring France within striking distance of India. In a swift maneuver Napoleon's army entered Cairo, but on the Nile his fleet was destroyed by the English under Admiral Horatio Nelson, and the Middle East proved too restive to control. Hearing that the Directory was about to fall, Napoleon abandoned his army of 12,000 men in Egypt and hurried back to France. He arrived in time to join in defeating the Directory and to gain a ten-year appointment as First Consul of the new republic in 1799. In his absence Austria had retaken Italy, and in 1800 he led an army that crushed Austria at Marengo. As a result almost all of north Italy was surrendered to France. In 1802 he signed a peace treaty with England, the Treaty of Amiens. Then, having been elected First Consul for life, he devoted himself to civil reform. He sold Louisiana to the United States to help pay French war debts, created the Bank of France to stabilize finance and currency, pruned and codified French laws (the Napoleonic Code which preserved the liberal gains of the revolution), and instituted universal education. He appointed the guileful Talleyrand minister of foreign affairs, clear evidence that the Treaty of Amiens was just a screen, and began to build flat-bottomed boats to carry troops across the Channel to invade England. In 1804 he declared himself emperor, and the pope officiated at his coronation at the Cathedral of Notre Dame. Characteristically, Napoleon took the crown from the pope's hands and placed it upon his own head.

England formed a coalition with Sweden, Russia, and Austria against the rising French menace, and Nelson, in command of the British fleet, kept so close a naval watch on the French coast that a Channel invasion was impossible. Only Spain, ruled by fumbling Charles IV and his debauched queen Louisa, supported Napoleon. In 1805 when French Admiral Villeneuve slipped past the English blockade during Nelson's absence, Charles reinforced the French fleet with Spanish ships. Nelson caught up with Villeneuve at the Spanish coast off Cape Trafalgar and annihilated his fleet, but he himself was killed during the battle. Napoleon then turned his attention away from England and toward the continent. In 1805 he defeated the Austrians at Ulm and entered Vienna. That same year he crushed a Russian-Austrian army at Austerlitz, and in the peace arrangements of 1806 he decreed the end of the Holy Roman Empire. He goaded Prussia into declaring war, destroyed her armies at Jena and Auerstädt, and entered Berlin. In 1807 he defeated a Prussian-Russian army at Friedland and deprived Prussia of half her territory. He was now at the zenith of his power. His empire was greater than that of Charlemagne. He made his brother Joseph king of Naples; he appointed his brother Louis king of Holland and his brother Jerome king of Westphalia. After he concluded an alliance with Czar Alexander, only England remained free of his domination. Through all of these triumphs Napoleon had retained his unerring sense of the possible: "I act only on the imagination of the nation. When this means fails me I shall be reduced to nothing." In the meantime he created new honors and titles for all who had supported him, and in 1807 his court could boast as many aristocrats as the court of Louis XVI.

The remainder of his career bears out the axiom that absolute power corrupts absolutely. "I am no ordinary man," he proclaimed, "and the laws of propriety and morals do not apply to me." To break England, he closed the ports of Europe to her, and she in turn blockaded European shipping, causing a rising shortage of food throughout the continent. In Spain Charles IV, menaced by a hungry mob, abdicated and signed the Spanish throne over to Napoleon, who declared his brother Joseph king of Spain. Napoleon marched scornfully against a weak Spanish army, declaring that Spain would not cost him 12,000 men, but an aroused countryside beat his army back and actually defeated it at Baylen. Concurrently, hunger and a spirit of revolt infected Austria, and although Napoleon won the bloody Battle of Wagram, the cost was considerable. In search of allies, and a dynasty, Napoleon divorced Josephine and in 1810 married the Archduchess Maria Louisa of Austria, a niece of Marie Antoinette, who gave him a son the following year. Suspicious of Talleyrand, Napoleon dismissed him and appointed a more malleable foreign minister. Czar Alexander objected to these policies, and so Napoleon invaded Russia in 1812 with an army of 600,000 men. The smaller Russian army retreated before him and he reached the gates of Moscow, but instead of a formal surrender he found an empty city. He occupied Moscow, taking up headquarters at the Kremlin, but soon fire, set by the Russians, gutted the city and forced his army to leave. When he tried to retreat by a southern route, an enormous Russian army forced him to return by the route he had come (which he had razed when marching in). Famine, the Russian winter, and guerrilla attacks decimated his army, and by the time he reached Germany it numbered 30,000 men. Russia, Prussia, and then Austria rose against him, and although he won one brilliant victory after another, they pursued him into France and captured Paris. The Paris mob cried *Vive Alexandre!* as the czar marched in. Napoleon abdicated in 1814 and was given the sovereignty of Elba, an island off the coast of Tuscany. The Bourbon Louis XVIII was restored to the throne of France, and diplomats met at Vienna to arrange the peace.

While they were meeting, Napoleon slipped away from Elba and landed at Antibes in southern France, where soldiers and civilians flocked to join him. For 100 days he fought with his old brilliance, but a combined British and Prussian force finally crushed him at Waterloo, in Belgium, on June 18, 1815. At the age of forty-six he was banished to St. Helena, 1200 miles off the west coast of Africa; he died six years later of cancer of the stomach. In his will he wrote: "I desire that my ashes repose on the banks of the Seine in the midst of the French people whom I have loved so dearly." Nineteen years later they were placed in the tomb of the Invalides, and time and distance have made them objects of sentimental reverence. But another Frenchman, the political theorist Alexis de Tocqueville, has kept sight of truth with this timeless epitaph: "He was as great as a man can be without virtue."

UNEASY PEACE: THE 1820s AND 1840s

With Napoleon gone, the Congress of Vienna embarked upon the most ambitious and widespread search for peace in the history of Europe. Its participants included prime ministers Castlereagh of England, Metternich of Austria, Talleyrand of France, and the rulers of Prussia, Russia, and

Denmark. Its policy was to restore the Europe that had existed before the nightmare of the French Revolution, and then to maintain a perpetual status quo. France was charged a war indemnity of 700 million francs and occupied for three years, but its boundaries were left intact; Holland and Belgium were reunited, as they had been in the seventeenth century; and each major power reacquired as much territory as it had held in 1805— except that Russia took another bite of Poland, including Warsaw, its capital city.

Two regulating alliances were formed: a Holy Alliance, promoted by Czar Alexander, which sought to bind all kings together in a Christian unity of charity and peace; and a more solidly based Quadruple Alliance, whereby England, Russia, Prussia, and Austria agreed to meet together regularly to maintain the peace. It was a peace derived from the will of nations rather than from a single conqueror, for nationalism had become a driving force.

A principal source of national pride were the feelings of superiority fostered by the fast-spreading industrial revolution. The steam-powered locomotive, invented by Stephenson while the Congress of Vienna was meeting, put the industrial revolution on wheels, facilitating cheaper, more widespread distribution. Factory towns altered the appearance of the European countryside, and the merchant capitalist became a major figure. He was probably freest to expand in the newly formed United States, and the royal heads of state at the Congress of Vienna declared themselves disturbed by the unsettling forces of democracy across the Atlantic. Actually, American government remained in the hands of its first families during its first forty years, but the westward trek had formed nine new states west of the Appalachians by 1828, and the skirmishes with England resulting from Britain's naval blockade during the Napoleonic wars (1812–1815) had produced a frontier hero, Andrew Jackson. His election to the presidency in 1828 led the way to universal manhood suffrage and to a rising belief that ability, not birth, qualified a man for political leadership. Even more unsettling, the new democracy declared itself ready to support other democratic revolutions. When the Holy Alliance pondered the invasion of South America to put a halt to rebellions there against Spain, President James Monroe stated in 1823 that such a move could not be interpreted "in any other light than a manifestation of an unfriendly disposition toward the United States." His Monroe Doctrine heralded a changing continent, and England, hoping for new trade markets in South America, supported American defiance. Thus while the Congress of Vienna strove to maintain the status quo, the ways of life it cultivated—nationalism and the industrial revolution—were essentially forces of change which would instigate the reforms and rebellions of the next twenty years.

In England, parliamentary government and an advanced industrial economy limited those reforms to peaceful ones. Liberal Tory leaders closed down "rotten" (underpopulated) boroughs and insured more democratic elections, with the result that the middle class began to share with the gentry the control of the House of Commons. In South America, France, Greece, and Belgium, reform meant revolution, and theirs were all successful. In the 1820s Brazil declared itself free from Portugal, and the Spanish colonies, led by Simon Bolivar, revolted and gained their independence from Spain: Chile, Argentina, Bolivia, Paraguay, Peru, Colombia, Ecuador, Venezuela, Guatemala, and Mexico became separate nations. Canada remained the only colony on the American continent. In France Charles X (1824–1830) abolished the constitution and strove to restore the king's absolute power. "I have either got to mount a horse or a death cart," he declared. He fled to England when he was overthrown after three days of fighting, and was replaced by the liberal Louis Philippe of Orleans, another Bourbon, who restored a constitutional monarchy. The French revolt prompted Belgium to declare herself independent of the Netherlands, and in 1839 a treaty signed by the Quadruple Alliance and France guaranteed her independence. Greece revolted against Turkey in 1821, and European pressure plus Greek persistence forced Turkey to grant Greece independence in 1829. In the Balkan peninsula Serbia fought free of Turkey by 1830.

Germany, Russia, Poland, Italy, and Spain also felt currents of reform, but shunted them aside. Austria dominated a loosely bound *Bund,* or confederation, of thirty-nine German states, whose leading policy maker, Prince Metternich, fought reform on every front. He created an army of secret police, muzzled the press, forbade printing the disturbing word "Protestant" ("Evangelical" was substituted), and succeeded in stifling all outbreaks during the 1820s. Czar Nicholas I (1825–1855) came to the throne of Russia at a time when that country still felt an echo of French revolutionary ideas. Personally neutral, Nicholas was shaken by an attempted aristocratic coup, the December Revolt of 1825, which tricked common soldiers into turning upon him. Thereafter he became the determined enemy of liberalism everywhere. When Poland revolted in 1831 he sent in an army of overwhelming size, and after cruel and lengthy reprisals decreed that "Poland shall henceforth be a part of the empire and form one nation with Russia." Italy in the 1820s began a series of uprisings instigated by secret societies like the *Carbonari* (charcoal burners), but Austria's hold was too strong to permit Italian unity. Even Spain demanded a democratic constitution in 1820, but it was a military junta that made the demand.

Social change, even upheaval, hung in the air. The industrial revolution gave Germany the first strong middle class in its history. England, in the forefront of the industrial revolution, saw its middle class advance to equal status alongside the aristocracy. The so-called Victorian Compromise provided for the comfortable coexistence of both groups and even allowed for modest factory reform; children under nine years of age could not in general be employed in textile mills, and children between nine and thirteen could work only nine hours a day. France, still in the vanguard of revolutionary ideas, theorized that greater equality of wealth and political representation offered the only road to Utopia. As early as 1825 the Count of Saint-Simon argued for a kind of Christian socialism wherein scientists would be the new priest class. Fifteen years later Pierre Proudhon preached that "property is theft,"[1] and Louis Blanc advocated national workshops to control the production and distribution of goods. All of these social changes and theories bore fruit in the upheavals of the 1840s, which saw revolts in France, Germany, Italy, Hungary, and, in milder form, in the United States.

The tepid Louis Philippe, who had replaced the white flag of the Bourbons for the tricolor of the revolution, was overthrown by a four-day civil war in 1848 and fled the country. He had been defeated by a small group, led by Louis Blanc, which set up machinery for national workshops and for the election of a president. The workshops soon proved unfeasible, and the president, elected by a nation that had been contented with its monarch, was Louis Bonaparte, grandson of the Empress Josephine. In that same year a revolutionary mob drove Metternich out of Austria, and a Frankfort Parliament, the "Professors' Parliament," sought guarantees for the rights of man and offered Frederick IV, King of Prussia, the throne of a united Germany. He refused, and the Austrian army soon suppressed the revolt at home and restored Germany to its former status. In Italy, Pius IX assumed the papacy in 1846, granted amnesty to political prisoners, and introduced social and industrial reforms. But he moved too slowly to suit Italian revolutionary fervor, and a mob drove him from Rome and proclaimed the city a republic. Meanwhile, Charles Albert, king of Sardinia, led a revolution against Austria in 1848 that was crushed so easily that he abdicated in favor of his son, Victor Emmanuel II, and went into exile. In 1849 a French army sent by Louis Bonaparte recaptured Rome for Pius IX. In America, the injustice of slavery had begun to make itself felt, and in 1848 a reformist Free Soil Party led by Martin Van Buren campaigned with the slogan of "Free Soil, Free Speech, Free Labor, Free Men."

NATIONALISM, UNIFICATION, AND PROSPERITY

The decade following the revolution year of 1848 was one of unparalleled prosperity. The industrial revolution had made Europe a commercial mecca, and gold discovered in California in 1848 and in Australia in 1858 poured new wealth into its coffers.

In 1852 Louis Bonaparte had himself elected Emperor Napoleon III. He created a glittering court where his empress, Eugénie de Montijo, lived as lavish and frivolous a life as Marie Antoinette had ever done. During his

---

[1] It is worth noting that while Proudhon could theorize freely in France, a Prussian journalist who attacked the middle class at this time was exiled from Prussia. His name was Karl Marx.

reign Paris became the showplace of the world, and French military prestige revived for the first time since the Treaty of Vienna. Czar Nicholas attempted to wrest the Balkan states away from a weakened Turkey, and in 1854 England declared war on Russia for threatening the balance of power. Napoleon allied France with England, and Italy sent troops to help the allies for her own long-range reasons. The outcome of the war revolved around the siege of Sevastopol, a Ukranian naval base in southern Crimea. The long, bloody seige was intensified by snow and cholera. In 1855 Sevastopol surrendered and Turkey retained the Balkans. The Crimean War produced Florence Nightingale, the Lady with the Lamp, who brought a touch of mercy to war by tending the wounded in the battle zone; otherwise it seemed almost a preliminary exercise for future wars.

Italy, still longing for unification, looked for guidance to Count Cavour, the dumpy, myopic "merchant with the umbrella" whose policy was to involve France or England in the next Italian revolt against Austria. He offered Napoleon Nice and Savoy to join in the war, and he promised to arrange it so that France's entry would seem justified. Austria, sensing intrigue, demanded Italian disarmament. Uprisings broke out all over Italy, and in 1860 France and Italy defeated Austria in the bloody and ghastly Battle of Solferino. Italian unity was accomplished and in 1861 Victor Emmanuel II became king of all Italy except Venice and Rome.

In that same year the United States began a struggle to reaffirm its unity. Throughout the 1840s and 1850s the slavery issue increasingly divided the North from the South and, on a deeper level, Northern industrialism clashed with Southern agrarianism. When Abraham Lincoln, a declared opponent of slavery, was elected president in 1860, the Southern states took steps toward secession, and the American Civil War began. Neither side could make substantial advances into the other's territory until, in 1863, General Ulysses S. Grant besieged and captured Vicksburg, Mississippi, thus driving a wedge between the eastern and western forces at the Mississippi River. Two years of scorched-earth warfare ended Southern resistance, and in 1865 the South surrendered and began to be penetrated by the Northern industrial revolution. Lincoln's assassination at the war's end brought to the South a twelve-year period of violent "Reconstruction" which delayed full-scale industrialization until the present century.

In England the Bill of 1867 insured all men the right to vote and ended the Victorian Compromise in favor of a new alliance between proletariat and aristocracy, which led to widespread social and political reforms. In Russia the moderately humane Czar Alexander II (1855–1881) liberated Russia's 47 million serfs in 1861, but since they were not able to pay taxes, liberation did little to better their lot. He also began to reform the judicial system. A Polish revolt in the midst of reform proved upsetting, if unsuccessful, and liberalism in Russia ended, apparently forever. Small extremist groups began to dream of more violent means of obtaining reform.

In Germany, Prussia began to emerge as the power fated to lead and to unify the nation. In 1818 Prussia organized the *Zollverein,* or customs union, a reciprocal tariff system which Prussia's archrival Austria refused to join. By 1853 almost all German states except Austria belonged to the *Zollverein,* and Prussia assumed German leadership. In 1861 King William I succeeded his vacillating brother Frederick William IV, and made the domineering and devious Otto von Bismarck his cabinet president. Bismarck dismissed the cabinet, assumed full control, and with the help of organizer Albert von Roon and a professor turned general, Helmuth von Moltke, he built a brilliant war machine. He tested it out by joining with Austria to regain two German provinces, Schleswig and Holstein, from Denmark. Then in 1866 he provoked Austria into declaring war on Prussia. Europe prepared to watch the famous Austrian whitecoats destroy Bismarck's army, and Italy agreed not to intervene on either side in return for a promise of receiving Venice from the victor. Austria, with its population of 35 million, mobilized an army of 540,000; Prussia, with 18 million, mobilized 550,000. Within five weeks von Moltke's war machine sent the Austrians flying from the field. Bismarck organized North Germany into a confederation run by Prussia while Austria, threatened by an uprising of her Hungarian subjects, granted Hungary equal status in her empire; by thus dividing herself into two nation-states she ceased to be a major power.

By 1866 Napoleon III had made France the leading European nation on the continent. New wealth, the growth of Paris, wartime triumphs, and an overseas empire that now included Algeria, Cambodia, and Cochin China, increased Napoleon's prestige and pride, and the failure of the French-supported scheme to make an Austrian, Maximilian, emperor of Mexico did not diminish this prestige. Angered at Bismarck because France had gained nothing for her nonintervention in the Prussian-Austrian war, Napoleon forced a willing Bismarck into a war over the succession to the Spanish throne. Again Europe expected a Prussian defeat and again the Prussian war machine ground its enemy to pieces. At Sedan Napoleon surrendered with his army of 104,000 men. The besieged city of Paris held out gallantly for a time (while the cafés served their patrons rats and cats), but by 1871 the Franco-Prussian War came to an end. William I was proclaimed emperor of the Second German *Reich,* or empire (the First *Reich* had been the Holy Roman Empire), in the Hall of Mirrors at Versailles. A now united Germany, directed by Chancellor Bismarck, took Alsace and Lorraine but left France her other eastern territory in return for her consent for Bismarck to make a triumphal entry into Paris. Italy drove the French army away from Rome and made that city the capital of its now wholly unified nation, while Pius IX retired to a separate domain within the Vatican. France became a republic headed by the first of a series of powerless presidents. Serbia and Montenegro revolted against Turkey, and a new Balkan nation, Bulgaria, emerged. By 1880, then, the Austrian and Turkish empires and the German and Italian city-states—that is, all those members of the Congress of Vienna which were not originally nation-states —had responded to the force of nationalism.

As nations they cultivated industry, so as to fulfill their claim of offering their citizens unique advantages. The Ruhr Valley, Piedmont, the Rhône Valley, the country north of Liverpool, and the heart of Belgium all became unbroken stretches of factories and mines. Across the Atlantic, a new colossus of industry rose up. American lumber, textile, and machinery output doubled in the decade following the Civil War; the number of its factory workers almost tripled; immigrants flooded in to work in these new industries, and population increased in the generation following the Civil War from 31 to 76 million. By 1890 the United States led all nations of the world in the production of coal, iron ore, steel, oil, and railroads. The industrial wealth that had built up a middle class in Europe aggrandized a special few in America: captains of industry like Jay Gould, Commodore Vanderbilt, and Andrew Carnegie. Inequities of wealth made for labor problems, in Europe as well as in America, but until the Franco-Prussian War, these were largely the concern of theorists like Karl Marx who protested that "All the peoples of the world are enmeshed in the net of the world market."

Science in the nineteenth century provided Europe and America with a new awareness and new distractions. Its chief concerns at this time were the exploration of new areas of knowledge, and inventions: Helmholtz and energy; Joule and thermodynamics; Lyell and geology; Ampère and electricity; Koch and Pasteur and a new knowledge of microbes all made the world a safer, more comfortable place in which to live. Nineteenth-century inventions included the telegraph, telephone, bicycle, trolley car, automobile, sewing machine, vulcanized rubber, raincoats, synthetic dyes, perfumes, fertilizers, and explosives. In America alone, 676,000 patents were taken out on inventions in the last decade of the nineteenth century.

As industrial production multiplied, a need for additional sources of raw materials and markets arose, and Europe began to look to other, less industrialized continents. Moreover, all the nations of Europe had now fulfilled their manifest destiny on that continent—at least the potent Chancellor Bismarck held that this was so and played a large part in encouraging Europe to expand elsewhere. France, already in Algiers, acquired Tunis in 1881 and Madagascar in 1884. Russia reached the Pacific and built a harbor at Vladivostok; now she could look out over East and West. America, like Russia, explored its own less industrialized areas, and by 1890 had closed its last frontier. Britain entrenched herself in India, Canada, Australia, and New Zealand, acquired a sizable region in South Africa, and bought the largest share of holdings of the Suez Canal. She also exploited the Orient, and the remainder of the Western world was quick to follow.

A war with China had given Hong Kong to Britain in 1842 and opened up the ports of Shanghai and Canton to British residence and trade. A second war, in 1856, opened up the Yangtze River to all foreign trade. By 1885 all of China that was accessible was converted into a province of western Europe. In 1854 the American Commodore Matthew Perry sailed into Tokyo Bay, his stated purpose to proffer a trade treaty. Japan, unlike China, offered no resistance and instead began to westernize itself energetically. England, Russia, and Holland followed the United States in obtaining trading privileges there, and by 1880 the once quaint kingdom of Nippon bustled with its own railroads, dockyards, postal system, telegraph lines, and industries.

By 1885 the nations of Europe seemed busy and satisfied. Germany and Italy, now wholly unified, began to enter the competition for world markets, a more fruitful outlet for a nation's energies than war. Wealth and comfort had multiplied geometrically throughout the century and showed every sign of continuing to do so. Prosperity and a community of interests made nations more willing than ever before to communicate and to live in peace. In 1885 the Grand Design of the Duke of Sully, for a United Nations of Europe, seemed to have been realized, which meant that the whole world would learn to live in peace—except that within the borders of each European nation strange, unprecedented tensions were building.

THE HUMANITIES APPROACH

Both the Age of Reason and the baroque were building toward Romanticism, which glowed brightest in Europe between the onset of *Sturm und Drang* and the revolutions of 1848, and persisted in America for a generation afterwards. As will be seen, its traits echo baroque traits and its ideas carry forward those of the Age of Reason. But it, too, has its own core of identity which distinguishes it, at least in close-up view, from its baroque and rational foundation supports. Unlike lower-case romanticism, which trails warm currents of exalting feeling, as in the *Odyssey* of Homer, the *Venus of Milo*, the Cathedral at Amiens, and Shakespeare's *Romeo and Juliet*, the Romanticism of 1770–1850 is the product of unique and special circumstances. These are the French Revolution, the industrial revolution, the rise of democracy, and the spread of economic imperialism, which together account for the *essence* of Romanticism.

Before the French Revolution the life of the serfs was brutal and hard. Russian landlords could beat them, imprison them, and, after 1785, send them to Siberia; a Polish noble who killed a serf had only to pay a small fine; Prussian Junkers caned their serfs for sport; France taxed them and starved them. During the French Revolution, which was fought in large measure to improve their lot, the serfs tended to resist reform. They backed the Vendée revolt, supported Royalist claims, and remained the most conservative group in the nation. The Romantic, then, had first to confront these two truths: that the serf suffered beyond measure and that he resisted change. The principles of the French Revolution caught up the youth of Europe:

> Bliss was it in that dawn to be alive,
> But to be young was very Heaven!

wrote the English poet William Wordsworth. But when the Romantic sought ethical support for that revolution he found instead another pair of truths: the cruel lot of the serf was bettered by the revolution; but the lofty principles of the revolution—liberty, equality, and fraternity—led to famine and the Reign of Terror. Out of evil had come good, but out of good had come evil. Napoleon, coming in the aftermath of popular revolution, set the seal of tyranny across Europe and re-established aristocracy anew; but he also reformed finance and education and unified and codified the law.

The Industrial Revolution provided luxuries in greater abundance and on a wider scale than ever before in history, but its mine and factory conditions created even worse living conditions than Medieval hunger and brutality had done. Asthma, blindness, lung diseases, distortion of the limbs, and typhus and cholera epidemics became common problems. The optimism inspired by scientific progress and by an increase in material goods was matched by the pessimism brought on by man's inhumanity to man.

Democracy confronted the Romantic with another double truth. It afforded more men a greater proportion of freedom than ever before, but it also required a more universal commitment to group life. That was the *general* democratic predicament. Some particular ones include the fact that the "Professors' Parliament" at Frankfort sought to insure its "fundamental democratic rights" by appointing an emperor to guard them; the fact that in England the greatest good for the greatest number led to the Malthusian (after economist Thomas Malthus) conclusion that since population increased geometrically and food arithmetically, the rich ought not to give charity to the poor, who would only have more children; and the fact that the most successful democracy on earth, the United States, rested on the labor of slaves.

Imperialism also provided opposing truths to confront the Romantic. By providing markets for manufactured goods it built up in Europe an optimistic sense of national pride; by exploiting African and Eastern natives it oppressed Europe with a sense of guilt and shame. Imperialist wealth brought the ideal of equality closer to reality in Europe, while it fostered inequality between Europe and the more backward continents. England produced opium in India and shipped it to China, thus increasing the number of Chinese drug addicts; when the Manchu emperor protested in 1850 England opened six more Chinese ports to opium trade—and England was the most humanitarian country on earth. What she did was for the betterment of her own people, but greater freedom for Europe meant harsher tyranny for Africa and Asia.

Revolt and conservatism; good from evil and evil from good; dictatorship and justice; optimism and pessimism; individualism and the communal yoke; pride and shame; equality and inequality; freedom and tyranny; all of these pairs were aspects of the Romantic complex, each factor true, each valid, each a necessary part of its opposite. As a result, the Romantic was torn between contrasts, unable to accept one side and reject the other. His state became an agony of striving with no hope of finding a proper solution or of ever coming to rest. This, then, was Romanticism: an endless tension between opposing truths, eternally dynamic, cropping up everywhere throughout the period and creating its special tone. The nineteenth-century middle class, at once a symbol of the status quo and of the drive toward liberal reform, is thus Romantic. The Victorian Compromise, whereby middle class and aristocracy coexist, is similarly Romantic. The pink socialism of François Fourier, whose *Theory of Universal Unity*, 1829, mixes religion, economic theory, and Pythagorian number symbolism, is the essence of Romantic thought. Cavour's "If we did for ourselves what we do for our country, what scoundrels we should be!" is a Romantic statement. Philosopher Immanuel Kant demonstrated that one cannot rationally prove the existence of God, and by the same token that one cannot rationally disprove His existence—which is the essence of Romantic dilemma. Georg Wilhelm Friedrich Hegel expounded a dialectic composed of a thesis and antithesis, which combine to form a synthesis, which in turn passes over into its opposite to form a fresh thesis and antithesis, and so on into infinity, which is Romantic dynamic tension in abstract form. "If the world were a paradise of luxury and ease, men would either die of boredom or hang themselves," is the Romantic observation of Arthur Schopenhauer. The Romantic archetype is Goethe's Faust, a brilliant scholar who finds reason inadequate and who gives himself up to a quest for a moment of perfect satisfaction. He journeys across space and time and in the end he dies still striving, still unsatisfied. Perhaps the man whose life came closest to Romanticism was George Noel Gordon, Lord Byron, who countered a career of vice with the purity of art and who ended a wastrel's life fighting for Greek independence. On his death bed at Missolonghi he wrote, *"Io lascio qualche cosa di caro nel mondo"* [I leave something dear (to me) in the world], to indicate that the striving was never over, that even the truth of death failed to cancel out the truth of life.

TRAITS AND IDEAS

Besides the Romantic essence of tension and striving forever unsatisfied, Romanticism had its shaping complement of traits and ideas. These, as stated earlier, derive from the Age of Reason and the baroque, but intensifying all of them is the Romantic essence, as the humanities approach that follows will show.

A salient Romantic trait is EMOTIONALISM, basically a carry-over from the baroque, but now bound up with Romantic agony. On the surface it emerged as a polar reaction to the so-called restraints of reason, and its champion, Jean Jacques Rousseau, hailed it thus: "I have only one faithful guide on whom I can count; the succession of feelings which have marked the development of my being." The cult word for Rousseau's emotionalism was "sensibility," a public display of emotion, of sorrow preferably, that marked the demonstrator as a higher, worthier being. Of Rousseau's own performances Hume noted: "He is like a man who was stript not only of his clothes but of his skin." Blatant though these public outbursts were, they generated a fresh wave of emotionalism that broke across the Romantic period.

This wave rose up at a time when the interior life of man had begun to seek out broader emotional outlets in religion. Methodist preaching had become so enthusiastic that congregations screamed and swooned; the Temples of Reason of the French Revolution owed more to Rousseau than to Voltaire. The external, political life of man also reflected the cult of sensibility. The Declaration of Independence edged political theory with rhetoric, and the French Declaration of the Rights of Man owed an even heavier debt to Rousseau. "The representatives of the French people," reads its preamble, "constituted as a National Assembly, believing that ignorance, forgetfulness, or contempt for the rights of man are the only causes of public misfortunes and of the corruptions of governments, have resolved to set forth in a solemn declaration the natural, inalienable and sacred rights of man."

In philosophy even Kant who probed the universe with the icepick of reason, turned at last for his subjective proof of God to an emotion: happiness. It was the "Happiness proportioned to . . . morality" that led man to "postulate the existence of God as the necessary condition of the possibility of the *summum bonum*." Hegel, in his philosophy of history, asserts that "Nothing great in the world has been accomplished without passion." His dialectic, which builds from one thesis-antithesis-synthesis triad to the next, ever higher, ever truer, ever more beautiful, has been summed up by the American philosopher Josiah Royce as "A logic of passion." But, among philosophers, it is Schopenhauer who articulates this trait most searchingly. For him, life is a Romantic agony and man the puppet of emotions, the chief among them being despair. Life "is like the alms thrown to a beggar, that keeps him alive today that his misery may be prolonged till tomorrow. So long as we are given up to the throng of desires with their constant hopes and fears, so long as we are the subjects of willing, we can never have lasting happiness and peace." Schopenhauer himself expounded a philosophy as emotional as Rousseau's polemics on occasion, especially in his essay on women, which reads in brief part: "It is only the man whose intellect is clouded by his sexual impulses who could give the name of the fair sex to that undersized, narrow-shouldered, broad-hipped, and short-legged race."

LITERATURE.   Rousseau's novel, *La Nouvelle Héloise* (1761), ushered in the man of feeling on a sea of tears. A married woman, in love with her tutor, is forced to live under the same roof with him. Since both of them are moral and respectable, they can only weep and suffer, until the lady dies. Goethe, in his youthful novel *Werther*, uses a similar plot, except that his weeping hero, Werther, kills himself. The scene in which Werther and his respectable, married lady-love read Ossian and merge their tears until Werther swoons, challenges credulity. The Russian poet Alexander Pushkin's *Eugene Onegin* contains a similar plot and emotional overflow. In England *The Man of Feeling* by Henry Mackenzie combines picaresque wanderings with Rousseau's sensibility.

The cult of sensibility arrested the Neoclassical revival and diverted it into Romantic channels. The poetry of André de Chénier and the dramas of Friedrich Schiller show this effect most clearly in literature. Chénier's Neoclassical clarity and classic references vie with oppressive melancholy, tender love of nature, and personal responses to the pain of love. Schiller,

Figure 8.1 HORACE WALPOLE, assisted by WILLIAM ROBINSON.   Strawberry Hill. Twickenham, England. (1749–1777).   A. F. Kersting: Art Reference Bureau.

in his drama *The Robbers,* combines a tendency toward reflective Sophoclean writing with tearful melodrama and an ending—in which the honorable robber gives himself up because stealing is a sin!—moral enough to suit even Rousseau. Goethe's *Faust,* Part Two, combines this same Neoclassic-Romantic mixture to achieve a loftier purpose; Part One, which tells the tragic love story of Faust for Gretchen, achieves the consistent emotional current that became a hallmark of Romanticism. Novalis' *Heinrich von Ofterdingen,* a novel depicting the life of a poet and his search for the Blue Flower, a Romantic symbol of the unattainable, has the same convincing emotional force as *Faust,* Part One. In France the novels of Victor Hugo (*Les Misérables, Notre Dame de Paris*) and of Alexander Dumas (*The Three Musketeers, The Count of Monte Cristo*) feed upon potent but plausible emotion. In England, the poet William Wordsworth finds in nature a source of powerful feelings. John Keats writes of melancholy, the nightingale, and bygone antiquity with passionate restraint. Percy Bysshe Shelley "shrieked, and clasped [his] hands in ecstasy!" at the sight of Intellectual Beauty. In America Henry Wadsworth Longfellow describes in *Evangeline* the deportation of the French from Acadia during the French and Indian Wars with Rousseaulike sensibility, and Nathaniel Hawthorne in his novel *The Scarlet Letter* places his heroine, Hester Prynne, at the apex of an emotional triangle Romantic in its equal and opposing play of forces.

ARCHITECTURE.   Sensibility even affected the practical art of architecture. Buildings were created for the specific purpose of achieving an emotional effect. Goethe's Werther read the third-century Gaelic poet Ossian, and wept because the past was so remote, and because it was all so sad. Horace Walpole, who wrote a novel with a Medieval setting in which ghosts walk and portraits come to life, *The Castle of Otranto,* built Strawberry Hill (Figure 8.1) to recapture the melancholy and strangeness of that nonexistent time. With the help of a professional builder, William Robinson, and a circle of amateur architects, Walpole redecorated and remodeled a basic rectangular plan until its salient appeal was emotional. The crenelated roof, the walls swathed in vines, the towers, the circled battlement, and the Gothic windows all convey a feeling of mystery and remoteness. Inside, gloomy, overdecorated chambers and hallways add to the hushed decaying effect so that feeling, not function, dominates both interior and façade. In a similar vein Fonthill Abbey, a country house, was designed by James Wyatt for a patron of sensibility. A 200-foot tower loomed above its narrow façade, and its foyer, perhaps larger than the rest of the house all together, resembled the interior of Amiens Cathedral, but with a staircase. It was shoddily built, with mood, not livability, as its purpose, and it crashed to the ground after a brief lifetime.

The popular etchings of Giovanni Battista Piranesi, which reproduced ancient buildings as exotic marvels surrounded by glowing life, gave impetus to a Classic-Romantic style of architecture akin to the writing of Chénier and Schiller. Its most fashionable practioner, Robert Adam, designed room interiors that blended classical formalism with rococo ovals, niches, and tracery in a way that satisfied both feeling and function. Widely popular in Britain, the Adam interiors became a standard feature of nineteenth-century New England homes as well. The Old Museum in Berlin by Friedrich Schinkel combines a regular Ionic façade with an exciting and original roof line. And the National Capitol in Washington, D.C., combines the Parthenon, Versailles, and the Dome of St. Paul's into a structure at once formal and emotionally compelling.

SCULPTURE.   Sensibility intensified by patriotic fervor are the ingredients of *The Departure of the Volunteers* by François Rude (Figure 8.2). Nicknamed *La Marseillaise* and placed on the *Arc de Triomphe,* this group statue depicts the Goddess of War trumpeting a call to arms (or perhaps singing the *Marseillaise*) and lunging forward in a thrust of motion taken up by the turning, twisting, striding group below her. Volunteers to defend their country in the days of the French Revolution, they include young and old as well as men of military age, and, as an added sensual fillip, the youth is nude. Like Strawberry Hill they hark back to a bygone age, not merely to 1793, but by their Grecian robes, Roman shields and helmets, and Medieval coats of mail, to all the glamour of war in ages past. The faces of the man and boy in the center, determined and aspiring, express all the ardent feeling that charges the work as a whole.

Less tempestuous and more an example of Classic-Romantic fusion is the *Washington* of the American sculptor, Horatio Greenough (Figure 8.3). A huge work, over eleven feet high, its seminude figure shares the solemn dignity of a Greek god with the elemental simplicity of Rousseau's noble savage; the face, too, wavers between classic majesty and Rousseauesque petulance. The *Bound Slave* by Hiram Powers, another American, contains the same classical-emotional fusion: the nude body is a close copy of the Medicean Venus, and the chained hands are a delicately sentimental reminder that Greece was still not free.

PAINTING.   The work of Jean Baptiste Greuze infused painting with unlimited sensibility. In his *The Prodigal Son,* for example, a dying father curses his stricken son while half a dozen relatives, and a dog, gyrate in paroxysms of horror and grief. The sensibility of Greuze added overtones of feeling to the Neoclassical paintings of Jacques Louis David. *The Death of Socrates* (Figure 8.4) has the solidity and decor of a work of classic sculpture. The outlines of the figures are precise and clear, the posed attitudes, togas, and crisp curls are studiedly Greek. Socrates, about to take the cup of hemlock, makes the same wooden gesture as does Greenough's *Washington,* and he sits illuminated by a light without warmth. But in jolting contrast to all of this formality are the grief-stricken attitudes of his disciples—there are twelve if we include the three on the stairs—which engulf Socrates' classic pose in a wave of powerful feeling.

Figure 8.2 FRANÇOIS RUDE. *The Departure of the Volunteers* (*La Marseillaise*).
Paris. (1836). [Archives Photographiques].

Figure 8.3 HORATIO GREENOUGH. *Washington.* (1832–1842). The Smithsonian Institution.

Figure 8.4 JACQUES LOUIS DAVID. *The Death of Socrates.* (1787). The Metropolitan Museum of Art, Wolfe Fund, 1931.

"There is not one touch in those Drawings and Pictures but what came from my Head & my Heart in Unison," wrote the Romantic poet-painter William Blake, thereby defining the role of emotion in the full tide of Romantic painting. Francisco Goya dramatized this mixture of head and heart in works of searing impact. His *May 3, 1808* (Figure 8.5) depicts the execution of a group of citizens of Madrid who had tried to revolt against Napoleon's army of occupation. The victims, placed between the curve of the hill, and the bayoneted rifles of the soldiers, stand pinned between man and nature. The neutral colors all around them form dramatic contrast with the splotch of dark red blood below the body of the foremost corpse. The fearful, despairing faces of those waiting to be shot are stark cartoons, the faces of men no longer living, while their executioners are faceless, men not really alive, toy soldiers shooting toy people—a universal image of the wartime game of life and death.

Romantic painters put emotion to a variety of uses. Blake (Figure 8.7) makes it contribute to a sense of wonder. Gainsborough and Corot infuse it into landscapes, making nature come alive according to the gospel of Rousseau. Delacroix (Figure 8.13) makes color convey emotion, as does Turner (Figure 8.8), who also uses emotion to comment upon history and nature. In America, the historical scenes of Benjamin West border on the

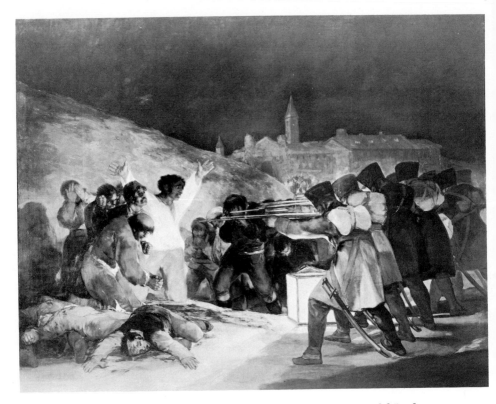

Figure 8.5 FRANCISCO GOYA. *May 3, 1808.* (1815). Museo del Prado.

verge of sensibility, and the nature scenes of Winslow Homer find endless drama in man's struggle with the elements.

MUSIC. Ludwig von Beethoven, like Schiller, Adam, Greenough, and David, marks the transition to Romanticism by combining, in his middle period, loose-fitting Classical form with a charged dramatic power never before heard in music. "Music," he wrote, "must strike fire," and to strike sparks he explored the resources of dynamics, of thumping repetition, of rhythmic energy, and of introspective lyricism in music that more or less followed the Classical sonata form and laws of tonality (pp. 257 and 265). The germinal four-note first theme of his *Fifth Symphony* has been likened to fate hammering at the door, and its final movement—in C major where the first movement began in C minor—to a triumphant outburst. His piano sonata, Op. 53, the *Waldstein Sonata,* opens with a similar explosion of power. The *Pathétique Sonata* sounds the depths of emotion, as do the slow movements of his *Fifth Piano Concerto (The Emperor Concerto)* and his *Violin Concerto.*

A similar blend of Classicism and Romanticism, adhering somewhat more closely to Classical form, shapes the symphonies, concertos, and oratorios of Felix Mendelssohn, the symphonies of Franz Schubert, and all of the music of Johannes Brahms, with whom the Romantic period comes to an end. Between Beethoven and Brahms, however, a Romantic style of music arose and flourished which, although keeping sight of Classical techniques, overstressed one or another—particularly melody—for emotional effect. Romantic melody tends to be lyric and moving, its beauty a distraction from Classical form; one result is that exposition tends to outweigh development in the Romantic treatment of the sonata form. To further enrich melody, Romantic harmony tends to grow more expressive, turning to new chordal relationships and progressions to achieve more colorful effects. With harmony more freely flowing, Classical laws of tonality begin to lose their hold, and new sounds and sonorities take precedence.

Romantic stress upon melody and harmony for heightened emotional effect occurs in the piano music of Frederic Chopin, Franz Liszt, and Robert Schumann; in the chamber music of Schubert (the second movement of his *String Quintet,* perhaps the most indispensable piece of music ever written, achieves pure Romantic tension between melodic flow and formal restraint); in the songs of Schubert, Schumann, and the American composer Stephen Foster; in the lyric operas of Vincenzo Bellini, Gaetano Donizetti, and Charles Gounod, the dramatic operas of Giuseppe Verdi, and the music dramas of Richard Wagner, whose *Tristan und Isolde* reaches peaks of passion that enlarge the vocabulary of music.

Baroque subjectivity continued into the Romantic period and, as in the case of emotionalism, deepened in intensity. It became more self-absorbed, more self-preoccupied, and with the onset of revolution, more widespread. It became a cult of INDIVIDUALISM, which, like every cult, became more insistent and intrusive as it grew. Rousseau sounded the keynote of Romantic individualism in the first page of his *Confessions.* "I am made unlike any one I have ever met; I will even venture to say that I am like no one in the whole world. I may be no better, but at least I am different. Whether nature did well or ill in breaking the mould in which she formed me, is a question which can only be resolved after the reading of my book." Napoleon was Romantic individualism unchained. Democracy became, among other things, a safeguard of Romantic individualism for the many. The American Bill of Rights, with its guarantees of free expression, religious liberty, and the right to bear arms, was a blueprint for individual self-expansion. The French Declaration of the Rights of Man was even more extreme, buttressing democratic safeguards with the defiance of Rousseau: "ignorance, forgetfulness, or contempt of the rights of man are the only causes of public misfortunes and of the corruptions of governments," reads its preamble in part.

In economics, Romantic individualism turned to the *laissez-faire* theories of Adam Smith, which favored free enterprise and opposed all restraint of trade. These theories, in practice, bred a class of captains of industry with a boundless capacity for self-expansion. In America, for example, such men as Vanderbilt, Cooke, and Gould absorbed railroads, bonds, and the United States gold reserve the way Napoleon had absorbed opposing armies. For better or worse Romantic individualism pervaded the age, despite attempts by Bismarck, Metternich, and Napoleon III to stamp it out. Napoleon III banished Victor Hugo and went so far as to order college professors to dress neatly and to trim their beards in an attempt to restore conformity, but despite his efforts France led all other countries in individualist expressions.

In philosophy, the first steps in Kant's *Critique of Pure Reason* lead to a proof of individualism. These are his "synthetic judgments," which bind a subject to another term not contained in it—that is, the chicken (subject) crosses the road (other term)—the binding representing an operation of the individual mind. Thus for Kant each mind brings its judgments to experience and thus determines man's view of the universe. In this way each man creates knowledge and, in a sense, reality. After Kant, Johann Gottlieb Fichte defined individualism as the creative activity of the ego. "The ego determines itself in part and is determined in part," and this makes for a society of "free individuals." For Hegel, the supreme form of government is metamorphosed into a "true individual." Schopenhauer, while contending that "the individual is only phenomenal," admitted that the individual's ceaseless struggle toward self-expansion was the basis for all of life's activities.

LITERATURE.   Goethe's Faust represents the Romantic individual in fullest dimensions. In his quest for a moment of perfect contentment, Faust grows ever more urgent and demanding, and is never satisfied. His tender love affair with Gretchen, his marriage with Helen of Troy, his return to his childhood in the Baucis and Philemon episode, and his creation of a brave new world only leave him with more expansive desires and a restless urge to assert himself. Goethe's novels about Wilhelm Meister, describing the artist as a Romantic individual, set forth a more selfish, more typical, less idealized example of individualism. Stendhal's Julien Sorel in *The Red and the Black* echoes Meister's preoccupation with self against the rigid sounding boards of army, church, and middle class. Pushkin's Eugene Onegin must be destructively himself, and like Schopenhauer's will-driven man must suffer for it. Herman Melville's *Moby Dick* makes Captain Ahab the hero, and victim, of his own Faustian quest. And Walt Whitman sounded his "barbaric yawp over the roofs of the world" in a "Song of Myself" that stretched and snapped the old ways of poetic form and content the way Beethoven's music had done.

ARCHITECTURE.   Although Romantic architecture turned up no Palladio or Wren to create a series of towering, trend-setting works, it did produce a number of one-of-a-kind structures of decided individuality. Strawberry Hill is uniquely bizarre, as is Wyatt's Fonthill Abbey. For the interior of the Bank of England, John Soane created inimitable swirling effects with iron and glass. Eugene Viollet-le-Duc, the foremost scholar-architect of his day, wrote: "If we would really have an architecture of the nineteenth century, we must, as a primary consideration, have a care that it is indeed our own, taking its form and characteristics not from precedent but from ourselves." Charles Garnier took the *Opéra* in Paris from himself, and its ponderous body, pale green rococo dome, and Christmas-tree ornamentation remain unique and oddly impressive. The "Wedding-Cake" House at Kennebunkport, Maine (Figure 8.6), reveals how Romantic individualism caught up the common man. The latticed entranceway, filigree façade, and knobby spires were superadded to a bare rectangular structure by an enterprising sea captain, and the result is a gingerbread-house unlike any other. The captains of industry in America and elsewhere sought this same originality through lavishness, and Biltmore, designed by Richard Hunt for the Vanderbilt family, boasts a hodgepodge façade and ornate furnishings typical of the atypicality of all such estates.

Figure 8.6   "Wedding Cake" House.   Kennebunkport, Maine.   (c. 1850).   [Wayne Andrews].

SCULPTURE.   The one major sculptor of the period, Auguste Rodin, flourished during its final phases and his individuality depended upon its later
stylistic innovations (Figures 8.10, 8.14, 8.18). Romantic sculpture proper
offered, as did architecture, some unique examples of individuality. *La
Marseillaise* has its own special vision and furious energy. *Jaguar Devouring
Hare* by Antoine Barye blends suggestion and realism in a unique way to
provide a chilling comment on the jungle. And the overcontorted gladiators,
animals, and personifications of the American William Rimmer produce an
individual if minor body of work.

PAINTING.   The Romantic artist was determined to convey *his* view of an
object and *his* feelings about it, and this desire bred a number of self-
consciously personal styles. Delacroix (Figure 8.13) claimed that "The
personality of the scientist is absent from his work; it is quite a different
matter with the artist. The seal that he imprints on his production is what
makes it the work of an artist," and he made color his special coat of arms. In
his paintings, color conveys mood and idea, and even becomes a means of
psychological analysis. Goya (Figures 8.5, 8.11) made stark form and revolutionary fervor his personal media. The American Washington Allston saw
nature with a glowing wonder unique to himself in canvases like *Moonlit
Landscape* and *Elijah in the Desert*. But it was a pair of English painters,
Blake and Turner, who carried individualism to its farthest extremes and
presented sights never seen before on land or sea. "I know that This
World is a World of imagination & Vision," wrote Blake. "I see Every
thing I paint In This World, but Every body does not see alike." What
Blake saw appeared in a series of watercolors and engravings, one of
which is *The Ancient of Days* (Figure 8.7). Taken from Proverbs viii: 27,
"When He prepared the heavens, I was there: when He set a compass on
the face of the depths," it portrays a divine being in the act of creation,
and the doubled-over body and single superextended arm suggest, but are
not, reality as we know it. The linear drawing, in contrast to the allusive
theme, blurs subject and object beyond logic; in this work we must rely not
on a frame of reference, but on our own intuition. For Blake, the creator of
the world was Urizen, an evil spirit, and yet the figure in this engraving, its
meditative eyes and flowing hair forming a Romantic tension of opposites,
seems anything but evil.

Where Blake saw visions that no other eye had seen, Turner changed
what the eye could see into visions. By using color with a fiery passion that
melted his objects into indistinguishable forms, Turner converted skies,
landscapes, cities, and railroads into windfall light. *The Fighting Téméraire*
(Figure 8.8) is half narrative, half vision. To the left, a famous old fighting
ship is being towed off to be destroyed, its graceful bow and masts in
poignant contrast to the dumpy, steaming tug. Around it settles a silver
dusk, while off to the right—a materialistic present? the future?—red
clouds and a yellow sun shroud the city making it seem a ghostly blur.

Figure 8.7 WILLIAM BLAKE. *The Ancient of Days.* (1794). Courtesy of the Trustees of the British Museum.

Figure 8.8 JOSEPH MALLORD WILLIAM TURNER. *The Fighting Téméraire.* (1839). Courtesy of the National Gallery, London.

MUSIC. Romantic composers too, prided themselves on expressing their own feelings and personalities, and all in all did the most to promote the cult of artist as individual. Beethoven, Liszt, and Wagner created the image of the artist as a new form of aristocracy, an image still operative today. The works and personality of Beethoven overshadowed the entire period. It was he who led music away from Classical forms and tonality, who first wrote for himself, eschewing patrons, and who, in his premature will, the "Heiligenstadt Will" written in 1802 when deafness first threatened, proclaimed his sacred mission as Artist: "Art alone withheld me [from suicide]; it seemed impossible to leave the world until I had produced all that I felt called upon to produce."

His *Third Symphony* is a conspicuous example of how he broke rule after rule to express himself. Subtitled the *Eroica*—originally written to honor Napoleon, whose coronation disillusioned and enraged the composer —it is music for titans. Its length was unprecedented; its overpowering first movement presents six themes instead of two or three; its second movement is a funeral march, strangely converted into a fugue at one stage; its finale consists of several variation cycles; and the heroic tone of the work as a whole is the legend of Napoleon cast in real and permanent form. In his final period, when deafness came, Beethoven broke the bounds of form, like the last works of Michelangelo, and in his final quartets and the daemonic *Grosse Fuge* (Op. 131, 132, 133), piano sonatas (Op. 106, 109, 110), *Missa Solemnis,* and *Ninth Symphony,* personal vision supersedes all custom or precedent. The *Ninth Symphony,* perhaps his most towering achievement, uses a *scherzo* second theme—in place of an *adagio*—whose chief motif consists of three notes supported rhythmically by kettle drums; an *adagio* third movement that connotes the Gates of Paradise; and a fourth movement that introduces the earlier themes, a chorus and four soloists, mixes two double fugues and a Turkish march, and culminates in a coda (tail ending) of unequaled massiveness and length.

Other manifestations of Romantic individualism include a new emphasis on solo songs, like those of Schubert and Schumann; the new prominence of virtuoso-composers like Liszt and Niccolò Paganini; new instrumental forms: fantasies, romances, and nocturnes in which the composer introspects aloud—Chopin's *Nocturnes* are among the finest examples of this style of writing; and the reshaping of a form as complex and public as opera to suit the composer's own desires. Richard Wagner, who claimed to believe in God and Beethoven, but who owed chief allegiance to himself, created giant music dramas purposing to summarize the soul of his people. If nothing else, they displayed the Wagnerian soul under a cosmic microscope. His use of *leitmotifs* (themes representing moods and characters) and of orchestral color was unique, and operas like the *Ring of the Nibelungs,* a tetralogy based on German folk myths, and *Tristan und Isolde* conveyed a solemn magic distinctively his own. His stormy life befitted the image of the Romantic Artist. The Philadelphia Exposition of 1876, recognizing him as a spirit kindred to captains of industry, offered him five thousand dollars to compose a single march.

In his *Apology for Sebonde* Montaigne expressed the central belief of the Renaissance (and of all previous periods) that institutions, faulty as they may be, represent the product of centuries of trial and error and should be adhered to as the best that mankind can produce. The propaganda of Francis Bacon challenged the validity of classical institutions for the Age of Reason and set in motion a questioning of all traditions. The Romantic period brought this questioning to a sharp climax by asserting that the status quo was wrong. Thus the ages-old institutions of Greek thought, Christianity, and aristocracy now came into decisive conflict with the rights of man. In politics, this conflict led to changes in the form of revolution, and during the Romantic period all of Europe and America felt its tremors. It gave rise to major innovations like American democracy, and to trivial ones like the renaming of playing cards during the French Revolution—jacks, queens, and kings became fraternities, equalities, and liberties.

The Congress of Vienna made a mighty effort to check the flow of change, but the world of the eighteenth century was slipping away.

The industrial revolution acceierated the change from agrarian to urban life, introduced a society in which men now worked for money instead of goods, and led to a series of changes in economic theory. The *laissez-faire* concept of Adam Smith gave way to the theories of Bentham and Sismondi that wealth must be considered in relationship to men. Mill suggested a compromise whereby production was determined by *laissez-faire*, and distribution by standards of equity. This in turn led to the roseate socialism of Saint-Simon and, at the close of the period, to the revolutionary communism of Karl Marx. In *Cosmos* (1858), the Baron von Humbolt was able to summarize all available scientific learning. A few years afterward every branch of science had changed and multiplied beyond reach, and Darwin, at the end of the period, introduced a science of changes: evolution. A view of CHANGE AS DESIRABLE AND NECESSARY so permeated the period that all aspects of life came to demand change which, once under way, continued.

In philosophy the world view of the universe changed from a mechanistic to an evolutionary one. Gotthold Lessing wrote a history of religion to show that all earlier religions were valid steps in God's progressive revelation. Johann Herder, in his history of mankind, claimed that everything ripened by a natural process of evolution, including art, language, politics, and society. For Hegel the universe was in continuous evolution, and he envisioned the course of history as a dual process of change through which man came to a consciousness of the world around him and God came to a consciousness of Himself.

LITERATURE.   Romantic literature initiated frequent changes in form and technique. Hugo in his play *Hernani* violated the unities and used run-on lines in place of the end-stop ones hallowed by Corneille and Racine, and thereby precipitated a riot. Goethe's Wilhelm Meister novels innovated the *Entwicklungsroman,* a novel in which a young, sensitive hero learns by absorbing ideas as well as practical experience. E. T. A. Hoffmann and Edgar Allan Poe transformed tales of mystery and horror into legitimate works of art. Byron's *Don Juan* blended epic, philosophy, and personal confession into an amalgam without precedent. And Whitman's poetry replaced traditional rhyme and meter with "free verse," concerned, like Romantic music, with shifting rhythmic and tonal effects.

In content, Romantic literature often sounded the revolutionary call to change. The *Sturm und Drang* movement was a protest against political as well as stylistic (Neoclassical) tyranny. Goethe's *Faust* saw man's predicament specifically as endless change: for a still point of peace, Faust offered to consign his soul to the devil. Schiller's *William Tell* is one of the great dramatic paeans to the spirit of revolution, and Byron's *Don Juan* includes a plea for the freedom of tyrannized Greece. Pushkin's *Boris Godunov* recounts in sympathetic accents the punishment of tyranny, and Whitman's *Democratic Vistas* voices an extended cheer for the changes about to come.

ARCHITECTURE.   "Having at our disposal new materials, machinery until now unknown, enlarged resources, requirements much more complicated than those with which the ancients had to deal in their architecture . . . we might then hope at least to lay the foundations of a true architecture of the nineteenth century, although perhaps we must leave to our successors the task of developing it to completion." So wrote Viollet-le-Duc prophetically in 1863. By that time the changing century had made commonplace such new types of buildings as exhibition halls, post offices, public schools, apartment houses, railroad stations, department store warehouses, mammoth factories, and that composite exercise in economy building, the factory town. Along with new types came new materials: stucco; hollow tile; iron used for floor beams and roof trusses; then steel columns and beams in post-and-girder constructions to form building frames; sheet glass of unprecedented size; and at the end of the period elevator shafts. Change in materials and techniques is reflected in Soane's glass and iron Bank of England interior; in the *Bibliothèque Sainte-Geneviève* by Henri Labrouste, a library using cast iron and glass to obtain a maximum amount of open space; and in the Crystal Palace by Joseph Paxton (Figure 8.9). Designed for the Great Exhibition of the Industry of All Nations, the first world's fair, the enormous structure consisted in the main of a cast-iron framework filled in with sheets of glass of standardized sizes whose plenitude lent the palace a fairy quality in glittering contrast to its geometrical factory-building outlines. Uniformity of size made for speedy construction, and the Crystal Palace went up in a few months, where it had taken Medieval buildings of comparable size centuries to complete.

Figure 8.9   JOSEPH PAXTON.   Crystal Palace.   London.   (1851).   Victoria and Albert Museum, Crown Copyright.

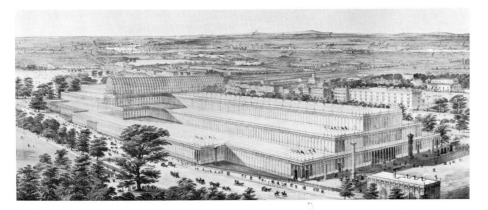

Nineteenth-century architecture was not only changed by new methods and materials but also by a swift succession of traditional styles: Gothic, Classic, Romantic, *Néo-Grec*, Victorian Gothic, and Eclectic, the latter a ceaseless search for novelty. A comparison of such Romantic works as Strawberry Hill, the "Wedding Cake" House, the Crystal Palace, the Houses of Parliament (Figure 8.12), and *Sacré-Coeur* (Figure 8.17) reveals how change, not consistency, supplied the architectural motif of this period.

SCULPTURE.   Little change occurred in sculpture until the end of the period, which accounts in part for its minor importance through most of the century. Auguste Rodin, the one major sculptor of the age, emerged during its final, impressionist phase, and the works of his middle period, such as *The Kiss* (Figure 8.10), usher in sculptural change. Using the new technique of modeling in clay while assistants translated the models into marble or bronze, Rodin concentrated upon the play of light and shadow, much as baroque sculptors had done. Sculpture for him was technically a matter of knobs and hollows, and by arranging these in proper relationship he sought to capture the essence of his subject. *The Kiss* was first intended to depict Paolo and Francesca, the lovers in Dante's Inferno, but Rodin's concern for the thing-in-itself changed the work into a universal expression of emotion. It vibrates with the movement of encircling arms, cast of bodies, knees that touch, and curling toes. It gains power from the tension of contrast: of faces vague and in shadow that vie with the hard clarity of smooth bodies; of bodies which in turn contrast with the rough stone on which they are seated. Despite its physical theme, the abstractions of movement and contrast dominate this work, so that not only does it introduce change in technique but also change in emphasis.

PAINTING.   Like literature and architecture, Romantic painting witnessed frequent changes in style and technique: the overflowing sensibility of Greuze; the Romantic Neoclassicism of David; the expressive coloring of Delacroix (Figure 8.13); the molten forms of Turner; the mystic primitivism of Blake; the art-for-art's-sake nudes of Jean Auguste Dominique Ingres—these, combined with the work of the realists and impressionists who close out Romanticism, provide styles and techniques varied enough to accommodate several periods.

As in literature, painting also recorded the sense of revolution that motivated change. In *Raft of the Medusa* Théodore Géricault depicted the agony of survivors from the ship *Medusa*, which the French government had licensed to leave port despite its damaged condition. *May 3, 1808* of Goya seethes against tyranny, and even his courtly scenes smoulder with revolutionary fervor. *The Family of Charles IV* (Figure 8.11) is a variation of *The Maids of Honor* of Velásquez (Figure 7.14) and like its source shows the artist at work before a canvas and flanked by royal visitors. But where

Figure 8.10   AUGUSTE RODIN.   *The Kiss.*   (1898).   Courtesy Musée Rodin, Permission Spadem 1968 by French Reproduction Rights, Inc.

Velásquez used the theme to explore spatial relationships, Goya uses it to dissect personality. A hard light sets the courtly figures in clear relief and highlights their jewels and decorations. In the foreground stands the king, resplendent in a costume whose brilliance belies the weak, flaccid face with its round, idiotic eyes. The queen mother, alongside the painter, has the same round eyes and a face whose years show nothing left but pettiness and dissipation. Queen Maria Luisa, notorious throughout Europe, stands in the center, her vanity and character apparent, and the face of her daughter at her side offers clear testimony to the future of the royal house. That Goya could thus portray the royal family attests to their ignorance and to the vigor of his own revolutionary sentiments.

MUSIC.   Here, too, the Romantic period witnessed rapid changes in forms and techniques. New forms introduced into serious music included the song cycle, waltz, mazurka, polonaise, fantasy, arabesque, nocturne, ballade, romance, tone poem, program symphony, and concert overture. New techniques included the introduction of new chords and chordal progressions, a drift away from Classical rules governing tonality, greater use of chromaticism, richer orchestral color through the addition of new instruments, and the division and subdivision of orchestral string sections.

Figure 8.11 FRANCISCO GOYA. *The Family of Charles IV.* (1800). Museo del Prado.

Beethoven altered the Classical sonata form often and freely; the first movement of his *Moonlight Sonata* is a free fantasy; for the third movement minuet he customarily substituted a *scherzo;* the coda that concludes his *Second Symphony* introduces a whole new theme; six themes form the opening exposition of his *Third Symphony;* his *Fifth Symphony* is the first symphony to use trombones; his *Ninth Symphony* introduces vocal soloists and a chorus; his *Quartet Opus 130* is in six movements; his *Piano Sonata Opus 111* contains only two movements; his *An die Ferne Geliebte* (to the far-off beloved), was the first of a multitude of Romantic song cycles—and these are only a few of his innovations. Other examples of Romantic stylistic novelties include Berlioz' first use of *leitmotif*, or recurring theme, in a symphony, his *Symphonie Fantastique;* the above-mentioned divided strings, devised by Carl Maria von Weber; and Wagner's extensive use of *leitmotif* and declamatory aria in his operas.

Romantic music also contained revolutionary content, and here again Beethoven predominated. His opera *Fidelio* celebrates the triumph of goodness over tyranny; his *Eroica Symphony* is a hymn to human heroism; and his *Ninth Symphony* uses Schiller's "Ode to Joy" (originally "Ode to Freedom"), with its glorious affirmation of man's goodness.

Beneath the literal events of this period churned one consistent underlying force: NATIONALISM. Empires split to form nations and city-states united to do the same. Revolutions brought twelve new American nations into being, and nations already created began to glory in their purpose. The nationalism of the Romantic period was a new and special kind. It meant a *personal* pride in one's country—earlier nationalisms had glorified empire or monarch—which now offered unprecedented freedom of opportunity, thanks to the industrial revolution and the rise of the middle class. In philosophy, Hegel erects a hierarchy of syntheses from individual to family to state, with the nation-state the most complete "individual" and Germany its most mature example.

LITERATURE.   The *Sturm und Drang* movement included a search for national identity, and the studies made by Herder of German folk poetry were attempts to establish the roots of a national culture; the nationalistic music dramas of Wagner magnified and intensified those efforts. In England the general call to freedom in the poetry of Shelley and Byron narrowed into nationalist propaganda in the poetry of Tennyson—in works, for example, like "The Charge of the Light Brigade." Pushkin and Mikhail Lermontov wrote poems whose theme was freedom, with an undercurrent of nationalism; Nikolai Gogol, despite the satiric tone of his fiction and drama, strove to inaugurate a truly national Russian literature. Giacomo Leopardi, at heart a melancholy lyricist, wrote many patriotic odes—"To Italy" is typical and powerful—in response to the spirit of the times. And

Walt Whitman in *Democratic Vistas* applauded the bright future of America in a tumbling torrent of prose:

The best culture will always be that of the manly and courageous instincts, and loving perceptions, and of self respect—aiming to form, over this continent, an idiocrasy of universalism, which, true child of America, will bring joy to its mother, returning to her in her own spirit, recruiting myriads of offspring, able, natural, perceptive, tolerant, devout believers in her, America, and with some definite instinct why and for what she has arisen, most vast, most formidable of historic births, and is, now and here, with wonderful step, journeying through Time.

ARCHITECTURE.   Many national monuments were built during this period, reminiscent of the self-glorying monuments of the Roman Empire: examples include the colossal *Arc de Triomphe* in Paris, the iron Liberation Spire designed by Schinkel in 1818 (to inspire a united Germany), and the Alexandrian Column in St. Petersburg. The rise and spread of Gothic architecture during the period gave more profound expression to its nationalism. Gothic models supplanted Greek and Roman ones—which nations began to look upon as alien—as each nation turned back to its particular Gothic or Medieval style, to its own past. Actual Medieval structures were remodeled, such as St. Ouen at Rouen and Cologne Cathedral, and a number of new "Gothic" structures were erected, conspicuous among them the Houses of Parliament (Figure 8.12). Built by Charles Barry but largely designed by Augustus Welby Pugin, author of books championing the Gothic style, its façade consists of two parts, like Chambord (Figure 5.5). The lower part is made up of symmetrical masses, neat, imposing, and of suitable magnitude. The upper part consists of an asymmetrical arrangement of pointed spires whose first-impression enchantment dims under close analysis. The pointed spire had the sanction of that influential art critic John Ruskin, who saw it as the symbol of Christian truth as well as architectural excellence. Parenthetically, American architecture, which had no Gothic past to fall back upon, turned to the designs of Pugin and to the theories of Ruskin for its own "Gothic," as in St. Patrick's Cathedral by James Renwick and Trinity Church by Richard Upjohn, both in New York City.

SCULPTURE.   Nationalism fostered the creation of an outsized number of commemorative statues, many of them compelling although they all fall short of greatness. Rude's monument to *Marshal Ney,* one of Napoleon's generals, has the same patriotic sweep and energy that characterizes *La Marseillaise.* David D'Angers, whose stated purpose was to make sculpture national, made formal and somewhat imposing monuments to French (and American) heroes and geniuses, including Racine and Corneille. Emmanuel Frémiet specialized in commemorative equestrian monuments, including Joan of Arc and Bertrand du Guesclin, a hero of the fourteenth-century wars against the English. In Germany Daniel Rauch created statues for the same avowed national purpose as D'Angers, and his best known work was

Figure 8.12   CHARLES BARRY AND AUGUSTUS WELBY PUGIN.   Houses of Parliament. London.   (c. 1836–1865).   [Central Office of Information, London].

an equestrian monument to Frederic the Great in Berlin. In America Greenough, William Rush, Henry Brown, and John Ward all made better than adequate commemorative statues of George Washington, while Irish-born Augustus St. Gaudens produced America's finest example of this kind of work, his pensive and spiritual statue of Lincoln in Lincoln Park, Chicago.

PAINTING.   After works like *The Death of Socrates* which extolled freedom in general, David lapsed into propagandistic nationalism in his capacity as official painter to Napoleon. His ponderous *Coronation of Napoleon I* typifies his work during this period. Antoine Gros did a series of Napoleonic scenes which also equated Napoleon with French nationalism. Delacroix, who founded the Romantic school of painting, disclosed the real spirit of French nationalism. His *Liberty Leading the People* (Figure 8.13) allegorizes the Revolution of 1830 which deposed Charles X. Liberty, with a rifle in one hand, the tricolor of revolution in the other, is flanked by an inspired youth and a top-hatted, frock-coated businessman. Behind them as they trample over barricades march workers, peasants, and even a soldier—in other words, all of France. Off to the right a misty Notre Dame, serene and static in contrast to the surging movement of the mob, lends the sanction of the church to this national revolution. Color adds its own emotional impact to the drama of this scene, the brilliant red at the tip of the tricolor a clarion call to passion and blood.

Figure 8.13 EUGÈNE DELACROIX. *Liberty Leading the People.* (1830). Louvre,
Paris. [Photographie Giraudon].

In Spain Goya sounded the same praise of freedom and national in-
tegrity in *May 3, 1808.* The Gothic loveliness of Turner's *Fighting
Téméraire* bespeaks his pride in England. In America the Washington portraits by Gilbert Stuart and Charles Willson Peale, the self-glorifying historical scenes by John Trumbull and Henry Sargent, and the love for the
American wilderness expressed in the work of George Caleb Bingham,
Asher Durand, and George Inness restate the pride and optimism of Whitman's *Democratic Vistas.*

MUSIC. Romantic music paid direct tribute to nationalism by cultivating
"national" styles toward the end of the period. "Politics, literature, people
. . . these reflections eventually find an outlet in music," wrote Schumann
in his music journal. Wagner composed his music dramas for the greater
glory of the German state and people. Verdi aimed to write operas that
were distinctively Italian, and his last name became a rallying cry for
Italian politics as well as Italian music—Verdi formed the initials for
Vittorio Emmanuele, Re D'Italia, Victor Emmanuel, King of Italy. In
Russia a group of five composers, Cesar Cui, Alexander Borodin, Modest

Mussorgsky, Mili Balakirev, and Nicolai Rimsky-Korsakov banded together to produce and promote Russian music in place of Western (European) music, and even a "Western" composer like Peter Tchaikovsky exudes the lush sentiment, the bombast, and the oriental opulence characteristic of his homeland. Isaac Albéniz and Miguel de Falla wrote music that glorified the accents of Spain; Edward Grieg did the same for Norway; Friedrich Smetana for Czechoslovakia; and in England William Schwenk Gilbert and Arthur Sullivan wrote operettas whose cozy satire was at heart complacent reassurance that all was well with the British empire.

In *Émile*, the landmark educational tract by Rousseau, the boy Émile ascends a mountain in company with the Vicar of Savoy, and at sunrise as they look out over the splendors of the Pô Valley the vicar expounds his religious philosophy. God is everywhere in nature, he asserts, and one can feel His presence there without need of any religious dogma. What the vicar expounds is PANTHEISM, a concept not original with Rousseau—although he contributed its sentimental, basis—but which, after *Émile*, spread throughout the age of Romanticism. Its immediate ancestor was the Deism of the Age of Reason, which shared with Romantic Pantheism an emphasis on moral optimism, and which differed from it mainly in its reliance upon reason. "I believe in God as fully as I believe in any other truth, because to believe or not to believe are the things in the world that are least under my control," Rousseau asserted. The quality of that statement is sufficient to reveal how close, yet how Romantically different, his Pantheism is from the serene logic of Shaftesbury.

In philosophy, Fichte posits an Absolute Ego, transcending the individual ego, which directs the "moral order" of the universe; not a being but a force, Absolute Ego infuses everything. The Hegelian chain of dialectic continues unbroken up to Absolute Spirit, which implies that a constantly striving and developing God motivates all struggle and change in nature. Goethe's Faust shocks Gretchen with his Pantheistic explanation of God, "Experiencing Him everywhere . . . Call it Happiness, Heart, Love, God,/I have no name for it./Feeling is all!" (The epic as a whole is more orthodox than its hero, as the Easter chorus which saves Faust from drinking poison makes clear.) Shelley sees God as the West Wind or, in his more philosophical mood, as Intellectual Beauty which "visits this various world with . . . inconstant wing." For all Romantic nature poets, God became at times the omnipresent emotional force glorified by the Savoyard vicar, and the late landscape paintings of Gainsborough capture a shadow of this force on canvas.

A corollary to Pantheism is the Romantic concept of nature as a physical force that of itself can breed goodness and inspiration. Derived from the rational concept of nature as matter, and harking back in part to the Renaissance view of nature as Eden, the Romantic idea of NATURE

AS BOTH TANGIBLE AND INSPIRING achieves a characteristic tension between reality and ideal. For Rousseau agriculture was "the most useful" and at the same time "the noblest" of human employments. For Wordsworth the colors and forms of nature were at first "an appetite," but in time revealed

> A presence that disturbs me with the joy
> Of elevated thoughts.

For Leopardi and Lamartine nature was at once a source of physical consolation and abstract melancholy. For Byron, in *Don Juan*, it evoked the full range of physical and spiritual feelings, from sensuality to foreboding, from nausea to prayer. For Henry David Thoreau, who spent his days in a hut by Walden Pond, the tangible and inspirational aspects of nature became the two sides of a common coin, and his writings blend physical and abstract nature images. "Time," he writes, "is but the stream I go a-fishing in. I drink at it; but while I drink I see the sandy bottom and detect how shallow it is. Its thin current slides away, but eternity remains. I would drink deeper; fish in the sky, whose bottom is pebbly with stars." And elsewhere: "I got up early and bathed in the pond; that was a religious exercise, and one of the best things which I did."

Corporeal nature conveys mood and mystery in the setting of Strawberry Hill. Turner in *The Fighting Téméraire* portrays nature—in this case sun and sky—as physical in color and abstract in shape. Blake on the other hand depicts abstractions like the Void with graphic exactitude. The physical qualities of the Vienna woods, the fields, the breezes, the birds overhead, and the muttering thunder inspired Beethoven to the supraphysical loveliness of the *Pastoral Symphony*. "When you wander through the mysterious forests of pine," he once wrote in a letter, "remember that Beethoven often made poetry there, or, as they say, composed." Von Weber in his opera *Der Freischütz* (the demon hunter), used a wolf's glen to evoke an effect as mysterious as Strawberry Hill.

Another corollary to the sentimental Pantheism of this period was the concept that since God infused all of nature, those who lived closest to nature became *ipso facto* the finest human beings. The spirit of liberalism, which discovered uncommon virtues in the common man, gave an ENNOBLING QUALITY TO RUSTIC LIFE. To this was added Rousseau's popularization of the noble savage, the unspoiled and therefore honorable primitive earlier lauded by Montaigne and by the Age of Reason. "It is the common people," Rousseau stated, "who compose the human race. What is not the people is so trivial that it is not worth taking into account. Before one who reflects, all civil distinctions disappear; he sees the same passions, the same feelings in the clown as in the man of note and reputation; he only distinguishes their language, and a varnish more or less elaborately laid on." Spurred on by this idea, Marie Antoinette and her ladies played at being milkmaids in the Trianon gardens of Versailles, and George III took pride in the nickname "Farmer George." Thomas Percy, convinced that art flowed purest in rustic sources, assembled what he thought was "people's poetry" in his *Reliques of Ancient English Poetry* (1765). Herder found the seeds of national identity in this poetry. Wordsworth, describing the making of his own sophisticated art, explained: "Humble and rustic life was generally chosen, because, in that condition, the essential passions of the heart find a better soil in which they can attain their maturity, are less under restraint, and speak a plainer and more emphatic language; . . . in that condition the passions of men are incorporated with the beautiful and permanent forms of nature." Faust finds catharsis in the frenzied folk rites of *Walpurgisnacht*. Keats turned Grecians into simple farmer peasants whose activities breathed truth and beauty. Chateaubriand in *Atala* lauded the nature-formed American Indian as the noblest work of God. Longfellow in *Hiawatha* celebrated a noble savage whose Indian lore is superimposed and accidental. And the life of Thoreau lent empirical conviction to the claims of this idea.

The "creative craftsmanship" of William Morris which placed artisan above factory, handmade furnishings above machine-made products, did so on the grounds that handmade work was morally purer. The Hungarian dances orchestrated by Lizst, the Slavonic dances of Dvořák, and Balakirev's collection of authentic Russian folk songs carry the Romantic concept of rustic life into its music, and the art ballads of Schubert and Schumann and the near-folk ballads of Stephen Foster do the same.

The conceptual mainspring of this period is a LIBERALISM that combined the social contract theory with the progressive ideas of the Age of Reason and extended them outward in all directions. It was expressed through faith in the individual, religious tolerance, constitutional government, and humanitarian economics. In concrete terms it gave rise to universal education and to the Declaration of the Rights of Man; to the freedom of worship guaranteed by the French Revolution and by the Bill of Rights; to the progressive revolutions that swept through Europe and the Americas. It produced the utilitarianism of Bentham and Mill which led in turn to the benevolent socialism of Fourier and Robert Owen, a factory owner who practiced the economic theories he preached. The examples set by men like Owen helped to confirm the view that liberalism was also the essential characteristic of Christianity. *The Life of Jesus* (1863) by Ernest Renan portrayed Jesus as a man nurtured by "the love of the people, the taste for poverty," whose creed is the liberal humanitarian one of loving and sharing. Novelist Charles Kingsley pushed this view a step farther: "Even the strangest and most monstrous forms of socialism are at bottom but Christian heresies."

Kant, for whom morality meant exercise of will not only for the good of the individual but for all mankind, wrote: "I am never to act otherwise than so that I could also will that my maxim should become a universal law." For Fichte morality involved revolt against the "aggressive few" who enslave the many, and the coexistence of free individuals whose maxim is "limit your freedom through the conception of the freedom of every other person with whom you can be connected." Schiller in *William Tell* converts these liberal ideas into ardent poetry. Vittorio Alfieri in his drama *Saul* shows how the liberal spirit of man demands its freedom even when the tyrant is God. Byron and Shelley were passionate liberals, the former giving his life for his ideals. "The abolition of personal slavery is the basis of the highest political hope that it can enter into the mind of man to conceive," wrote Shelley in "A Defence of Poetry," and: "our own will be a memorable age in intellectual achievements, and we live among such philosophers and poets as surpass beyond comparison any who have appeared since the last national struggle for civil and religious liberty."

Goya propagandized for humanitarian benevolence in savage terms. Géricault in *Raft of the Medusa* and Turner in *Slave Ship* urged government reform and tolerance respectively. Beethoven made music the vehicle for humanitarian ideals in his opera *Fidelio* and in the choral section of his *Ninth Symphony*. Liszt, who redefined sacred music as "Humanitarian," wrote symphonic poems commemorating such liberal spirits as *Mazeppa*, *Prometheus*, and *Tasso*.

The Age of Reason concept of TWO PUBLICS, one discriminating, the other ignorant, persisted through Romanticism, and beyond. The intellectual art critic John Ruskin deplored the fact that *"public* taste seems plunging deeper and deeper into degradation day by day"; and Robert Schumann wrote of music: "It is characteristic of anything unusual that it cannot be easily understood; the majority is always tuned to the superficial." The sudden emergence of a large middle-class public in this period did more than confirm the pessimism of Ruskin and Schumann—it alienated the artist from a class which though well-meaning was as yet ill-prepared to comprehend him. As a result, half in defiance, half in self-defense, the artist set himself apart and adopted the pose of a superior being in this middle-class society. The esthetics of Romanticism gave the artist ample support for the role he chose to play. According to Hegel art alone shows man to himself as he really is, because it brings the subjective and objective viewpoints into a more perfect balance. The Will, the eternal life force, claimed Schopenhauer, can be objectified and made visible only through art. Art "plucks the object of its contemplation out of the stream of the world's course, and has it isolated before it. And this particular thing which, in that stream, was a small perishing part, becomes to art the representative of the whole, an equivalent of the endless multitude in space and time." As art embodies the universal, it incorporates the beholder: "In esthetic contemplation the particular thing becomes the idea of its experiences, and the individual contemplating it becomes the pure subject of knowledge." For Friedrich Schelling art alone conveyed absolute objectivity, and only through art could nature complete itself and be revealed in all its fullness.

Judgments like these reinforced the claims of Shelley that "A poet, as he is the author to others of the highest wisdom, pleasure, virtue, and glory, so he ought personally to be the happiest, the best, the wisest, and the most illustrious of men." Regarding the function of the poet he could say: "But poets, or those who imagine and express this indestructible order, are not only the authors of language and music, of the dance, and architecture, and statuary, and painting: they are the institutors of laws, and the founders of civil society, and the inventors of the arts of life, and the teachers." The Wilhelm Meister novels of Goethe and *Heinrich von Ofterdingen* of Novalis translate these views into works of fiction. The activities of Goethe and Byron, Beethoven and Wagner carried them over into life. Commemorative statues of artist-heroes mushroomed in the cities of Europe: they included in Paris, one of Racine by D'Angers, of Balzac and Victor Hugo by Rodin; and in Vienna, an elegant Mozart by Victor Tilgner.

We are close enough to Romanticism to make special categories of the variations that color its final stages. In fact, those variations have been studied in such depth that they seem to take on the weight and self-containment of separate periods. It is not uncommon to hear of the realistic "school" that flourished in the mid-nineteenth century and of the *new* phenomenon of impressionism that invaded its final quarter. Yet any broadscale survey of realism and impressionism reveals that while their stances differ superficially from Romanticism, their bases do not. In the following humanities approach to realism and impressionism we will see how both consist of the same traits as Romanticism: emotionalism, individualism, change as desirable, and nationalism; both are, in short, Romanticism masked.

REALISM

Where Goethe's Faust ranges across time and the universe in search of a sense of fulfillment, Emma Rouault in the novel *Madame Bovary* by Gustave Flaubert engages in a similar search by means of a series of drab extramarital affairs. Like Faust she is locked in a world too small for her;

like him she strives desperately to overcome the tension of opposites that increases as the years go by, and she remains restless, struggling, and unsatisfied to the very end. Her state sums up realism in capsule form. *It is Romanticism in essence but with the glow of hope dimmed, acted out on a smaller scale, in the here and now.* Factory life, life in the mines, the new way of working for money instead of for a livelihood, and the stifling communal requirements of liberal reform cut back horizons and pointed up the mediocrity of most lives, a mediocrity exemplified by the new superior group, the middle class. For the realist the factories, mines, materialism, and middle-class outlook combined to make life sordid, and he depicted it that way in meticulous detail. But he was no more literal than his Romantic forebears; *Huckleberry Finn, The Burghers of Calais, The Third-Class Carriage,* and *I Pagliacci* are arranged in as careful and contrived a manner as any previous works. Even the gloom spread over them is measured out in due proportion.

LITERATURE.   Both *The Red and the Black* and *The Charterhouse of Parma* by Stendhal chronicle the career of a youth detached from all classes of society, whose struggle to remain true to himself turns into a ceaseless struggle for survival. In each novel this Romantic situation is played against a cool, ironic backdrop realistic in its pessimism and limiting dimensions. But the paradoxical misfortunes of Julien Sorel and Fabrizio del Dongo stir the emotions as deeply as the aspirations of Faust. Both heroes are the quintessence of individualism; both are instantly ready to accept change—indeed, both symbolize changes in society that their own worlds have not yet caught up with; and Sorel as Frenchman, Fabrizio as French rationalist coupled with Italian Romantic (the legacy of his mixed parentage), also symbolize the best that each nation has to offer, nationalism in action. In *Great Expectations* Charles Dickens uses the little world of social distinctions to frame a story of such emotional power that his contemporary readers pressured him to lighten its ending. Lower-class Pip strives, sometimes shamefully, to be an individual (a concept he conceives in terms of class), and his tragedy is to be caught in a shifting quicksand of social change. There is also a current of nationalism in this novel, but subdued and associated solely with the lower classes. In *The Brothers Karamazov* by Feodor Dostoevski the brothers Ivan, Dmitri, and Alyosha all pursue their own Faustian quest within the oppressive world of czarist Russia. Passionate, as alienated as Sorel and Fabrizio, and caught up in crosscurrents of social change, all of them, the best and the worst, exemplify the author's fierce sense of national pride. *Huckleberry Finn* by Mark Twain is realistic in its homespun setting and pessimistic view of mankind in general. But despite its surface casualness, its appeal is largely to the emotions, its hero the prototype of the individual, its world charged with post Civil War changes, and Huck as American lights up every page.

ARCHITECTURE.   With its solid grounding in the practical concerns of construction, architecture is the art least liable to respond to fluctuations in stance. But factory conditions did ring in some changes in construction that might be labeled realistic: for one thing, new techniques of building, such as using iron trusses to support and enclose vast spaces, made for more pragmatic and less "artistic" effects—as in nineteenth-century railway stations and the *Halles Centrales,* the bare rectangular Paris food market. Also needed was a new building complex, the industrial town, as pedestrian and depressing a place as the society of Emma Bovary. Here is Dickens' classic description of one: "It was a town of red brick, or of brick that would have been red if the smoke and ashes had allowed it; but as matters stood it was a town of unnatural red and black like the painted face of a savage. . . . It contained several large streets all very like one another, and many small streets still more like one another, inhabited by people equally like one another. . . ."

The realist influence can also be seen on the Crystal Palace, which resembled a giant greenhouse and functioned as a spacious showroom and nothing more, and on the new interest in engineering which resulted in structures like the Brooklyn Bridge. But apart from these few external symptoms, architecture throughout the Romantic period practiced many styles concurrently. There was never one dominant Romantic architectural style, only a state of seeking, and in that sense nineteenth-century architecture was consistently Romantic. Realism did brush against it, but was not enough of a force to make a conspicuous impact.

SCULPTURE.   Realism affected the purpose and subject matter of sculpture in several ways. Realist concern for the here and now influenced the female nudes of Alexandre Falguière, who aimed only to provide a realistic visual experience. Other works contemporary with Falguière portrayed the drab, confined life of the common man with equal photographic literalness: *Return of the Miners,* a relief by the Belgian sculptor Constantin Meunier, and the statues of laborers by the Spaniard Miguel Blay are grim and tragic, although like Falguière's work essentially calculated to stimulate the emotions.

Rodin explored realism in his early work, and *The Burghers of Calais* (Figure 8.14) is an outstanding example. It depicts the surrender of the city fathers to Edward III after his successful siege of Calais during the Hundred Years' War. The sackcloth robes and gnarled feet and hands are lifelike and arresting, but the essence of realism is in the faces. Grim with despair, their every craggy line expresses realistic contemplation of the here and now. The sustaining force in this work is emotion, the bitter resignation of the elders emanating sorrow and foreboding. Each of the five burghers is shrouded in his own thoughts, his individuality enhanced by the fact that Rodin intended each figure to be a separate work. Style here has undergone a drastic change, as a comparison with the fluid lines and grander-than-life aura of *La Marseillaise* and *Washington* makes clear. To the nationalism of the theme itself Rodin adds a timeless national appeal by making these Frenchmen immediately real.

PAINTING.   In painting as in literature the widespread influence of realism stimulated work of the first rank. Realist painters refused to paint angels unless they could see them, and a few retired to the country where they could better study the actual effects of light and color in nature. Known as the Barbizon school, after the name of the village to which they retired, the group, including Jean François Millet and Théodore Rousseau, painted country scenes with a subdued simplicity that led straight to the more sophisticated art of Gustave Courbet, who first defined this kind of work as realism. Courbet's statement sums up the basic tenet of the school:

Figure 8.14 AUGUSTE RODIN.   *The Burghers of Calais.*   (1884–1886).   Calais, France.   [Archives Photographiques].

Figure 8.15   GUSTAVE COURBET.   *Funeral at Ornans.*   (1850).   Louvre, Paris.

"Imagination in art consists in knowing how to find the most complete expression of an existing object, but never in imagining or in creating the object itself." Restricted like all realists to the here and now, Courbet in *Funeral at Ornans* (Figure 8.15) depicts the burial of his grandfather. Its commonplace nineteenth-century trappings challenge the heroic funerals of past tradition. A humble man is being buried, and his mourners are a throng of peasants, shown as they really are, some weeping, some posing, some looking as unconcerned as the dog in the center of the scene. As the priest intones the service the acolytes behind him fidget with impatience while behind them rises a serene statue of the crucified Christ. A horizontal ridge of stone encloses the group and binds it to the earth. For all its matter-of-factness, *Funeral at Ornans* is ordered with as much attention to symbolic composition as *The Death of Socrates*. Like the latter work its content is emotional, the artist's style is individual and represents a drastic change from existing styles, and it projects the aspect of nationalism most characteristic of France after the Revolution—humanitarianism.

The realism of Courbet led to visual experience for its own sake, in the work of Édouard Manet. His *Déjeuner sur l'herbe,* picnic on the grass (the double meaning of this title seems to have been overlooked), shows two fully clothed men sitting in the woods in the daytime with a naked model, while another model is undressing behind them. Here realism is restricted to fresh perceptions for the eye. In contrast, *The Third-Class Carriage* by Honoré Daumier (Figure 8.16) uses the resources of realism with the broadest possible purpose. In heavy linear outlines which make technique as well as subject literal, Daumier depicts a group of common people riding in a train. The figures in the front row join to form a triangle, which is ironic since each is isolated: the mother brooding over her baby, the patient old woman, and the sleeping boy. Behind them, in what at first seems like a horizontal line, are three additional groups, the outsiders—the world outside ourselves?—apparently communicating, or perhaps just staring at each other, while the center pair stares searchingly at the viewer, as alone as the figures on the front row. In the enforced close quarters of a third-class carriage Daumier raises to light the threadbare and timeless isolation of the human condition. His deep-felt concern for humanity, his awareness of the individual predicament and of social as well as artistic change make *The Third-Class Carriage* a product of its own time and perhaps the surest piece of evidence that realism is the legitimate offspring of Romanticism.

MUSIC.   Realism entered into instrumental music by way of program music, and into vocal music by means of a school of opera known as *verismo*. Program music, wherein music is made to express tangible things, was anticipated by Berlioz. In his *Symphonie Fantastique* Berlioz purported to be narrating an episode in the life of an artist, but aside from a *leitmotif* that represents the artist's lady love, the work depicts a succession of feelings rather than objects. Wagner used *leitmotifs* more programmatically. In his *Ring of the Nibelungs* they represent things and places,

Figure 8.16   HONORÉ DAUMIER.   *The Third-Class Carriage.*   (c. 1860).   The Metropolitan Museum of Art, Bequest of Mrs. H. O. Havemeyer, 1929, The H. O. Havemeyer Collection.

people, and states of being—Wotan's spear, the gold guarded by the Rhine Maidens, the Rhine, Valhalla, Siegfried, Brünhilde, Freia, sleep, death, and redemption through love. Liszt, in a new form of music which Wagner labeled symphonic poem, offered musically realistic portraits of character (*Faust Symphony, Dante Symphony*), of landscape (*Les Préludes*), and of events (*Battle of the Huns*). In another new form, the symphonic suite, a variant of the baroque symphonic suite of dances, nationalist composers narrated programmatic stories, such as Rimsky-Korsakov's *Scheherazade*, Tchaikovsky's *Nutcracker Suite,* and Grieg's *Peer Gynt Suite.*

Veristic opera aims at heightened dramatic effects and in general uses a sordid story as framework. *I Pagliacci* (the clowns) by Ruggiero Leoncavallo and *Cavalleria Rusticana* (rustic chivalry) by Pietro Mascagni are outstanding examples of the genre. Mention should be made of the operas of Giacomo Puccini which endure in spite of critical disapproval and which fuse *verismo* with an eloquent, sometimes too eloquent, Romanticism, particularly in their portraits of women: Tosca, Madame Butterfly, Manon Lescaut, and Mimi in *La Bohème.* Needless to say, *verismo* and program music both reflect the same emotionalism, individualized style, changing form, and nationalism that we find in the other realistic arts.

IMPRESSIONISM

In that landmark of impressionist poetry, "The Afternoon of a Faun" by Stéphane Mallarmé, a drowsy faun at midday recalls his past experiences. His mind vaguely roams the world of his desires, seizes for a time upon the memory of twin nymphs whom he ravished only to lose them at the moment of perfect peace, and then trails off into dreamy indifference. The "heavenly potency of wine" and the nagging question, "Did I love a dream?" dim the fervor of his desire and blur the edges of its reality. Like Faust the faun is driven by yearnings, which, half formed and half perceived, drift away. Impressionism, then, is Romanticism in the act of breaking up, where the tensions slacken and become obscure desires, subjective, fluctuating, and evocative. Dream and mood take the place of passionate longing, and an unreal faun supplants Goethe's "Man in essence good, though darkly driven." Beauty, wrote Charles Baudelaire, the forerunner of impressionism, is "something ardent and sad, a little vague, leaving free play to conjecture." Romanticism began with the artist communicating his own ideas of truth and beauty; impressionism concludes with the artist enclosing his ideas in vague forms that only hint at what he means: a sentence fragment, a sculpted curve that leads nowhere, a floating, half-formed musical phrase. With impressionism we are moving toward an age in which form will take precedence over content.

LITERATURE.   The most considerable impressionist literary work is the drama *Pelleas and Melisande* by Maurice Maeterlinck. Its plot follows in outline that of *Tristan und Isolde:* a pair of lovers, knowing permanent happiness is impossible because of the lady's marriage, stay together to meet their death. But the Maeterlinck drama is shrouded in vagueness. Melisande's abrupt appearance out of nowhere in the middle of a wood, her mysterious origin, her elliptic statements, a grotto, a magic fountain, and a mysterious golden crown make the story seem at every turn something other than it appears to be. Even Melisande's affair with Pelleas is ambiguous, and may not have really happened. In keeping with Romanticism, the appeal of *Pelleas and Melisande* is emotional; sadness and mystery darken every scene, almost every line. Melisande possesses an individuality unique even in fiction, and her drama produces more than enough stylistic and technical changes to satisfy the age. While this work and impressionism in general do not lend themselves to nationalism, an implied nationalism unifies almost all impressionist works. Impressionism is a French movement; its semiofficial language is French, its chief practitioners are all French (even Americans like Vielé-Griffin resided in Paris and wrote their impressionist verse in French), and its delicate flutter is essentially French, stemming from the rococo of Louis XV.

The other principal impressionist authors are the poets Paul Verlaine, Arthur Rimbaud, and Stéphane Mallarmé, whose works typify emotionalism, individualism, and change respectively. "Music ahead of everything," begins Verlaine's *Art poétique,* and Rimbaud explained himself thus: "I attuned myself to simple hallucinations. I used to see monsters, mysteries. . . . Then I expressed my magic sophisms in verbal hallucinations."

ARCHITECTURE.   Architecture, so eclectic in style at this time and by its nature so unsuited to the fluctuating evocations of impressionism, almost ignored the movement. One can perceive, however, in certain late nineteenth-century buildings, if not evidence of, at least an impression of contact with impressionism. The clearest example is the church of *Sacré-Coeur* (Figure 8.17) designed by Paul Abadie. Seen at close range it looks like a church, but placed as it is upon a crowning hill and viewed from a distance its cluster of white domes and turrets suggests the faery magic of *Pelleas and Melisande,* and in the shifting dusk forms that are unique and unresolved.

SCULPTURE.   Rodin raised impressionism to a notable level of achievement. *The Kiss* subordinates realism and even meaning to an emotional impression achieved through movement. In *The Thinker* (Figure 8.18), a more static work, Rodin gives impressionist sculpture its richest statement. A bronze statue some twenty-eight inches high, the figure is muscled and tensed like the work of Michelangelo, whom Rodin idolized, and its pose recalls the crouching figure staring out from Michelangelo's painting of *The Last Judgment.* Its *contrapposto,* again from Michelangelo, is germane

Figure 8.17   PAUL ABADIE.   Sacré-Coeur.   Paris.   (Begun 1874).   Courtesy of the French Government Tourist Office.

to the theme, the tension of the body matching the straining effort of the subject's mind. But this thinker is a primitive man, his flat-featured face dull and troubled with the effort of thought. Like the faun of Mallarmé, the thinker—perhaps a pessimistic view of modern man—is on the verge of lapsing into brooding. The contrast between the thinker's realistic face and torso, and the smooth masses that are his hair and the backs of his hands, conveys an impression of fluctuating reality. The play of light and shadow across the curved figure adds shifting impressions of clarity and blur. Yet despite these technical achievements the theme, a thinker's earnest stupidity, is miniature in contrast to the work of, say, Rodin's favorite, Michelangelo—*The Kiss* too has slight significance. From the work of Rodin, of Maeterlinck, and of Mallarmé, we may generalize that as Romanticism reduced itself to impressions it dwindled in stature.

Figure 8.18   Auguste Rodin.   *The Thinker.*   (1879–1889).   The Metropolitan Museum of Art, Gift of Thomas F. Ryan, 1910.

PAINTING.   Impressionism in painting gained its start, and the name for the entire school, from a painting by Claude Monet shown in Paris in 1874 entitled *Impression, Soleil Levant* (impression: sunrise). *The Cathedral of Rouen* (Figure 8.19) typifies the movement as a whole. It is one of twenty-six views of the cathedral painted by Monet at different times of the day. They were all done outdoors to catch the different aspects of light upon the building, for the impressionist painter considered all objects as forms suffused in light and depicted all forms as objects which reflected light. Instead of literal reproduction, he offered impressions of the play of light across the scene, and since light was forever changing these were fleeting impressions, and therefore blurred. To achieve his impressions, he spaced short dabs of color at intervals, thus obtaining brighter, more light-filled effects than a flat application of color could achieve. These separated dabs made brightness (light) seem to flow back and forth across the canvas, without definite purpose, like the thoughts of Mallarmé's faun. A final characteristic: in a painting which emphasizes content like *The Maids of Honor* by Velasquez (Figure 7.14), what the eye would focus on at first glance is vivid; the remainder of the scene is blurred; in *The Cathedral of Rouen* the same misty atmosphere envelops all parts, for it is not the subjective eye that is of prime importance but the objective form. Impressionist uses of light were tried earlier,[2] but Monet brought them to complete fruition, and after him impressionism had to seek out variant forms. In *Prima Ballerina* (Figure 8.20) Edgar Degas views his subject from an unusual angle so as to suggest the impression of spontaneity. He uses the new medium of pastel (oil-base sticks of powdered pigment) for sharper emphasis on line and for fetching color effects. From the new discovery of Japanese art he had learned to use broad diagonals, here formed by the ballerina's arms, and to place his principal subject off center, thus isolating her in space. The scene at the rear is blurred in the style of Monet, with the landscape backdrop a jumble of hints and allusions: The tree trunks are cut short by the edge of the canvas lest their completed outlines make them seem too real. The prima ballerina is drawn as if poised for flight, her carriage giving the impression of continuous motion. Less a person than an impression of gracefulness, she hardly seems real, and in truth the purpose of this work is only to give a fleeting impression of movement. Romantic individualism and responsiveness to novelty are apparent here, and in the cathedral of Monet, and in both works visual sensation conveys a certain emotional impact, but feeling is beginning to give way in both cases to concern with form. Pierre Renoir, who follows Degas, will show still more preoccupation with form, especially in his later paintings of bathers.

---

[2] The impressionist discovery that shadows were not black or gray but were colors complementary to the object casting a shadow had been made earlier by Titian, Rubens, and Watteau, among others.

384

Figure 8.19   EDGAR DEGAS.   *Prima Ballerina*.   (c. 1876).   Louvre, Paris.

Figure 8.20   (left)   CLAUDE MONET.   *The Cathedral of Rouen* (in the morning). (1894).   The Metropolitan Museum of Art, The Theodore M. Davis Collection, Bequest of Theodore M. Davis, 1915.

MUSIC.   Impressionism in music is most concerned with shifting color and an emphasis on shifting mood. Color is achieved by new uses of the orchestra and by the introduction of unusual instruments; pastel colors are the ones most often sought, so that the orchestra is made smaller, and instruments like the *glockenspiel* and celesta play prominent parts. Mood is evoked by themes made to sound incomplete, as though their outlines are blurred, and by surge after surge of repetition to suggest the sea, or flocks of clouds, or the mind's turning over a reverie or desire. Amorphous or shifting rhythms, like the phrases of Mallarmé, add undercurrents to mood, and harmonic chords previously considered dissonant enrich orchestral color with unusual atmospheric effects.

The outstanding impressionist composer was Claude Debussy, who in the main took the program music of the realists and adapted it to the idioms of impressionism. At heart a Romantic, his music rests mainly on emotional appeal, his style attains an individuality almost inimitable, and his technical innovations were as thoroughgoing as those of any composer since Beethoven. Harmonic practices that dispensed with tonality; extensive use of chromatic and whole-tone (six-note) scales; human voices murmuring wordlessly to suggest instruments—these, plus the impressionist focus upon mood and delicate coloring, set his works apart. His *Prelude to the Afternoon of a Faun* (1894), matched Mallarmé's poem with comparable music and launched orchestral impressionism. Its dreamy, multicolored texture and its half-formed theme introduced by a solo flute, have all of the indistinctness and shimmer of Monet's *Cathedral of Rouen*. Subsequent tone poems such as *Nocturne* and *La Mer* (the sea), continued and developed this evocative style. His opera *Pelleas and Melisande*, based on the play by Maeterlinck, cloaked even the visual art of music drama in cloudy obscurity. Hushed declamatory arias more like broken phrasings and a veiled and dappled orchestral background surround the work with a vaporous atmosphere. Like Mallarmé, Maeterlinck, Rodin, Monet, and Degas, Debussy for all his innovations fell short of producing works of supreme greatness. Coming at the end of a period whose origins lay in the sixteenth century, impressionism was the art of an exhausted tradition.

FORMS AND TECHNIQUES

Most Romantic forms are carry-overs from the Age of Reason and baroque forms, and can be studied as such. The distinctive nature of Romanticism, however, did give rise to a number of special techniques.

EXOTICISM: The use of strange and far-off elements to add a touch of mystery and glamour to Romantic works was called exoticism. Chateaubriand in *Atala* and *René* uses his imagined version of the American Indian to typify the philosophical savage; Baudelaire in "Exotic Fragrance" thrills to "the scent of the green tamarinds"; the bulbous, vaguely oriental domes of *Sacré-Coeur* are exotic, as is Nash's Royal Pavilion at Brighton, inspired by the Taj Mahal, and the Egyptian touches in Haviland's Tombs Prison in New York. In painting, there are the Japanese elements in *Prima Ballerina* and the subject matter in Delacroix' *Women of Algiers* and Ingres' *Odalisque* (Turkish harem slave). Oriental elements were inserted by Puccini in *Madame Butterfly* and *Turandot*, by Gilbert and Sullivan in *The Mikado*, and by Rimsky-Korsakov in *Scheherazade*.

MEDIEVALISM: This gave a rose-tinted view of the Middle Ages sometimes to promote nationalism but in the main to lend an aura of glamour. Victor Hugo sets *Notre Dame de Paris* in a melodramatic Medieval past, Keats sets "La Belle Dame sans Merci" in a mysterious Medieval time; Poe's "The Masque of the Red Death" makes the Middle Ages the setting for luxury and terror; Fonthill Abbey and the Houses of Parliament glamourize the Middle Ages, as do Delacroix in *Entrance of the Crusaders into Constantinople* and Wagner in *Die Meistersinger* (the master singers), and *Parsifal*.

SUPERNATURALISM: Sometimes bound up with Medievalism, supernaturalism always has the separate purpose of adding mystery, sometimes with religious implications. Supernaturalism is used in ghost-filled Gothic novels such as Walpole's *Castle of Otranto* and *The Mysteries of Udolpho* by Ann Radcliffe; in the *Faust Walpurgisnacht* scenes; in the poems and tales of Poe, the tales of E. T. A. Hoffmann, Coleridge's "The Rime of the Ancient Mariner," and Hawthorne's *The Marble Faun;* in Strawberry Hill; in the gargoyles on Notre Dame Cathedral, almost all of them carved in the 1850s; in the nightmare canvases of Fuseli and Böcklin; in Mendelssohn's *Midsummer Night's Dream* overture; and in numerous operas including Meyerbeer's *Robert the Devil*, von Weber's *Der Freischütz* and *Oberon*, Wagner's *Ring of the Nibelungs*, Offenbach's *Tales of Hoffman*, Rimsky Korsakov's *Le Coq d'Or* (the golden cockerel), and Debussy's *Pelleas and Melisande*.

ECLECTICISM: A commingling of styles, eclecticism accounts for the swift stylistic changes of the period. Eclecticism is apparent in the Neoclassical, Romantic, and Italian *reali* (Medieval popular epics) elements of Byron's *Don Juan;* the gamut of traditions that parallel Fabrizio's series of love affairs in *The Charterhouse of Parma;* the classical and Renaissance elements in Goethe's *Faust;* the romanesque, oriental, and sheer imaginative elements of *Sacré-Coeur;* the classical-Renaissance-baroque-oriental mixture that is Hunt's Biltmore; the *Opéra* of Garnier; the classic, baroque, and Romantic elements in Dalou's statue of Silenus; Delacroix' merger of the fleshy figures of Rubens, Venetian coloring, and Dutch genre painting in *Liberty Leading the People;* and Puccini's merging of sensibility, *verismo,* and impressionist techniques in *Tosca* and *Turandot,* all reflect eclecticism.

The Romantic period, then, had its own essence, but by and large its traits derive from the baroque. If it achieved greater intensity than the baroque, it was often smaller in scope. If we compare Milton and Racine with Goethe and Hugo; Wren with Pugin; Bernini with Rodin; Velásquez, Rubens, and Rembrandt with Goya, Delacroix, and Degas; Bach and Mozart with Beethoven and Wagner, the latter in each case seem overshadowed by their baroque forebears. Only the novel, not in full development until the Romantic period, surpasses its baroque origins. Romanticism as the second wave of a single age seems to lack the size of impact of the first wave. Its ideas, bred first in the Age of Reason, lend substance to its institutions and to its works of art, but at the same time they make Romanticism still more dependent upon the earlier period. Even the vaunted Romantic revolt against rationalist science is a surface gesture only. Opposing Tennyson's popular charge that Darwinism left "nature red in tooth and claw," are the wide-ranging scientific speculations of Goethe and the tributes to science by Hugo, Berlioz, Novalis, Schiller, Shelley, Coleridge, and Stendhal, to mention but a few. Science, in fact, became the underlying faith of the Romantic period. Frazer's *The Golden Bough* and Strauss' *Life of Jesus* explored myth scientifically. Kant used inductive logic to investigate problems of God, the soul, and the universe. Comte considered science the chief prop of human life. Père Laugier in his influential *Observations sur l'Architecture* (1755), stressed scientific logic above all else in building and in city planning, and his doctrines were in the main adopted by the French *École des Beaux Arts* and by all Western architects throughout the nineteenth century. The impressionist painters developed their theories of light and color from the researches of physicists Helmholtz, Maxwell, and Chevreul. Scientific improvements in the piano—stronger frames (developed via the laws of physics), tougher strings, felt hammers to produce optimum acoustical effects—gave it a new sonority and variety without which the piano music of Beethoven and Chopin would not have been possible.

Romanticism thus forms part of a total complex with the

Age of Reason and the baroque. Only in its final variation, impressionism, do we detect a loosening of the bonds that suggests the intrusion of something new.

SELECTED BIBLIOGRAPHY

History

Beard, Charles, and Mary Beard. *The Rise of American Civilization.* 2 vols. New York: Macmillan, 1927.

Brinton, Crane C. *A Decade of Revolution, 1789–1799.* New York: Harper Torchbooks, 1963.

Gershoy, Leo. *The French Revolution, 1789–99.* New York: Holt, Rinehart and Winston, 1932.

Gottschalk, L. R. *The Era of the French Revolution (1715–1815).* Boston: Houghton Mifflin, 1929.

Hall, W. P., and W. S. Davis. *The Course of Europe Since Waterloo.* New York: Appleton, 1941.

Schapiro, J. Salwyn. *Modern and Contemporary European History, 1815–1934.* Boston: Houghton Mifflin, 1934.

Social and Intellectual Background

Aiken, Henry. (Ed.) *The Age of Ideology.* New York: Mentor, 1956.

Babbitt, Irving. *Rousseau and Romanticism.* Boston: Houghton Mifflin, 1919.

Barzun, Jacques. *Romanticism and the Modern Ego.* Boston: Little, Brown, 1943.

Binkley, Robert C. *Realism and Nationalism, 1852–1871.* New York: Harper & Row, 1935.

Bowra, C. M. *The Romantic Imagination.* New York: Oxford Galaxy, 1961.

Hayes, C. J. H. *The Historical Evolution of Modern Nationalism.* New York: Richard R. Smith, 1931.

Lindsay, Alexander D. *The Philosophy of Immanuel Kant.* London: Jack, 1934.

McDowell, A. S. *Realism; A Study in Art and Thought.* London: Constable, 1918.

Mead, George H. *Movements of Thought in the Nineteenth Century.* Chicago: University of Chicago Press, 1949.

Merz, John T. *A History of European Thought in the Nineteenth Century.* 4 vols. Edinburgh: Blackwood, 1896–1914.

Nettels, Curtis P. *The Roots of American Civilization.* New York: Appleton, 1939.

Praz, Mario. *The Romantic Agony.* New York: Oxford University Press, 1933.

Roubiczek, Paul. *The Misinterpretation of Man; Studies in European Thought of the 19th Century.* New York: Scribner, 1947.

Stace, W. T. *The Philosophy of Hegel.* New York: Macmillan, 1924.

Wolf, A. A. *A History of Science, Technology, and Philosophy in the 19th Century.* London: G. Allen, 1938.

Literature

Abrams, Meyer H. *The Mirror and the Lamp.* New York: Norton, 1961.

Brandes, George. *Main Currents in Nineteenth-Century Literature.* 6 vols. London: Heinemann, 1901–1923.

Frye, Northrop. (Ed.) *Romanticism Reconsidered.* New York: Columbia University Press, 1963.

Kermode, Frank. *Romantic Image.* New York: Vintage, 1964.

Lukacs, George. *Studies in European Realism.* New York: Hillway, 1950.

Matthiessen, F. O. *The American Renaissance.* New York: Oxford University Press, 1941.

Neff, Emery E. *A Revolution in European Poetry.* New York: Columbia University Press, 1951.

Omond, T. S. *The Romantic Triumph.* New York: Scribner, 1905.

Parrington, Vernon. *Main Currents in American Thought.* 3 vols. New York: Harcourt, 1930.

Simmons, Ernest. *Introduction to Russian Realism.* Bloomington: Indiana University Press, 1964.

Symons, Arthur. *The Symbolist Movement in Literature.* New York: Dutton, 1957.

Willoughby, L. A. *The Romantic Movement in Germany.* New York: Oxford University Press, 1930.

Architecture, Sculpture, Painting

Bell, Clive. *The French Impressionists.* Greenwich: New York Graphic, 1957.

Clark, Kenneth. *The Gothic Revival.* New York: Scribner, 1950.

Friedlaender, Walter F. *David to Delacroix.* Cambridge, Mass.; Harvard University Press, 1952.

Hamilton, George Heard. *Manet and His Critics.* New Haven, Conn.: Yale University Press, 1954.

Hitchcock, Henry-Russell. *Architecture: Nineteenth and Twentieth Centuries.* Baltimore: Penguin, 1958.

Holt, Elizabeth G. (Ed.) *From the Classicists to the Impressionists: a Documentary History of Art and Architecture in the 19th Century.* Garden City, N.Y.: Anchor, 1965.

Larkin, Oliver W. *Art and Life in America.* New York: Holt, Rinehart and Winston, 1960.

Leymarie, Jean. *Impressionism.* 2 vols. New York: Skira, 1955.

Newton, Eric. *The Romantic Rebellion.* New York: Schocken, 1962.

Novotny, Fritz. *Painting and Sculpture in Europe, 1780–1880.* Baltimore: Penguin, 1960.

Raynal, Maurice. *The 19th Century: New sources of emotion from Goya to Gauguin.* New York: Skira, 1951.

Rewald, John. *The History of Impressionism.* New York: Museum of Modern Art, 1946.

Music

Abraham, Gerald. *A Hundred Years of Music.* London: Aldine, 1964.

Barzun, Jacques. *Berlioz and the Romantic Century.* 2 vols. Boston: Little, Brown, 1950.

Brion, Marcel. *Schumann and the Romantic Age*. New York: Macmillan, 1956.

Burk, John N. *The Life and Works of Beethoven*. New York: Random House, 1946.

Carse, Adam. *The Orchestra from Beethoven to Berlioz*. Cambridge: Heffer, 1948.

Dannreuther, Edward. *The Romantic Period*. New York: Oxford University Press, 1939.

Einstein, Alfred. *Music in the Romantic Era*. New York: Norton, 1947.

Thompson, Oscar. *Debussy, Man and Artist*. New York: Dodd, Mead, 1937.

Ways, Max, *et al*. *The Story of Great Music: The Romantic Era*. New York: *Time*, Inc., 1965.

CHAPTER 9
THE AGE OF
ANXIETY

EVENTS

BACKGROUND OF WORLD WAR I

The two decades that closed the nineteenth century in Europe seemed as placid as any in history. Germany, the chief land power, having fulfilled its territorial needs in the Franco-Prussian War, now concentrated on schemes to bolster German industry and to maintain a vigilant peace throughout the continent. When in 1890 the new young emperor, William II, removed Chancellor Bismarck and ruled absolutely, the rest of Europe sighed with relief. Britain, the chief sea power, had reached its peak of wealth and possessions and was basking in the late glow of Victorian optimism. France devised a workable constitution in 1875, and her Third Republic at last managed to satisfy a majority of the people. With calm came prosperity, and French luxury products—wines, silks, gowns, gloves, china—became a byword in the capitals of the world. Russia concentrated on keeping the peace within her own borders, and Czar Alexander III contained his growing intelligentsia (professional people) with Siberia and the whip. Alien groups were made to conform under threat of pogroms (persecutions), which stimulated the emigration of large numbers of Russian Jews to America. Nicholas II, who succeeded Alexander in 1894, was a mild, adaptable monarch and under his rule tensions subsided for a time. Austria-Hungary maintained its oil and water equilibrium under the cynical, compromising rule of aging Emperor Franz Joseph I. Italy survived a shaky, corrupt fiscal policy and began to take on self-confidence in 1900 when Victor Emmanuel III assumed the throne.

The threat of eruption existed only in the Balkan peninsula, the buffer between Turkey, Russia, Austria-Hungary, and Germany. The independent state of Serbia with its population of 4 million resented the bondage of two thirds of its fellows in Austria-Hungary and Turkey; and among the Turkish-held Balkan states, Bosnia, Rumania, Macedonia, and Bulgaria agitated steadily for independence. To keep them in check the major powers, dominated by Bismarck, had devised a system of alliances that stalemated threats of war. In 1881 Bismarck formed the *Dreikaiser Bund*, or three emperors' league, consisting of Russia, Germany, and Prussia; in 1882 the Triple Alliance of Germany, Austria-Hungary, and Italy was formed against Russia; this led in 1894 to the Franco-Russian alliance against Germany. Meantime, to siphon off hostile aggressions there was the solace of imperialism, and during these years Europe carved up Africa and the Middle East at will. Germany entered the imperialist race late—a reluctant Bismarck saw little value in it—but annexed a strip of southwest Africa in 1884 and Kenya a year later, a territory of several million square miles. Belgium gained control of the Congo Free State, a rich central section containing a million square miles. England occupied Nigeria, South Africa, Egypt, and the Sudan. France added West Africa, including the Sahara Desert, to its Algerian possession and took steps to annex Morocco as well. Italy took what was left, the thin eastern slices of Eritrea and Italian Somaliland, so that in Africa by 1900 only Morocco and the inaccessible highland territory of Abyssinia remained outside European control.

By 1900 the 400 million people of Europe and the 100 million people of European descent living elsewhere comprised one third of the world's population. Among them they controlled virtually the entire globe except for a distraught and divided China and the tiny, efficient island of Japan. That they were ignorant of the Orient was made clear in 1895, when Japan attacked China and defeated her in a matter of months to the delighted astonishment of the West. "Jap the Giant-Killer," the British newspapers hailed the victors, and no objections were raised when Japan declared Korea independent and took possession of the island of Formosa. But when Japan also claimed the peninsula of Liaotung including the strategic naval base of Port Arthur, Russia, Germany, and France demanded its return. Japan obeyed without a murmur, but when Russia seized Port Arthur for itself in 1898, Japanese distrust of the Western world deepened. For the present, however, she concentrated on literacy—compulsory education was begun in 1872—industry, and the stockpiling of Western-type military equipment.

Another brief war that seemed negligible to Europe at the time involved another fringe of the world. In 1895 Cuba revolted against Spain, and a Spanish army of 200,000 men moved in and took savage countermeasures. Over 100,000 civilians were herded into stockades and murdered. The United States, shocked by these cruelties so close at hand, and concerned for its huge investments in Cuba, began to protest. Spain ignored the protests and when in 1898 the American battleship *Maine* was blown up in Havana harbor, the United States declared war. It was over within ten weeks. The American fleet under Admiral Dewey advanced upon the Spanish fleet, which it outranged, and at the Admiral's command, "You may fire when you are ready, Gridley," wiped it out (in spite of bad marksmanship) without the loss of a single American sailor. The ground fighting was just as brief and one-sided, with more Americans dying from tainted meat than Spanish bullets. Cuba was declared independent, and Puerto Rico and the Philippines were ceded to the United States. Spain, like China, was a second-class power, and the American victory, marked as it was by clumsy tactics, made little impression upon Europe. Yet the United States had become a major power almost overnight. In a single generation following the

Civil War the Napoleonic tactics of the captains of industry had industrialized the nation from coast to coast, accomplishing in thirty years what had taken Europe two centuries. By 1890 the last American frontier was closed, and despite her bent toward isolation she was forced to look outside her boundaries for further expansion. Puerto Rico and the Philippines were a start, and in 1899 Secretary of State John Hay affirmed the Open Door policy of equal trade opportunity for all with China.

With hindsight one can see that by 1900 forces had emerged that were changing the course of the world. Despite its surface serenity Europe had reached a point where its centuries-old dominance of the globe was coming to a halt. With the emergence of America and Japan as major powers, commercial supremacy began to shift to the opposite ends of the earth. With the partition of Africa all escape valves were now closed and the European nations were forced to turn upon one another for release. The first half of the twentieth century acts out the tragic consequences of these changes.

In 1899 Europe attended the First Hague Peace Conference, called by Czar Nicholas. As it opened war broke out between England and the Boer Republic, a Dutch settlement in South Africa. The outnumbered Boers fought long and hard to oust British commercial interests attracted by the discovery of gold and diamonds, but defeat came in 1901 and Britain annexed the Boers a year later. In China a group of fanatics and hoodlums calling themselves the Fists of Righteous Harmony—the Western world dubbed them Boxers—rebelled against all foreigners in 1900 and murdered many. An international police force marched on Peking, crushed the rebellion, and dictated humiliating terms to China. Japan, still smoldering over the Russian occupation of Port Arthur, and anxious to save face in Asia, attacked and destroyed a large segment of the Russian navy in 1904, besieged the Russian army at Port Arthur, and captured the port. Russia fought back on several fronts with little success, and in 1905 accepted Theodore Roosevelt's offer to act as mediator for peace. Japan obtained Liaotung peninsula, a part of Manchuria, and Russia's guarantee of the independence of Korea, a bridge territory into China which Japan coveted. Russia suffered humiliation which turned into rage when a procession of workers petitioned the czar for better conditions. They were fired upon by the army and 1500 were killed, but out of that massacre and the Russian military defeat came agitation that resulted in the appointment of three Dumas (Parliaments) in 1906–1907. Debates in them between the intelligentsia and the militant Socialists, led to a great deal of rhetoric and no reform. After the squabbles of the third Duma, Czarina Alexandra, a neurotic, domineering woman, stirred Nicholas to take action, and this threat drove several Socialist leaders to seek refuge in Switzerland, including Nikolai Lenin and Joseph Stalin.

In the meantime the nations of Europe formed more extensive and binding alliances. England, alarmed by Russian encroachments in China, signed a treaty with Japan in 1902, thereby drawing away from its nineteenth-century policy of political isolation and assuring Japan of German neutrality in the upcoming Russo-Japanese war. England also formed the *Entente Cordiale*, or cordial agreement, with France in 1904 and an entente with Russia in 1907. With Bismarck's Triple Alliance (Germany, Austria-Hungary, Italy) reconfirmed and with the Triple Entente of England, France, and Russia in the making the battle lines were drawn. The tensions, *with no external outlet*, were already building; they required only the proper incident.

France had backed England's claim to Egypt and the Sudan in return for British backing of the French claim to Morocco, but now Germany, a late entry in the imperialist race, desired Morocco. A twelve-power conference at Algeciras, Spain, in 1906 decreed that a Franco-Spanish task force would protect that kingdom, to the disappointment of Germany. In 1907 a military revolt against the Turkish sultan, organized by a Committee of Union and Progress, more popularly known as the Young Turks, overthrew the sultan and established a chaotic dictatorship. Austria-Hungary took advantage of the turmoil to annex two of Turkey's Balkan provinces, Bosnia and Herzegovina, thus placing another million Serbs under Austria's imperial banner. Serbia called for Russian aid in a war with Austria-Hungary, but Russia was in no position to oblige. With Czarina Alexandra under the spell of a macabre holy man, Rasputin, with the nobles corrupt and discontented, and with the Socialists resorting to terrorism, the czar was hard-pressed to maintain even a semblance of order, and a widespread war was out of the question. Serbia was forced to accept the annexation of Bosnia-Herzegovina in 1908, giving the Triple Alliance a moral victory and disappointing the Triple Entente. In 1911 the Sultan of Morocco, menaced by a military revolt, asked for French protection. Germany sent a cruiser to the Moroccan port of Agadir to "protect" her Moroccan interests, but was forced to back down by France and England. France established a protectorate in Morocco, and in this case the Triple Entente gained a point over the Triple Alliance. In 1912 Greece organized the other Balkan states of Serbia, Montenegro, Bulgaria, and Rumania into a league against Turkey, and with Turkey thus occupied, Italy pounced on the Turkish province of Tripoli and added it to her African empire. In the meantime the Balkan countries defeated Turkey with surprising ease and obtained their independence as separate states. Serbia then joined all liberated Serbs together to form the state of Yugoslavia. Balkan independence deprived the major European powers of the buffer of Turkish-held dependencies and left them facing one another directly. Moreover, Yugoslavia kept the pot boiling by terrorist agitation for the freedom of its 8 million fellows still ruled by

Austria-Hungary. An abortive war between Bulgaria and the other Balkan states in 1913 added fuel to the war-feeling that seethed across the continent. An American visitor to the continent that year, Colonel House, assessed the situation as militarism running stark mad.

WORLD WAR I

On June 28, 1914, the Archduke Franz Ferdinand, heir apparent of Austria-Hungary, and his wife were assassinated at Sarajevo, capital of Bosnia, by a youthful member of the Serbian terrorist organization, the Black Hand. A month later Austria-Hungary delivered a savage ultimatim to Belgrade, and despite an immediate submissive Yugoslavian reply, declared war on July 28. Russia began to mobilize, and Germany, along with England the least desirous of conflict at that moment, declared war on Russia August 1, on France August 3, and invaded Belgium August 4, the day England declared war on Germany. The British foreign secretary, Lord Grey, lamented the onrush of war with prophetic words: "The lamps are going out all over Europe. We shall not see them lit again in our lifetime."

Once committed to the war, Germany set in motion its Schlieffen Plan, which called for first the overrunning of Belgium, then a swift descent upon France, and finally a concerted turning east to knock out Russia. As the German forces surged through Belgium, and then down across northern France the kaiser promised: "By Christmas we will be home." But a line of French and British troops met the six-pronged German advance north of Paris along the Marne River in a bloody battle and drove them back thirty miles. The French lost 300,000 men doing so, but it was a sacrifice which changed the course of the war. The Germans dug an arc of trenches stretching from the northern French border to Switzerland—in the east passing just above the French fortress city of Verdun—and held off all further Franco-British advance. The Allies dug in too, and a stalemate ensued. Japan declared war on Germany at this time, but offered the Allies little in the way of material support.

Soon after the start of the war Paul von Hindenburg was appointed German commander-in-chief, and he made the brilliant tactician Eric Ludendorff his chief of staff. Between them they defeated the Russians at Tannenberg in East Prussia and captured 200,000 prisoners. The Russians, strong in numbers but short on supplies and ammunition, retaliated by beating the Austrians back across Galicia. The year 1914 ended with a deadlock on the western front, with Germany entrenched in western Poland, and with Russia in possession of Galicia.

In 1915 Turkey entered the war by attacking Russia without warning. She then blocked the Dardanelle Straits, thus closing off the western supply route to Russia via the Black Sea. A British-Australian force besieged the Gallipoli Peninsula, adjoining the Dardanelles, but by the end of the year, with over 100,000 killed or wounded, the British had to evacuate the peninsula. Italy, whose commitment to the Triple Alliance extended only to "defensive" wars, sold herself to the Entente for the promise of Trieste and a segment of the Austrian Tyrol, and declared war on Austria-Hungary. The deadlock persisted on the western front all that year, but in the east Germany drove the Russians far back into their own territory. Then Bulgaria entered the war on the German side and, with German help, captured Yugoslavia.

By 1916 the populations of both sides had begun to feel the effects of this new "total" warfare. The British blockade of Germany and Austria-Hungary meant starvation and poverty among the civilian population, while the Franco-British need for war materials and the inept Russian industrial policy meant similar hardships for the other side. In addition, new weapons made the new-style total war still more terrible: by 1916 machine guns, airplanes, armored tanks, submarines, and poison gas were all in use, as well as barbed wire, an American device for restraining cattle, which was now strung between the trenches. Pressured by dwindling supplies, Germany mounted a full-scale offensive against Verdun, calculating that defeat there would discourage the French and force them to surrender. In the fiercest battle of the war the Germans and French fought deadlocked as casualties reached staggering proportions. To relieve the French, the British launched a counterthrust to the west along the Somme River where their own casualties the first day were 60,000 dead. When the fighting subsided both sides retained their original positions, although their losses totaled over a million men. Rumania now entered the war on the Franco-British side and Germany defeated her in record time, confiscating her grain fields and oil wells; this last minute reprieve of supplies gave Germany materiel to continue the war. Germany also made a final attempt to break the British naval blockade, at the Battle of Jutland off the Danish coast, but was unsuccessful.

Two offsetting changes came in 1917: Russia quit the war and America entered it. In Russia the forces of revolution, choked since the mid-nineteenth century, finally erupted. The people, supported by Cossack troops, marched on Czar Nicholas while a few exasperated members of the nobility poisoned Rasputin, shot him, and flung his body into a canal. A frightened Nicholas abdicated at once, and in February[1] control of the government passed into the hands of Socialist liberals led by Alexander Kerensky, his group bolstered by a new force, the Soviet (council) of

---

[1] The Russian calendar lagged thirteen days behind the Western calendar until 1918, and these events occurred in March according to Western calculations. Since they are prominent in Russian history as the February Revolution, they are so dated here.

Workingmen's and Soldiers' Deputies led by Nikolai Lenin. The Russian army, demoralized, began deserting the Austrian front in droves, and in October[2] the Soviet or Bolsheviks, the many, as they called themselves then, ousted Kerensky. They assumed control of the government and signed a peace treaty, The Treaty of Brest-Litovsk, with Germany in 1918. Its harsh terms stripped Russia of forty-four percent of her population, twenty-seven percent of her land, and thirty-three percent of her manufactures and iron production, but as Lenin put it: "It is a question of signing the German terms now or of signing the death warrant of the Soviet Republic three weeks later."

Unable to break the British blockade, the Germans had resorted to submarine warfare to harass enemy shipping. The sinking of American merchant ships and of the British liner *Lusitania* with over a hundred American passengers aboard, resulted in American protests and a German promise to restrict its submarine warfare. But in January 1917 after a winter of near starvation, the kaiser ordered unrestricted submarine warfare. Eight American vessels were soon sunk, and these incidents plus the revelation of a German plot to involve the United States in war with Mexico and Japan led to a declaration of war against Germany on April 6, 1917. More influential than these immediate causes, however, were a long-standing friendship with France—Colonel Stanton's "Lafayette, we are here," was no mere piece of rhetoric—; common cultural ties with England, reflected in President Wilson's "the world must be made safe for democracy"; and the American purchase of a billion and a half dollars worth of Allied war bonds. In 1917 America was the most potent economic power in the world, but nine tenths of its product went to insure Americans the highest living standard in history. On the surface isolationist, which was what the kaiser had counted on, America was drawn into the conflict by the nature of her new economic position. American conscription was a slow process, however, and she took little or no part in the war in 1917, a year of German-Austrian victories. Besides the Russian demise, a French offensive failed, a British offensive failed, and the Austrian army overran the Italians at Caporetto, a Yugoslavian village at the northeast Italian border, and sent them in full retreat. To the British-American peace feelers of January 1918, the kaiser replied: "We must bring peace to the world by battering in with the iron fist and shining sword the doors of those who will not have peace."

In 1918 Ludendorff hurled his armies at the Franco-British lines for the finishing blow. In four drives the Germans were back along the Marne. But then with all Allied armies under the skillful command of Marshal Foch, including a million fresh American soldiers in the field, the Germans

[2] The epoch-making October Revolution occurred in November according to the Western calendar. See the previous footnote.

were forced back. By November the Germans were back where they had started in 1914, and meanwhile the Italians rallied outside of Venice and turned the tide against Austria. Austria surrendered on November 3 and on November 10 the kaiser fled into Holland. On November 11 in a dining car in the Compiègne Forest the German representatives signed the terms of peace. World War I was over. It had cost over 8 million lives, plus 20 million wounded—a shocking forty percent of those engaged in fighting— and $337 billion, all of it spent on destruction, to say nothing of the desperate misery of civilian populations. But it was not the climax of the tragedy, only the exposition.

As an aftermath in Russia the Bolsheviks, now renamed Communists, moved their capital back from St. Petersburg to Moscow, made the Kremlin their administrative center, and prepared for a civil war with czarist loyalists, landowners, and military adventurers, who called themselves the Whites, in distinction to the Reds, the color of the Communist flag. As the Whites advanced in 1918 the czar and his family, still prisoners of the Reds, were dragged into a cellar and shot. By 1920 the Whites, without a leader or a unifying cause, were defeated and 150,000 of them went into permanent exile. A Communist Party numbering no more than 30,000 had determined the destiny of some 150 million people.

BETWEEN WORLD WARS: TENSIONS AND DEPRESSION

When the victorious leaders met at Versailles to confer on peace terms, President Wilson urged the acceptance of his earlier announced Fourteen Points to guarantee a lasting peace. The European representatives, their countries devastated by total war, instead sought reparations, and to gain them fixed upon Germany the blame for the entire conflict. Article 231 of the Versailles Treaty proclaimed: "The Allied and Associated Governments affirm and Germany accepts the responsibility of Germany and her allies for causing all the loss and damage to which the Allied and Associated Governments and their nationals have been subjected as a consequence of the war imposed upon them by the aggression of Germany and her allies." As a sop to Wilson his fourteenth point, the establishment of a League of Nations—to arbitrate disputes instead of resorting to war—was adopted, but the main concern of the treaty was German reparations. The Germans lost Alsace-Lorraine and gave up their Saar Valley and upper Silesian coal mines (one third of their total coal output) to France for fifteen years, gave a sizable portion of their fleet and railroads to the Allies, and agreed to pay heavy damages—the initial demand of $52 billion was later whittled down to $32 billion. Wilson returned to America to seek ratification of the League, but the Senate rejected it on the grounds that Article XIV required all members to contribute military aid in case of another war. Wilson took his cause to the American people, who in 1920 declared for Warren G. Harding and his slogan of "back to normalcy," and America settled back into isolation and left Europe to handle its troubles by itself.

The next few years were marked by tense and edgy reactions to four years of total war. Germany paid $250 million in reparations in 1921 and made another payment the following year, but then the bottom dropped out of its economy and no payment was made in 1923. A straitened French government sent its troops into the Ruhr Valley, the heart of German industry, to threaten reprisals unless production were increased. The Germans resisted passively, by means of a general strike, and a frustrated French army had no recourse but to leave. Then German currency, reflecting German insolvency, got caught in a spiral of inflation. Within a few months it took 750 billion marks to purchase what one mark had bought a year ago, and the postwar German Republic with its seat in Weimar, abode of Goethe, rather than in Prussian Berlin, floundered amid the struggles of its Nationalist, Communist, and Socialist delegates. Britain at this time was little better off. Its empire in 1920 included 13 million square miles and a population of 500 million, the largest empire in history. But the war had loosed a new spirit of nationalism: the dominions (Canada, Australia, New Zealand, South Africa) began to demand equal status, Ireland became the independent Irish Free State in 1922, and Asia and Africa were stirring. In addition, acute unemployment at home, which bred poverty and hunger, intensified postwar misery. In Russia the Communist economy floundered, and Lenin was forced to introduce a New Economic Policy (NEP) which offered concessions to foreign capitalists wishing to invest in industry in Russia. Poland, declared a republic in 1918, was sinking under corruption as well as poverty. The economic plight of Austria rivaled that of Germany. In America a rash of strikes in 1919, fear of a Communist takeover, and the depression of 1919–1921 gave the nation a bad case of nerves and the Ku Klux Klan a membership of 4 million by 1924. Italy furnished the seedbed for a new kind of answer to Communism, a totalitarianism based upon supranationalism instead of economics. Italy called it Fascism, from the Latin *fasces*, a bundle of sticks tied round an axe and used in ancient Rome as a symbol of authority. With resentment at its small prizes at Versailles, inflation, weak politicians, brigandage in the south, and Communist uprisings in the north, Italy was as demoralized after the war as the defeated countries. Moreover its large middle class, rootless amid this turmoil, was ripe for a new experiment. Fascism with its black shirts, Fascist dagger, and Roman salute provided it. Sparked in 1922 by Benito Mussolini, an ex-Socialist and a master of bluster, 50,000 Fascists marched on Rome (though Mussolini remained discreetly behind) where an abject king appointed Mussolini prime minister. Parliament voted him dictatorial powers for a year, after which he controlled the country. By 1924 Fascists controlled all key government posts, and their opponents had either fled the country or been killed.

By 1925 European production reached its prewar level and kept rising, bringing Europe a higher standard of living than it had ever known. The United States, Japan, and now Latin America made inroads into the world market, which slowed the upward pace, but in the later 1920s Europe and the rest of the world seemed well on the way to recovery. Mussolini introduced the corporative state, a syndicate of employers and a syndicate of workers forbidden to disagree and required to turn over excess profits in the form of taxes to the state. Protests, severely dealt with, soon ceased, and a nationwide public building program gave Italy the outward appearance of success. Beggars were driven from the streets and the trains ran on time. The Lateran Treaty of 1929 reconciled church and monarchy at last: Mussolini ceded some hundred acres in Rome, the Vatican, to the pope as the church's inviolable domain and established compulsory Catholic education in the schools; the pope in turn recognized and agreed to support the kingdom of Italy. In Russia Lenin died in 1924 and his succession was disputed by an intellectual internationalist, Leon Trotsky, and a shrewd Georgian farmer, Joseph Stalin, a nationalist whose policy was to concentrate on building up Russia from within. Supported by Lev Kamenev and Grigori Zinoviev, hardheaded nationalists, Stalin emerged victorious and Trotsky fled into exile. In 1928 Stalin scrapped the NEP and inaugurated his first Five Year Plan, an all-out effort to build up Russian agriculture and industry through cooperative farms and factories. In China Sun Yat-sen, an enlightened Social Democrat, introduced reforms and a measure of prosperity to that disorganized country by means of the Kuomintang (southern nationalist party). His disciple, Chiang Kai-shek, continued a program of liberal reforms after the death of Sun Yat-sen in 1925. The various factions in the Weimar Republic coalesced in 1925, elected Von Hindenburg president, and Germany's industrial output grew until by 1929 it was surpassed only by that of the United States. In England conservative prime minister Stanley Baldwin kept the country on an even keel, though heavy industrial production lagged. France under conservative Aristide Briand also showed signs of recovery. In America the upswing was sharpest and most flamboyant, and the boom of 1924–1929 raised the standard of living and of leisure to new levels. The motion picture, the radio, and the automobile furnished delightful toys for an emancipated middle class. Land booms, stock market speculation, and installment buying spread wealth and goods like jam from Maine to California. American self-sufficiency became a source of national pride, and by 1926 tariff laws reached their highest point in American history. Calvin Coolidge, a symbol of *laissez-faire*, was president, and America kept cool with Cal by practicing isolationism and self-indulgence. In 1925 England, France, and Germany agreed in a treaty signed at Locarno, Switzerland, to guarantee Germany's frontier at the Rhine—no more Ruhr incidents—and to demilitarize a zone fifty kilometers east of the Rhine. Germany entered the League of Nations and Briand proclaimed: "Peace for Germany and France: that means we have ended the long series of terrible and bloody conflicts which have stained the pages of history." In 1928 the Kellogg-Briand Pact, between America and France, renounced war as an instrument of national policy.

On October 29, 1929, prices on the American stock market fell with a crash: blue chip stocks lost as much as 200 points a week, and by the end of the year stock values had declined by $40 billion. As the life savings of millions were wiped out, 5000 banks closed their doors, and unemployment rose to 12 or 15 million. Panic swept the country along with a chilling realization that the excitement of the twenties had been a flush of fever, that wealth and prosperity had been a hectic dream, and that financial security might well be gone forever. Clutching at straws, America stopped foreign buying altogether, stepped up its demands for payment of war debts to countries struggling toward recovery, and called in its short-term loans, a bulk of which had been used to back German industry. The 1930s in America was a decade of depression, a decade during which the rest of the world reacted in a grim variety of ways.

In 1930, with American loans to Germany stopped, German banks began to close and factories laid off increasing numbers of employees. In the elections that year, with Von Hindenburg still president, the Communists gained a modest percentage of votes while those of a troublesome minority party, the *Nazional-Socialistisch deutsche arbeiterpartei* (German national socialist workers' party), skyrocketed. Called Nazis for short, they first gained notoriety in 1923 when an Austrian ex-corporal, Adolph Hitler, called for a demonstration parade in Munich. Headed by General Ludendorff, who had become a violent right-wing militarist, it was halted by police fire and Hitler was jailed. There he wrote *Mein Kampf* (my struggle), a fuzzy harangue whose contentions would enflame the world. "The great masses of the people," states *Mein Kampf,* "will fall victim more easily to a big lie than to a small one." The burden of the book is that the Jews had ruined Germany, with help from the Communists, and that the pure Aryan *Volk* must rise again. With financing from wealthy industrialists, who found the Nazis useful in fighting Communists, Hitler captivated a demoralized society with his hypnotic, shrieking tirades. In the presidential elections of 1932 the eighty-five-year-old Von Hindenburg was reelected and Hitler, who ran second, was appointed chancellor at Junker insistence. In 1933 the *Reichstag* (parliament) was burned by a feebleminded Dutch youth, and Hitler used this "threat" to grant himself emergency dictatorial powers. He withdrew Germany from the League of Nations, and with the death of Von Hindenburg in 1934 he became president. Hitler now declared himself Führer, leader, and his new regime the Third *Reich* (the Holy Roman Empire and that of Bismarck being the first two.) Nazi brown shirts and swastikas (an Indian fertility symbol) began to cover Germany, and within the next few years the Nazis systematically persecuted the Jews, placed all labor and almost all industry under state control, and began to rebuild and rearm the German war machine; in German-speaking Austria a pan-German party began calling for *Anschluss*, annexation, with Germany. In Italy Mussolini, like Hitler, assumed total control and launched a rearmament program.

Hungary, Rumania, and Bulgaria established Fascist-type military dictatorships in the 1930s. Joseph Pilsudski set up a benevolent one in Poland to save it from political ineptitude, as did Kemal Ataturk in Turkey and Rheza Khan in Iran (formerly Persia). In Greece Yanni Metaxas became prime minister with dictatorial powers; in Portugal Antonio Salazar did the same; in Spain a military dictatorship from 1923–1930 was followed by a liberal republic, but in 1936 a military junta headed by Francisco Franco threatened civil war.

In Russia Stalin turned to a Union Police Force, the NKVD, to implement results. His second Five Year Plan, 1933–1937, industrialized half the nation and raised the standard of living to pre-World War I levels. By 1939 agricultural output and employment tripled, compared to 1913; 38 million students attended school, compared to 18 million in 1913; and women had rights equal to men. In 1936 a new constitution was passed—the Third Constitution—which guaranteed freedom of speech and universal suffrage. Since Russia was now a classless society, Stalin declared that rival parties were no longer needed, and a Great Purge of dissidents occurred during 1936–1938. Between 7 and 14 million persons were killed or imprisoned during those years, with Kamenev and Zinoviev among those executed.

In 1929 the Communist segment of the Kuomintang broke with Chiang Kai-shek, and a civil war began, but was interrupted by the encroachments of Japan. Japan, now dominated by a militarist faction, occupied Manchuria in 1931 and set up a puppet government there. Condemned by the League, Japan withdrew its membership, pushed into the Chinese mainland, and took possession of five north Chinese provinces including Peking by 1937.

When the depression first struck America President Herbert Hoover favored a Reconstruction Finance Corporation to put business back on its feet, but vetoed schemes to put the government in business. By 1932 there were 30,000 bankruptcies, and Franklin Delano Roosevelt was elected president for the first of four terms. His New Deal established government control of business and sought security for workers and farmers. Relief was meted out to the unemployed; the Civilian Conservation Corps created jobs for the youth of the nation, and Public Works Programs did the same for adults; the Federal Housing Administration stimulated building; the Security Exchange Commission regulated the sale of stocks; the National Labor Relations Board insured labor the right to collective bargaining; and the Social Security Act provided for permanent care of the aged. France and England—and the United States too—flirted with Fascist solutions to the economic crisis, but like America settled for more strongly centralized governments which nevertheless rested on a democratic base.

If the root direction of this age was government control in greater or lesser measure, its mainstay and prop was applied science. A genie loosed from the bottle, the science of 1880–1945 could serve all masters, and as in the case of totalitarian governments a few men and a few groups served, and dominated, the rest. Science now proffered the benefits of the X-ray, insulin, sulfanilamide, penicillin, streptomycin, and cortisone; of nylon and artificial silks, dyes, and perfumes; of lucite and plexiglass; of the electric light, electric furnace, telephone, and airplane. It entertained and coddled by providing the radio, movies, television, and the automobile. It produced new weapons: improved tanks, guns, cannon, and fighter planes; and jet engine rockets and radar to defend against them. But above all it dissected and mastered the tiniest and deadliest structure in the universe: the atom.

In 1935 Mussolini made clear the long-range intentions of Fascism. With the approach to the highlands of Abyssinia made possible by improved airplanes, Mussolini attacked that country and annexed it to the Italian empire the following year. When the League objected, Italy withdrew from membership. In 1936 German troops entered the demilitarized zone of the Rhine and then crossed the river. "We have no territorial demands to make in Europe, but the Russian menace is intolerable," Hitler explained. That year a Spanish Civil War erupted and soon became a struggle symbolic of Fascism versus Communism. German and Italian volunteers assisted Franco's air force in the saturation bombing of the Basque city of Guernica, the first such experiment in modern warfare, and the Civil War ended in 1939 with Franco assuming dictatorial powers. In 1936 Hitler and Mussolini formed a Berlin-Rome Axis, and Germany and Japan signed an Anti-Comintern Pact, which Italy also signed the following year. Japan then launched a full-scale war against China, capturing Shanghai, Chenchow, Sinyang, Hankow, Canton, and Nanking, the Chinese capital, in the course of which 2 million Chinese soldiers were killed and 60 million civilians displaced from their homes. The Japanese now identified themselves as descendants of the Sun Goddess obligated to spread superior Japanese culture throughout Asia. In 1938 they announced the "New Order in Eastern Asia": its object was to make Asia self-sufficient. Japan at that time attacked an American gunboat in the Yangtze River, and American-Japanese friction continued thereafter until in 1940 America refused to renew a commercial treaty with Japan.

In 1938 Hitler marched into Austria and annexed it; by a plebiscite, 99.75 percent of the Austrians then approved the *Anschluss.* He next turned toward Czechoslovakia, ringed on three sides by Germany and containing over 3 million Germans. Czechoslovakia appealed for aid to France and Britain. France, with over a dozen political parties struggling for supremacy, followed the lead of Britain. The new British prime minister was Neville Chamberlain, a timid, indecisive man and like his cabinet old and weary of war. Bullied and cajoled by Hitler, he agreed to abandon Czechoslovakia, "a far-away country of which we know nothing," as the price of lasting peace. Germany, Poland, and Hungary dismembered Czechoslovakia, with Hitler getting the valuable Skoda armament works.

Inside the Polish Corridor, that strip of eastern Germany given to Poland after World War I, lay the German-speaking free city of Danzig. Its existence, plus Hitler's announced Eastern policy of acquiring "the necessary soil for the German people," furnished him with reasons enough to invade Poland. In August 1939 Hitler and Stalin signed a nonaggression pact, and with Russia thus nullified, with France and England indecisive, and with the remote United States having left the field clear by the passage of Neutrality Acts in 1935 and 1937, Hitler prepared to take over Poland. On September 1, 1939, Germany marched on western Poland while Russia, as per agreement, overran and occupied eastern Poland. But Chamberlain had guaranteed British aid if Poland were invaded, and this time he did not back down. Britain and France declared war on Germany, and World War II began.

WORLD WAR II

Germany crushed Poland within a month and in so doing introduced a new term into the world's vocabulary: *Blitzkrieg,* lightning war. Germany then held still while Russia invaded Finland in November 1939 for refusing to form a part of the Russian defense zone. The League of Nations thereupon expelled Russia (its final act), and a stubborn Finland fell the following March. Next Hitler brought *Blitzkrieg* to Scandinavia where his armies overran Denmark and subdued Norway by means of air power and by betrayal from within organized by Vidkun Quisling, a former defense minister. Norway added to Germany's food and timber supply and provided air bases from which to attack England. Its fall also brought in Winston Churchill to replace Chamberlain as British prime minister.

On May 10, 1940, Germany once more launched the Schlieffen Plan. Holland fell in five days, the better prepared Belgians in a week, and by June 4 German thrusts had penetrated into northern and southern France and moved to encircle France in a giant pincer. This time there was no Marne resistance, and on June 10 Mussolini felt bold enough to declare war on France and England as German troops were sweeping across Paris. Two weeks later the French accepted the German terms for their surrender in the same dining car that the victorious Foch had used after World War I. A French puppet government was set up under Marshal Philippe Pétain at Vichy, and only a corps of French soldiers now in North Africa under General Charles de Gaulle remained in active opposition. The one solace for England in this French debacle and defeat was its improvised rescue of some 365,000 British and French troops encircled at the northern French port of Dunkirk. Hitler spent a month insuring the complete subjection of France while his *Luftwaffe* (air weapon), moved to take command of the British sky. British pilots, vastly outnumbered but aided by radar and by the superiority of their Hurricane and Spitfire fighter planes, managed to hold their own. Bombing raids on London and its vicinity damaged or destroyed over a million houses, but the people stood firm and the air force continued its resistance. Churchill, himself a symbol of resistance, declared that "Never in the field of human conflict was so much owed by so many to so few." America, despite her neutrality, enacted Lend Lease legislation that provided England with destroyers and supplies, and for a year England held out alone against the Axis.

Italy attacked the English base at Egypt, but General Archibald Wavell, with two divisions, drove the Italians back across Libya, wiping out ten Italian divisions in the process. German troops under General Erwin Rommel reinforced the Italians and created a stalemate in North Africa. Unable to penetrate England's air defenses, Hitler turned to the Balkans. He conquered Yugoslavia in eleven days, captured Crete by means of the first airborne invasion ever launched, and the Balkans were his. In September 1940 Germany, Italy, and Japan signed a ten-year military pact, and on June 22, 1941, Germany invaded Russia without warning. By November German troops had covered 400,000 square miles of Russian territory, were bombarding Leningrad (formerly St. Petersburg) and Moscow, and in the south overran Kiev and the Ukraine. Winter halted their march on Stalingrad, while Finland, Rumania, and Hungary all declared war on Russia.

America began sending Lend Lease to Russia, but a sudden turn of events diverted American attention elsewhere. In October 1941 Japan replaced its premier with the militant General Hideki Tojo, and on December 7, 1941, Japan attacked the American Pacific fleet at Pearl Harbor, Hawaii. Germany and Italy declared war on the United States. In six months of *Blitzkreig* the Japanese navy captured 3 million square miles of Pacific territory, including Guam, Wake Island, and Corregidor, and in Southeast Asia occupied Burma, forcing the British back into India and thereby cutting them off from China. So far the Axis powers seemed unbeatable, but in 1942 came indications of a change. American planes crippled the Japanese fleet at Coral Sea and Midway Island, thus preventing a Japanese landing at Australia. General Bernard Montgomery out-maneuvered Rommel in North Africa and defeated him at El Alamein. At Stalingrad, the gateway to the valley of the Volga, the Russian army made a last ditch stand. In May 300,000 seasoned German troops from the French front advanced upon Stalingrad. Artillery bombardment smashed three fourths of the city the first day, covering the streets with rubble and making them impassable to tanks. As the Germans marched in the Russians met them hand to hand, and bloody street battles raged for months. Winter came and the German high command wanted to retreat, but Hitler refused to allow it. Like Napoleon his rise was marked by a gift for anticipating events, while his decline was marked by efforts to shape events to fit his liking. The most able of the Russian generals, Georgi Zhukov, forced the Germans in Stalingrad into a closed pocket, and those who were left surrendered in January 1943. It was Hitler's first failure and the most disastrous single defeat in German military history.

Stalingrad was the turning point of the war, but even so the end could not come swiftly. World War II was global and total in a way that dwarfed all previous wars. Every continent and every nation was involved directly or indirectly. Even Latin America, with at most a tangential concern with European affairs, responded to its new egalitarian treatment by a maturing United States. At a Pan American Conference in Rio de Janeiro in 1942 all Latin American countries except Chile and Argentina broke off relations with the Axis powers and some of them declared war. Civilians were enmeshed in this war as never before, at work in war production, involved in bombing raids, and displaced as refugees as the tides of battle shifted. Jews were savagely slaughtered in all Nazi-occupied territories, and other civilians were executed to keep the majority in check. Eight million of them were imported as slave laborers to work in German factories under inhuman conditions.

A combined British-American force under General Dwight Eisenhower landed in North Africa and secured an Axis surrender there in May 1943. One continent was cleared, and it provided a launching place for a strike into southern Europe. Sicily was invaded, cleared in six weeks, and Mussolini fell from power. The king of Italy signed an armistice, but the Germans moved swiftly to defend the Italian peninsula against an Allied advance. Russia swept all German troops from its borders. In the Pacific the American marines took the tiny atoll of Taiwan, one of the Gilbert Islands, from a Japanese army dedicated to holding it at any price. The costliest battle in United States marine history, it marked the turning point of the war in the Pacific. On June 6, 1944, the Allies launched a full-scale invasion from England into northern France, landing 250,000 troops on the first day. After fierce coastal fighting the German defenses broke, and the Allied advance surged forward forty miles a day. Paris was retaken on August 25 and by September 1 western Germany was invaded. An invasion army under de Gaulle landed at Marseilles and cleared out southern France. The Russians swept across the Balkans and by September they had penetrated eastern Germany. America now dominated the Pacific waters, and under the command of General Douglas MacArthur began to take one strategic Japanese-held island after another. British, Chinese, Indian, and African divisions cleared the Japanese forces out of Burma and reopened the Burma Road into China.

In Europe the Allied air force bombed German cities and factories. The German army launched a final desperate counterthrust against Antwerp in December, but American troops checked them at nearby Bastogne, and the Allied advance continued. Russia overran East Prussia and halted forty-five miles outside Berlin. The western Allies crossed the Rhine, entered the Ruhr, and German troops began surrendering at the rate of 50,000 a day. Russian and American troops met at the Elbe River, as per an agreement between Stalin and Roosevelt, who had died unexpectedly on April 12. On April 28 Mussolini, the "Sawdust Caesar," was caught and executed near Lake Como by Italian partisans. Hitler, who had been directing imaginary armies from an air raid shelter under the chancellory building in Berlin, shot himself on April 30, and on May 7 Germany surrendered.

America now turned full attention toward a desperate and unyielding Japan, entrenched on its island, its fleet and oil supply wiped out. A two-stage invasion was planned, but science had solved the method of unleashing nuclear energy. After Japan refused an ultimatum to surrender, the first atomic bomb was dropped on Hiroshima on August 6, 1945. It destroyed over four square miles and killed 70,000 people. Japan still refused to surrender and Russia declared war against it on August 8. On August 9 a larger atomic bomb was dropped on Nagasaki, obliterating six square miles and a population still uncounted. On September 2, six years and one day after the start of the war, Japan surrendered to General MacArthur on the deck of the USS *Missouri*.

The statistics of this epitaph to the Age of Anxiety are as follows: cost of armaments—$1,117,000,000,000; property destroyed—$2,235,000,000,000; soldiers involved—70,000,000; soldiers killed—10,000,000; civilians killed—22,000,000.

THE HUMANITIES APPROACH

In no other period have underlying forces done so much to motivate events as in this one. The crises, wars, depressions, purges, and upheavals of 1880–1945 reverberate with the tensions of anxiety; and while this age has no monopoly on such tensions, their frequency and virulence here exceed all limits and baffle all attempts to read them on the surface. With no major power anxious for war in 1914, why should World War I have started? Why should the chain of events leading to World War II seem so rhythmic and inevitable? The reasons seem to stem—and this is partly surface explanation too—from the influential theories of three men, locked into place by those of a fourth.

In 1859 Charles Darwin (1809–1882) published *The Origin of Species by Means of Natural Selection*. In it he details the one true and unchanging law of nature, which governs organic life as surely as the laws of science govern matter. The law, of "struggle for existence," finds all creatures struggling to adapt to changes in environment and at the same time struggling with other species and, more fiercely, with one another in order to survive. Nature turns out to be a battleground, and what seems alluring veils the actual cruelty of the struggle. In Darwin's words: "We behold the face of nature bright with gladness, we often see superabundance of food; we do not see or we forget that the birds which are idly singing round us mostly live on insects or seeds, and are thus constantly destroying life; or we forget how largely these songsters, or their eggs, or their nestlings, are destroyed by birds and beasts of prey." The world of nature thus became no longer a Romantic refuge but an alien enemy.

Karl Marx (1818–1883) viewed the world of everyday society as a continuous struggle for existence. "The history of all hitherto existing society is the history of class struggles," begins the *Communist Manifesto* written in 1847 in collaboration with Friedrich Engels, and in a preface to the *Manifesto* forty years later, Engels makes Communism common cause with Darwinian evolution. "The whole history of mankind . . . has been a history of class struggles, contests between exploiting and exploited, ruling and oppressed classes; . . . the history of these class struggles form a series of evolutions." For Marx, changing methods of production change human conditions, and as the majority of mankind, the proletariat, seeks to adapt itself to these methods, social changes march in inevitable progression. "Circumstances make men just as much as men make circumstances": far from being in control of his fate, man is the product of economic forces which determine his conduct, his society, and the predictable course of his history. With the upsurge of socialism and Communism, mankind in the Age of Anxiety had to face not only the onslaught of alien forces in the world around it but of alien forces beyond its control in the world it had made.

As for the world it never made, Søren Kierkegaard (1813–1855) discovered there even more fundamental causes for anxiety. To be free, he contended, man must choose himself, not God, and in thus choosing freedom, the *summum bonum* of this life, man is alienated from God. "In that way man is left juggling with a phantom—freedom of choice." Man left to himself has no spiritual recourse other than an absurd leap of faith into a blind unknown, terrifying because of its illogic and leaving men the helpless victims of ignorance and dread. The works of Kierkegaard, ignored during his lifetime, became the breeding ground for thinkers a generation later who, like Kierkegaard, saw "the predicament of the existing individual" as the cause of endless anxiety. And while these Existentialists found few if any solutions in common, all were agreed that mankind, "situated in existence," found itself alienated from a God who, challenged by the logic of science, may or may not exist. Thus for the Age of Anxiety the world beyond joined with the worlds of nature and society to evoke, in Kierkegaard's words, fear and trembling.

With all avenues of outlet grown dark, the Age of Anxiety might have sought solace in its own interior resources, but Sigmund Freud (1856–1939) revealed to it that the mind was as much a battleground as Darwinian nature, as ineluctably determined as Marxian society, and as unknowable as Kierkegaard's God. With repressed feelings struggling for existence in the unconscious, with a superego unable to contain them and therefore unable to maintain free will, and with the unconscious hidden away from conscious awareness, the mind reinforced all facets of anxiety. And when the functions of mind interlocked with those of society, the results could only be alarming. As Freud himself concluded: "Since culture [here used in the Germanic sense of total human preoccupation] obeys an inner erotic impulse which bids it bind mankind into a closely knit mass, it can achieve this aim only by means of its vigilance in fomenting an ever-increasing sense of guilt."

While Darwin presented the fullest exposition of the struggle for existence, and while his followers exploited it in his name, he did not spring fully armed out of a void. James Burnett, Lord Monboddo (1714–1799), had pondered evolution earlier, and Goethe had anticipated all of the findings of Darwin in more general terms. The social theories of Marx form a direct line of development from the writings of Saint-Simon, Fourier, and Owen. The absurd leap of Kierkegaard finds an early counterpart in the advice of Beatrice to Dante in the *Paradiso* of the *Divine Comedy*, and his concept of man's alienation from God echoes Medieval and Deistic philosophy, and in turn is echoed with harsher overtones by Nietzsche. Inspired pathfinder that he was, Freud still found bases for his conjectures in the writings of Jean Charcot and Joseph Breuer, to say nothing of Sophocles and Shakespeare. We tend today to credit Darwin, Marx, Kierkegaard, and Freud as spokesmen for these ideas because their explications were the richest and most impressive and because they appeared when Romanticism was drawing to a close. They spearheaded a revolt against Romanticism which was smoldering behind the bland façade of 1880–1900. They were not solitary voices, however, but gifted and prophetic interpreters of the age that created World War I and the chain of reactions that followed—the Age of Anxiety.

TRAITS AND IDEAS

Anxiety forms the nucleus of this period, and all contemporary traits and ideas revolve around it in sympathetic relationship. Close as we are to the age, we can detect a dozen or more overlapping aspects of anxiety, each of which yields its harvest to the humanities approach: guilt, alienation, suffering, and abandonment are a few of the more common ones. The present survey of anxiety limits itself to three traits, which at once encompass anxiety and provide an adequate basis for further inquiry. They include *despair,* which best represents the inner nature of anxiety; *violence,* which mirrors its outward physical appearance; and *depersonalization,* a bulky but precise description of its most potent and universal effect.

Perhaps the *Angst,* dread, of the philosopher Martin Heidegger best defines the DESPAIR of this period. "All things," Heidegger writes, "and we with them, sink into a sort of indifference. But not in the sense that everything simply disappears; rather, in the very act of drawing away from us everything turns toward us. This withdrawal of what-is-in-totality, which then swarms round us as dread, this is what oppresses us. There is nothing to hold on to." All things seemed to conspire to alienate themselves from, yet impinge upon, the life of man during this period. Foremost was war with its new and ghastly weapons; also encirclement by technology, the twilight of imperialism, and the increased constraints brought about by rising populations. These gave twentieth-century man the feeling that there was no way out of this shrinking yet inescapable world. Fascism and Communism erected further barriers, the depression yet another, and as Freud perceived, these causes of despair perversely bred in mankind a desperate sense of guilt.

In philosophy Kierkegaard prophesied the coming growth of despair: "One might say perhaps that there lives not one single man who after all is not to some extent in despair, in whose inmost parts there does not dwell a disquietude, a discord, an anxious dread of an unknown something, or of a something he does not even dare to make acquaintance with, dread of a possibility of life, or dread of himself." Friedrich Nietzsche echoed Kierkegaard, but from his own turbulent frame of reference: "Our whole European culture has been moving for some time now, with a tortured tension that is growing from decade to decade, as toward a catastrophe: restlessly, violently, headlong, like a river that wants to reach the end, that no longer reflects, that is afraid to reflect." The Existentialists found twentieth-century man abandoned in this alien world and proclaimed the inevitability of despair. Heidegger dissected the trait and Karl Jaspers saw it as attacking the mind, body, and spirit to the point where "*Angst* increases to such a pitch that the sufferer may feel himself to be nothing more than a lost point in empty space." Existentialist Jean Paul Sartre explained that twentieth-century man is not only isolated by his anguish but also responsible to the unreachable society around him, so that private despair evolves into a sense of universal helplessness. Bertrand Russell, whose concern was not Existentialism but the "powerful instrument" of mathematics, nevertheless sounds like Jaspers when contemplating the psyche of his age: "Brief and powerless is Man's life; on him and all his race the slow sure doom falls pitiless and dark. Blind to good and evil, reckless of destruction, omnipotent matter rolls on its relentless way."

LITERATURE.   An early major statement of twentieth-century despair is *Jude the Obscure* (1896) by Thomas Hardy. Tragic as is Jude's own life, with its grinding failure and disappointments, the universal meaning of the novel emerges from the suicide of "Father Time," Jude's prematurely aged son. "It is," explains a doctor brought into the novel for this very purpose, "the beginning of the coming universal wish not to live." With this flash of intuition Hardy envisioned the political desperation, twentieth-century *Angst,* and the Freudian death wish that still lay beyond the horizon.

Anton Chekhov in *Uncle Vanya* sees the world overcome by the failure of nerve, and his six major characters all sink into gloomy, hopeless apathy. Henrik Ibsen sets vital heroines like Nora (*A Doll's House*) and Hedda (*Hedda Gabler*) amid the encroaching Age of Anxiety which overcomes them. In *The Castle* Franz Kafka shows Everyman abandoned by society and God; in *The Trial* the anonymous K. wanders hopelessly through mazes of bureaucracy and his own unconscious; and the grotesque humor that laces both these works depends upon our recognizing despair as an accomplished fact. Marcel Proust uses the new stream-of-consciousness technique in his *Remembrance of Things Past* cycle of novels to present the stale message that all striving is hopeless, that the sometimes boorish, sometimes contemptible middle class will swallow up society and disfigure love, honor, beauty, and even middle-class morality. Ernest Hemingway uses a deceptively simple style to anatomize twentieth-century *Angst. The Sun Also Rises* is a study of impotence, physical, moral, and creative, in a postwar world immobilized by emotional paralysis. *For Whom the Bell Tolls* exposes idealism to the Spanish Civil War and shows how it leads at last only to a desire for death. In Hemingway's most famous short story, "The Killers," Ole Andreson explains that "There ain't anything to do," as he waits listlessly to die in the town called Summit. In *Absalom, Absalom* William Faulkner contemplates a microcosm in which everything is foreordained to crumble: family ties, the barren middle class, the old South and the new (actually not the South at all but the Age of Anxiety played out against a regional backdrop). In "The Waste Land" T. S. Eliot presents the twentieth century as an age wrung dry, where living dead men throng city streets or slump in pubs or mansions waiting for the final knock upon the door. And Sartre in *No Exit* offers the crowning irony: man's punishment in hell will be an eternity of despair.

ARCHITECTURE.   Despair and the trait of violence that follows from it deal with the expressive qualities of anxiety; the third trait, depersonalization, deals with its formal quality. Architecture, because of its formal nature will seize upon the latter trait to the virtual exclusion of the first two, though one can find a few side effects of despair and violence in its productions. The population explosion of the twentieth century and the overcrowded cities spurred profiteers to build cheap, high-rise apartment houses on sunless narrow streets, with small, stifling rooms and instant disrepair which made them symbols of proletarian despair. The *Art Nouveau* style (its trademark is a whiplash design) in vogue up to World War I marked a violent protest against the whole nineteenth-century world. The *Grand Palais des Beaux Arts* in Paris and the New Amsterdam Theater in New York have Art Nouveau exteriors, and both seemed dated by 1930. Art Nouveau decor is more successful in interiors, such as those by Henry van de Velde and, a notable example, Hvitträsk, the Finnish studio home of architect Eliel Saarinen.

SCULPTURE.   The work of Aristide Maillol, the most eminent follower of Rodin, furnishes a view of the gradual transition to anxiety. In his famous allegorical statue, *La Méditerranée* (the Mediterranean), the lady's somber brooding face and attitude foreshadow the coming impact of despair. In the full tide was a group of early twentieth-century German sculptors whose chief spokesmen were Ernst Barlach, who specialized in ponderous sorrowing figures done in wood, and Wilhelm Lehmbruck. Lehmbruck's *Seated Youth* (Figure 9.1) is almost faceless, and therefore tragically incapable of vigor or zest. The bowed head, slumped shoulders, drooping hands, and even the set of the feet connote despair. The body is stretched beyond logic or endurance, and yet seems in proportion, as though this new age requires a new shape. Lehmbruck is often called a Gothic sculptor, and like his Medieval forebears (see the *Gero Crucifixion*, Figure 4.24) and the Existentialists of his own time he concretizes the griefs of the universe within the shape of life here on earth. This solitary figure— so much of the sculpture of this age depicts figures in isolation—suggests at once Medieval contemplation and Heidegger's "All things, and we with them, sink into a sort of indifference."

The theme of despair persists throughout the drastic changes in

Figure 9.1   WILHELM LEHMBRUCK.   *Seated Youth*.   (1918).   Art Museum Duisburg, Germany.   [Gabriele Basch-Hauck: Städelesches Kunstinstitut].

Figure 9.2   HENRY MOORE.   *Recumbent Figure*.   (1938).   The Tate Gallery, London.

sculptural technique during this period. In Cubist sculpture Naum Gabo captured timeless grief in the sharp geometrical shapes of his *Constructed Head, No. 2.* And abstract sculpture at times probed the essence of despair. *Recumbent Figure* by Henry Moore (Figure 9.2) carries the isolation of Lehmbruck into the misty unknown. Where *Seated Youth* is at least realistic in outline, *Recumbent Figure* is only so by implication, and life as we know it has disappeared, replaced by something heavy and mysterious, hopeless of solution.

PAINTING.   Like Thomas Hardy the Norwegian artist Edvard Munch sensed the current of anxiety early, and he too portrayed the shattering impact of despair. *The Scream* (Figure 9.3) depicts the nightmare anguish of a drab Everyman, shapeless and alone beneath an alien sky. The swirling background traces the whiplash curve of Art Nouveau design, and the token features of the victim anticipate the mere indentations in the sculpture of Moore.

In Paris Pablo Picasso, whose work pursued all traits and techniques of the Age of Anxiety, focused upon despair during his blue period, 1901–1904. In it he exploited the psychology of the color blue, connoting depression, in themes to match. *La Vie* (Figure 9.4) sees life as despair even at its moments of greatest potential happiness. At the left a couple, in the first flush of love, are nonetheless isolated from one another by melancholy; on the bed in the background they symbolize the isolating disappointment of carnal love. At the right the aging wife, now a mother, eyes her past with hostility, while in the lower center the aging husband sits bowed with grief like a carving on a tomb, his pose reminiscent of Lehmbruck's *Seated Youth.* Other Paris-based painters deeply influenced by despair include Amedeo Modigliani, whose stylized women with their elongated faces all project a similar wistfulness; and Georges Rouault, whose religious figures seem steeped in personal sorrow, recalling the gloomy rationalization of theologian Nicholas Berdyaev that "The failure of history does not mean that history is devoid of necessity or relevance. Similarly the failure of Christianity does not mean that Christianity is not the highest truth."

In Italy Giorgio de Chirico painted eternity and infinity as hopelessly alien and remote. In America Max Weber painted nature and city life as composed of forlorn and isolated elements, and Edward Hopper explored the muted sadness implicit in mass-produced American living. *Early Sunday Morning* (Figure 9.5) might be retitled "quiet scream"; the façade is as flat and two dimensional as Munch's protagonist, as though the dwellers in the houses had no depth whatsoever. The apparent differences in the groups of second story windows underscore the uniform drabness of all of them. The contrast of glaring light against muted coloring spotlights the emptiness of this Sunday morning world in which even the barber pole and fire hydrant proclaim their own isolation.

Figure 9.3 EDVARD MUNCH. *The Scream.* (1893). National Gallery, Oslo. [O. Vaering].

MUSIC. Probably no art gave itself up to anxiety with such abandon as music, as a single hearing of what we still call modern music will make clear. Where other arts, and earlier music, interacted with their ages, modern music so subordinated itself to anxiety that its major achievements, although not ugly, cannot be described as beautiful. To convey anxiety modern music broke with old techniques and established new ones: the removal of tonal centers so that the listener had a feeling of being cut adrift, the frequent use of dissonance, and the use of arid melodies built out of wide skips were among the most common and effective despair techniques. Dissonance in Igor Stravinsky's *Le Sacre du Printemps* (the rite of

Figure 9.4   PABLO PICASSO.   *La Vie.*   (1903).   The Cleveland Museum of Art, Gift of Hanna Fund, 1945.

Figure 9.5 EDWARD HOPPER. *Early Sunday Morning.* (1930). The Whitney Museum of American Art, New York.

spring), conveys a poignant harshness. In *Pierrot Lunaire* (young moonstruck Peter), Arnold Schönberg employs *Sprechstimme*, speaking voice, a crooning sound that only approximates song and pitch, thus making for dissonance and lack of a tonal center. In combination with a chamber orchestra that provides eerie Rorschach responses to the text, the net effect is gloomy and disturbing. Schönberg's *Die Erwartung* (the expectation), joins eerie dissonance to painful themes. The famous dissonantal Mystery Chord which pervades the work of Alexander Scriabin—C, F sharp, B flat, E, A, D— makes more of a sorrowing than a mysterious sound.

Music expressed the despair of the period by its choice of content as well as through techniques. Eric Satie penned the following description, typical of him and his work, to one of his piano pieces:

> This vast region of the world is inhabited by one man: a Negro—He is bored to death with laughing—Million year old trees cast a shadow showing 9:17 A.M. The toads call each other by name. To think better, the Negro holds his cerebellum in his right hand, his fingers spread. From a distance he looks like a distinguished physiologist. Four anonymous serpents charm him, hanging from the tails of his uniform, which is tattered from trouble and solitude. On the edge of the river an old mangrove tree is slowly washing its roots, fouled with filth—This is not the time for love's sweet surrender.

In opera, Richard Strauss transformed Biblical story and Greek myth into gloomy studies of Freudian abnormality. *Salome* with its incessant dissonance and shrieking woodwinds bespoke a world without hope. *Elektra,* even more dissonant, added overtones of madness to the general effect.

No opera encapsulated its age so well as Alban Berg's *Wozzeck*, which portrays a thirty-year-old army private helpless in an alien world. As captain's orderly, doctor's guinea pig, prostitute's cuckold, and sergeant's butt, he drifts off into madness as the only solution. Berg used *Sprechstimme* and the new compositional devices to achieve a devastating, almost unendurable effect.

World Wars I and II, Fascism, Nazism, and the Communist purges of 1936–1938 all dramatized the VIOLENCE that formed the surface image of anxiety. Tabloid newspapers and crime magazines, introduced during this period, reveled in it, and the new mass audience that read them absorbed this violence into its daily life. In describing that audience the sociologist José Ortega y Gasset observed: "In the disturbances caused by the scarcity of food, the mob goes in search of bread, and the means it employs is generally to wreck the bakeries." But such conduct and reading matter were more effects than causes. Violence had emerged early in the period as a shaping trait out of a nineteenth-century movement known as Nihilism, which swept across Russia and filtered through the continent. Its thesis, which bred the assassination of Czar Alexander II, held that: "What can be smashed must be smashed. Whatever will stand the blow is of use. Whatever is smashed to pieces is rubbish. At any rate smash right and left. No harm can come of that." In the same vein was the Darwinian struggle for existence and Marx's contention that "not only has the bourgeoisie forged the weapons that bring death to itself; it has also called into existence the men who are to wield those weapons." *Reflections on Violence* (1915) by Georges Sorel contended that national socialism could only come about through acts of violence: Mussolini was a close student of Sorel, and Hitler made use of him with grisly variations. "Our age wields an axe," wrote Trotsky, and Freud stated its motto as "the hostility of each against all and of all against each."

In philosophy Nietzsche defined life as the will to power, and power was obtained by smashing one's neighbor. "Not contentment, but more power; not peace at any price, but war," he wrote, and: "I welcome all signs that a more manly, a warlike, age is about to begin." Bergson saw mankind evolving, extending itself, "by an increasingly violent effort," and John Dewey held that all human activity was a "surging, explosive discharge—blind, unintelligent." But more seminal than any of these, the trait of violence bred its own unique philosophy of war. In *On War* (1873) Karl von Clausewitz dissected war and violence with dispassionate logic. He set forth such tenets as: war ought to be short and decisive and to be so must involve the total civil population. Armies must attack, always attack, "use force unsparingly without reference to the bloodshed involved," so that entire nations feel the pressure, the *Schreckligkeit* (intimidation) of total war. Violent feelings must be whipped up in advance by propaganda so that "The passions which burst forth in war already have a latent existence in the people."

LITERATURE.   As *Jude the Obscure* heralded the despair of the Age of Anxiety, *Fathers and Sons* (1861) by Ivan Turgenev anticipates its violence. Its hero, Bazarov, is a Nihilist—the term was popularized by this novel—who "does not take any principle on faith," and his cynical, aggressive life and absurd death shook his readers' complacency. In *The Plumed Serpent* D. H. Lawrence takes a Nihilistic view of Christianity so as to make room for his own version of Aztec primitivism. War and totalitarianism gave rise to a number of novels reflecting on their violence. Chief among them were *All Quiet on the Western Front* by Erich Maria Remarque, which exposes the senseless and tragic brutality of World War I; *Bread and Wine* by Ignazio Silone, with its glimpses of Mussolini's Fascists stomping people to death; and *Darkness at Noon* by Arthur Koestler, where cellar interrogations are the catechisms of a world in which force has triumphed over spirit.

America, less directly affected than Europe by the violence of the age, could therefore stomach more of it in literature, and American Age of Anxiety literature abounds in explicit descriptions of brutality. In his *U.S.A. Trilogy* John Dos Passos presents a movie-speed panoramic view of a savage and turbulent America. In his *Studs Lonigan* trilogy James T. Farrell narrows the focus to a few big city scenes and people, but his New Year's orgy is a searing picture of violent America that holds its own with Dos Passos' more crowded canvas. In *Elmer Gantry* Sinclair Lewis has the average man take to the whip when his religious beliefs are challenged. Eugene O'Neill has him revel in cruelty in *The Emperor Jones.* In *Sanctuary* Faulkner chronicles a mob hero, Popeye, who sublimates his impotence into a lust for death. As a child Popeye cut up live kittens; as an adult he murdered with frequency and indifference; and at the end, respected even by his jailer, he welcomes the hangman's noose as a friend, the transition from Darwin to Freud almost too pat to ring true.

All the arts of this period turned with a will toward another kind of violence: a blistering attack on the values and principles of the middle class—see Ezra Pound's broadside that all poetry over twenty years old ought to be burned. Spearhead of this attack was *Ubu Roi* (1896), a play by Alfred Jarry. It opens with an obscene travesty of *Macbeth* and proceeds to spit upon a long list of the world's classics. King Ubu, the epitome of the middle class, has a pear-shaped head, a grotesque and swollen face, and a huge gourd of a stomach. He is greedy, lecherous, cowardly, dishonest, and, when he can be, sadistic. His gods are gold, sex, and power and his language is a steady flow of four-letter words. His wife is a shade less attractive and even more sulfurous than he. These bourgeois cartoons and gutter expletives furnished models for the Dadaists and Futurists of the Age of Anxiety.

ARCHITECTURE.   See page 415 for the slender evidences of violence and despair in the architecture of this period.

SCULPTURE.   Like Jarry, the Dadaists and Futurists who flourished around World War I struck out at the middle class. The Dadaists centered their attention on painting, although they did exhibit toilet seats and urinals as works of sculpture, while the Futurists, machine oriented as they were, stressed sculpture. Futurism was born in wartime Italy and prefigured Mussolini, who encouraged it during his regime. It celebrated the machine as the force that could liberate art from the cloying esthetics of the middle class. The chief Futurist propagandist, Filippo Marinetti, explains the movement as follows: "A racing car with its trunk adorned by great exhaust pipes like snakes with an explosive breath—a roaring car that seems to be driving under shrapnel, is more beautiful than the *Victory of Samothrace*." "We want to glorify war, the only hygiene of the world . . . . We want to demolish museums, libraries, fight against morality, feminism, and all opportunistic and utilitarian cowardices." "For art can be nothing but violence, cruelty, and injustice." A masterwork of Futurist sculpture is *Unique Forms of Continuity in Space* by Umberto Boccioni (Figure 9.6). Its striding figure suggests the dynamic movement of a piston, and like a moving piston the figure persists in time. The total effect of this temporal unity-in-plurality is further complicated by the jagged planes that crisscross and shoot off in a rush of movement: as time seems to be stretched, space seems to be exploded. Other sculptors affected by Futurism include Alexander Archipenko, Jacques Lipchitz, and, second in merit only to Boccioni, Raymond Duchamp-Villon.

One interesting sidelight in art history is the reaction of the public to the New York Armory Show of 1913, where a mammoth collection of modern sculpture and painting was revealed for the first time to large American audiences. Tabloids shrilled headlines, public figures turned art critics, and the crowds attending the show seemed always on the brink of rioting. These reactions, it might be pointed out, have implications far deeper than the slow formation of American culture. The audience was responding in kind, and perceptively, to the violent attack upon it from Age of Anxiety artists.

PAINTING.   Dadaism, the *Ubu Roi* of painting, flung its defiance in the faces of the middle class. Dada, a word composed of infantile nonsense syllables, also, and not without design, connotes father. Its principal spokesman, Tristan Tzara, propounds its creed in part as follows: "Every product of disgust capable of becoming a negation of the family is Dada; a protest with the fists of its whole being engaged in destructive action: Dada; knowledge of all the means rejected up until now by the shamefaced sex of comfortable compromise and good manners: Dada." In its extreme form Dadaism produced the *Merzbilders*, trash pictures, of Kurt Schwitters, composed of cut-out pieces of trash paper and postage stamps pasted on a canvas (works of this type became known as *collages, colle* being the French word for paste). In modified form Dadaism influenced such signifi- cant painters as Max Ernst (*The Gramineous Bicycle, The Little Tear Gland That Says Tic-Tac*) and Marcel Duchamp, whose ready-mades were painted everyday utensils retitled *The Bride, The Bachelors,* and so forth. Duchamp also exhibited a photograph of the *Mona Lisa* on which he had drawn a moustache, and dabbled in a technique akin to Futurism for his *Nude Descending a Staircase* (Figure 9.7), the *cause célèbre* of the armory show. Dubbed "explosion in a shingle factory," a witticism rooted in perception, *Nude* launches a flow of power through space and time. Many of its shapes resemble pipes and engine casings, a link with Duchamp's ready-mades. The clashing, more violent rhythms at the top of the canvas settle down into a more subdued and fluid rhythm below, giving the work a satisfying variety of speeds. The precise staircase and lettering (the title of the painting) in the lower left suggest the serious grounding and intention of this work, which is indeed a brilliant exercise in structure, motion, and turbulent defiance of the status quo.

The earliest twentieth-century school of French painters, *Les Fauves* (the wild men), were so dubbed because of their primitive drawing and subject matter, and also because of the shocking intensity of their colors, primary colors for the most part laid raw in sweeping strokes upon the canvas. Prior to *Les Fauves* the harbinger works of Vincent van Gogh seethe with whirling lines and turbulent color. The *Brücke,* or bridge school in Germany added violent subject matter to the shocking coloring of the French school. Picasso fused this same violence and raw color in a series of paintings of women he made in the 1930s, but his epic to the violence of the age was done in black, white, and grey. *Guernica* (Figure 9.8) commem- orates the razing of that city (see p. 406) and at the same time condemns the ferocity of all war. The shapes in this work are unreal, yet a reality pulsates from them that jolts the senses and, if the clearly guided movement from viewer's right to left is followed, reveals a deliberate and cosmic plan. To the right a bombed figure is entrapped in a hellish blackness. Beside him (and hell?) a door opens conveniently into this world at war. Here desper- ate faces contemplate wreckage, a sky which rains down bombs, and the pitiful illumination for this world, a single electric bulb. A bomb sticks in the throat of a screaming horse—not even animals are spared the horrors of war—while broken monuments strew the ground, shards of a past forever lost. At the left a shrieking woman holds her dead child, in gro- tesque caricature of the *Pietà,* staring up into the face of a bull, symbol of so many ancient religions, but in his present hideous and implacable guise more a symbol of "brutality and darkness" (Picasso's own description). Alongside the bull, in the upper left corner, a charred grotesque arm seems to be raising the curtain on man's future.

Figure 9.6 UMBERTO BOCCIONI. *Unique Forms of Continuity in Space.* (1913).
The Museum of Modern Art, Acquired through the Lillie P. Bliss Bequest.

Figure 9.7 MARCEL DUCHAMP. *Nude Descending a Staircase.* (1912). Philadelphia Museum of Art.

Figure 9.8 PABLO PICASSO. *Guernica.* (1937). Collection of the artist; on extended loan to The Museum of Modern Art, New York.

In North and Central America a group of Mexican artists depicted man's struggle for survival on the battlefield of capitalism. In canvases and murals of impressive power, David Siqueiros, Diego Rivera, and José Orozco voiced protests against the callous ferocity of the age. The latter's *Christ Destroying the Cross* (Figure 9.9) portrays a god of wrath returned to earth, his clenched fist and worker's axe twin symbols of the violence etched in his face. Behind him lie the cross he has hacked down, a broken Buddha, a classical column, and a tangled heap of munitions—all of the ancient gods now overthrown by the primitive worker's God who stands before us. Clashing reds, yellows, and oranges and crisscrossing lines of force add to the powerful impression of outrage in this work.

MUSIC.   Twentieth-century musicians also made Dadaist attacks on middle-class sensibility. Alexander Mossolov waggled a piece of sheet steel at his audience during the performance of his *Iron Foundry*. Satie's ballet, *Parade,* includes the following Ubuesque sequence: "The Chinese magician draws an egg from his braid, eats it, digests it, and finds it at the toe of his sandal. He breathes fire, burns himself, hops around to put out the sparks. The young girl comes on stage, rides a bicycle, imitates Charlie Chaplin, chases a thief with a revolver, boxes, dances to ragtime, falls asleep, is shipwrecked, rolls in the grass on an April morning, takes a picture."—all this to dissonantal music whose score provides for the frequent accompaniment of stamping feet. In his *Ballet Mécanique* the American composer George Antheil included the sounds of automobile horns, airplane propellers, and

Figure 9.9 José Orozco. *Christ Destroying the Cross.* (1932–1934). Courtesy of Dartmouth College.

anvils. Forays such as these account in large part for the Armory Show type response to Stravinsky's *Le Sacre du Printemps.* The first night Paris audience howled, whistled, and spat in one another's faces. In this serious and epoch-making work Stravinsky sought to convey the turbulence of the age through blaring orchestral colors, harsh dissonances, and above all through driving, fluctuating rhythms. The elemental plot line—a girl must dance herself to death to appease primitive gods—adds to the turmoil, but rhythm is foremost here in suggesting pure ferocity. A number of later composers delved as did Stravinsky into rhythmic chaos: Bela Bartok in his early piano work, *Allegro Barbaro;* Carl Orff in his secular cantatas, *Carmina Burana* and *Catulli Carmina;* Maurice Ravel in his explosive piano *Concerto in D for the Left Hand;* Walter Piston in the first movement of his *Second Symphony.*

As Stravinsky had in his *Sacre* and *Petrouchka* ballets, opera composers turned to librettos whose plots lent themselves to the violence of the age. Their tragedies were not the tender ones of Romanticism but morbid probings into psychological or physical horrors. Strauss' *Salome* flirts with the bloody head of John the Baptist and kisses it on the lips, and an appalled Herod orders her crushed to death. Strauss' *Elektra* rages with mounting insanity and dies of joy over the death of her mother—and Strauss' music amplifies these passions. Berg's *Wozzeck*, the victim of universal violence, drowns himself in water tinged with his murdered mistress' blood. In the opera *Lulu* Berg's music plumbs the depths of sadism. In a scene typical of the work as a whole the youthful composer, Alva, succumbs to the temptress Lulu and admits his love for her, whereupon she tells him while fondling him, "I poisoned your mother."

In a landmark work of this period, *The Decline of the West*, the sociohistorian Oswald Spengler interpreted the Age of Anxiety as the death rattle of Romanticism, a final phase in which all culture gave way to an arid technology that reduced everything to what he called "forms." By forms Spengler meant physical qualities whose shapes blotted out, or at least overshadowed, the vitality, soul, and life they represented. This reduction of everything to form spelled out for him the death of Western civilization. "The grand ornamentation of the past," he wrote, "has become as truly a dead language as Sanskrit or Church Latin. Instead of its symbolism being honored or obeyed, its mummy, its legacies of perfected forms, are put into the pot anyhow, and recast in wholly organic forms." Written just after World War I *The Decline of the West* came too early to assess the full scope of the Age of Anxiety, but it did manage to seize upon what is probably the principal trait of the period—DEPERSONALIZATION, the stripping of individual identity from members of the body politic, from human conduct and desire, from the everyday actions of life and the aspirations of art.

In politics Fascism demanded the complete surrender of the individual will to the overriding requirements of the state. The Germany of Bismarck provided the breeding ground for such a view. Nicknamed the land of *Verboten*, it regulated the hours for music practice in apartments, the size of beer mugs, even the number of pedestrians allowed to walk abreast in city streets. The Nazi twenty-five point program, issued in 1920, included the following statement: "The activities of the individual may not clash with the interests of the whole but must proceed within the frame of the community and be for the general good." The creed of the Communist Third International, issued in 1919, expressed a parallel drive toward uniformity and proposed to banish "all inequalities based on sex, religion, and nationality." In an America blighted by the depression the leveling share-the-wealth program of Huey Long swept Louisiana, nor was its influence confined to that state; and aspects of the New Deal also restricted individual expansion.

Determinism, the view that life was determined by forces outside the individual's control, ruled much of the thought and conduct of the age. Darwinian nature was deterministic, as was Marxist economics. "In every historical epoch," the *Communist Manifesto* states, "the prevailing mode of economic production and exchange, and the social organization necessarily following from it, form the basis upon which is built up, and from which alone can be explained, the political and intellectual history of that epoch." As economics determined society, so according to Freud unconscious drives determined individual conduct. Unknowable and uncontrollable, these drives made each of us will-less victims of social pressures, themselves the inevitable products of economic forces, if Marx was to be believed. And on top of depersonalization in politics and conduct, the machine production of technology reduced industrial workers to so many standardized parts. The new phenomenon of universal education came to resemble mass production, and "whole children" emerged like sausage links from the institutions of learning. In an environment like this, popular culture bloomed, sprouting formula entertainment via radio, the movies, and slick magazines, and thus the trait became self-generating: depersonalization, at first imposed, became a general craving.

In the case of depersonalization too, Kierkegaard intuited a coming trend by deploring the rise of what he termed the crowd. "A crowd in its very concept is the untruth, by reason of the fact that it renders the individual completely impenitent and irresponsible, or at least weakens his sense of responsibility by reducing it to a fraction." Ernst Haeckel based his philosophy of materialism on the new encirclement of individuality. "Comparative and genetic psychology," he stated, "has shown that there cannot be an immortal soul; and monistic physiology has proven the futility of the assumption of free will. Finally, the science of evolution has made it clear that the same eternal iron laws that rule the inorganic world are valid too in the organic and moral world." Edmund Husserl, whose Phenomenology may well anticipate our own age as Kierkegaard did the Age of Anxiety, sees all men with similar environments locked inside a uniform spatiotemporal fact-world. And the logical positivism of Rudolph Carnap would reduce all knowledge to cold, impersonal definitions.

LITERATURE.   Kafka in *The Trial* presents an interior view of depersonalized twentieth-century man. K. is pressured by forces beyond his control and, since they are often symbols from his unconscious, beyond his capacity to understand. In the end they destroy him without his ever really knowing why—in large part because the "me" in K. has never really existed. Thomas Mann in *Mario and the Magician* shows how a hero-villain, Cipolla (onion)—Mussolini in transparent disguise—may forge all classes in twentieth-century society into a unit mass which he shapes and directs at will. Hermann Hesse in *The Bead Game* holds that depersonalization is the highest ideal of our century's culture and reduces all aspects of civilization to a series of formal patterns which may be arranged in various ways. As a result all knowledge and aspiration become an impersonal exercise, a bead game. In *The Plumed Serpent*, D. H. Lawrence advocates his own twentieth-century version of religion, wherein one can find God only through the complete submersion of one's individuality: depersonalization here becomes the *summum bonum*. In *Brave New World*, Aldous Huxley carries the consequences of this trait to their logical and shocking extreme. In his world of the future all babies are classified in units and their qualities and capacities prearranged like so many IBM cards. Thus the intrusive problem of personality is disposed of in advance. Sinclair Lewis' George F. Babbitt and Lowell Schmaltz, in *Babbitt* and *The Man Who Knew Coolidge*, dispose of their personalities themselves, electing to stifle all individuality in order to mesh with the crowd. Schmaltz, a spookily accurate caricature, enjoys the results of his self-performed lobotomy with never a moment's qualm.

Depersonalization in the other arts appears as form rather than content, and poetry, the genre closest to sculpture, painting, and music, best reflects the dominance of form in Age of Anxiety literature. The most form-conscious poet writing in English during this period was T. S. Eliot, whose "objective correlative" anticipated Hesse's bead game. Simplified, objective correlative means that a poetic image or phrase correlates with one interpretation only, which all readers should be made to arrive at objectively, regardless of their personal backgrounds. For example, the metaphor "April is the cruelest month"—from "The Waste Land," a large-scale presentation of the objective correlative—means, as Eliot's notes make clear, that April, in primitive agricultural societies a time of rebirth (of the soil), is most cruel in the Age of Anxiety because this age, far from meriting rebirth, is better off dead. Thus one image yields one meaning and no more, depersonalizing poem and reader alike. In his *Pisan Cantos* Ezra Pound uses the objective correlative with uneven success, basing his poems on a vast, unwieldy objective frame of reference: man's racial unconscious. W. B. Yeats conformed to the spirit of the time by developing his own objective form, a series of "gyres," or corkscrew turnings, each corresponding to 2000 years of history divided into twenty-eight segments like the phases of the moon.

ARCHITECTURE.   Large-scale group housing made up of standardized apartment units flourished at this time, and major architects like Walter Gropius in Germany and J. J. P. Oud in Holland sought to give these projects at least the beauty of precise and functional forms. Assembly-line factories took on a slick and faceless appearance in keeping with their function. A pioneer in this style was Peter Behrens, architect-in-chief of the German General Electric Company, whose spacious geometric designs—

for example, the General Electric Turbine factory in Berlin—pave the way for such crowning accomplishments in factory architecture as the Johnson Wax Company plant by Frank Lloyd Wright.

Function dominates ornament in the architecture of this period, and sometimes, as during its early break away from Romanticism, function dispenses with ornament altogether. A pioneer of this new functionalism was the American architect Louis Sullivan, whose Wainwright Building (Figure 9.10) exemplified his own dictum that in architecture, "Form follows Function." In America the rapid growth of cities and the soaring cost of center city property made tall buildings desirable; steel framework and the invention of the elevator in 1871 made them possible. In 1885 William Jenney completed the first skyscraper, the ten-story Home Life Insurance Building in Chicago, its façade ornamented in four separate clusters like a checkerboard. A year later, also in Chicago, Henry H. Richardson completed the Marshall Field Warehouse whose spare rugged façade and bunched windows expressed its function as warehouse and nothing more. Four years later Sullivan brought the structure of Jenney and design of Richardson into sudden and correct focus; the Wainwright Building inaugurated the functional skyscraper. In outline it is a clean rectangular structure whose vertical piers and horizontal borders mirror in general the steel skeleton within. Its walls, used not for support but as membranes to protect against the weather, also serve as a diagram for the interior of the building; they present one appearance for the lower stories, used as shops and meeting rooms, and another for the offices in the upper stories. Identical windows above suggest the standardized layouts of the offices, and at the top a cornice juts out forming the same flat perpendicular as the rooftop.

In the Wainwright Building horizontal bands provide some minimal decoration. The International Style that flourished in the 1920s dispensed with even that. Here form and space unite in pure geometric patterns whose aim, as a Dutch artist, Theo van Doesburg put it, is "a collective style . . . beyond person and nation." The guiding spirits of the International Style were Gropius, Oud, Miës van der Rohr, and Charles Jeanneret, who called himself Le Corbusier. The *Bauhaus*, or structure house, built by Gropius was a cluster of arts and crafts buildings whose function determined their form. The Shop Block (Figure 9.11) consists of ground floor offices with workshops above, their different appearance diagramed by the walls, as in the Wainwright Building. The two parts are separated by a cantilever, a horizontal slab with a vertical support, its bare rectangular surfaces in keeping with the design of the whole. The glass windows in the upper part push as close to the outer wall as possible to achieve the effect of planar surfaces. Subdivided into countless cubes they repeat the overall form of the upper part, and their obvious function, to let in light but to furnish no support, lends them an air of cold detachment.

Figure 9.10 Louis Sullivan.
Wainwright Building. St. Louis.
(1890–1891). Hedrich-Blessing.

Figure 9.11 Walter Gropius. The Shop Block (*Bauhaus*). Dessau, Germany.
(1925–1926). Courtesy of Walter Gropius.

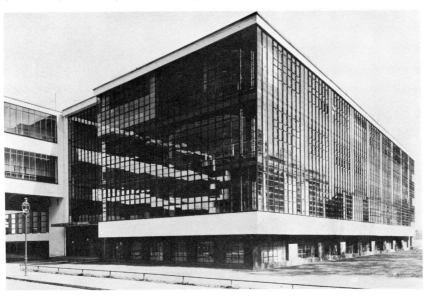

Le Corbusier brought this same impersonality into the home, which he defined as a "machine for living." His Villa Savoye (Figure 9.13) is in outline a cube supported on pillars of reinforced concrete. The rectangular bands of the main story are bisected horizontally by bands of windows that also form rectangles. Some are enclosed by glass, others open to allow the inhabitants of the Villa to commune directly with the fields and trees surrounding it. The cylinder shapes on the roof conceal ramps and gardens behind their impersonal form. Inside, the rooms are rectangular blocks of space separated only by glass walls, so that all seem to mesh like the parts of a machine.

An ultimate step in depersonalization in architecture was taken by architectural groups like MARS and TECTON, who not only employed the International Style but added to it the anonymity of group enterprise. And the early achievements of Frank Lloyd Wright, such as the Robie House in Chicago, owe a major debt to the geometric forms of the International Style, despite their prairie expansiveness.

SCULPTURE.   In theory Cubism holds that all visible objects are essentially composed of cubes, cones, and cylinders, and that to restate those objects as those forms is to portray their essence. In practice Cubism restated objects in terms of all kinds of geometric shapes, a majority of them four sided. Cubism began in 1908, and the following year Picasso gave impetus to it in sculpture with his *Head of a Woman*. Such subsequent sculptors as Archipenko, Lipchitz, and Henri Matisse explored its possibilities more fully. Matisse, who according to one apocryphal story gave Cubism its name, experimented with the formal construction of the human back in four successive works, of which the third comes as close as any work to the Cubist ideal. *The Back III* (Figure 9.14) represents the head as a cleft cube and the remainder—shoulders, arms, spinal column, and legs—as blends of cone and cylinder. The back is identifiable as such, but the elemental forms composing it dominate the subject matter.

Where Cubism focused on forms at least identifiable as geometrical shapes, a subsequent style of sculpture, Constructivism, took the ultimate step into impersonality of form. Begun in Moscow by Vladimir Tatlin and dispersed throughout Europe after the Russian Revolution, Constructivism created forms to which none of the spectators' personal experiences could be correlated; these were simply abstract forms occupying space. To remove their sculpture still farther from a personal frame of reference, the Constructivists made use of untraditional materials such as sheet metal, glass, celluloid, catgut, and plastics. Naum Gabo and Antoine Pevsner rank with Tatlin in the forefront of the movement, and Gabo's *Spiral Theme* (Figure 9.12), an exercise in movement through space, typifies Constructivist form.

The synthesis of the two foregoing styles is the work of Constantin Brancusi, which mediates between the traditional form of Cubism and the nonobjective form of Constructivism, making form express essence. *Bird in Space* (Figure 9.15) may be defined as abstract geometry, its shape as precise as a cone or cylinder, its function to suggest bird and motion not as visible things but as abstract concepts akin to the objective correlative of T. S. Eliot. Its chief merit lies in Brancusi's flair for seizing upon the vital essence of his subject. Similar to his work in theory, but less vital, are the "concretions" of Jean Arp, which often search out the essence of organic forms, as in his *Human Concretion* and *Shell and Head.*

PAINTING.   In a classic statement made about painting in 1890, critic Maurice Denis averred: "We must never forget that a picture, before being a warhorse, a nude woman, an anecdote or what not, is essentially a flat surface covered with colors arranged in a certain order." Certainly painting best lends itself to a tidy classification of all the uses which this period makes of form. Age of Anxiety painting applies form to the visible world in one of two ways: either (1) it strips an object of all features except those essential to convey inner meaning, a simplification down to form often called Primitivism and found in the work of van Gogh, Gauguin (Figure 9.22) and *Les Fauves;* or (2) it rearranges the surface of an object in clusters of geometric forms, which is the technique of Cubism developed by Picasso and Georges Braque. Painting also interprets the invisible world, the world of essences, in terms of form, a technique called Expressionism. The formal means it uses to depict those essences vary, and give rise to subcategories of Expressionism—Abstractionism, Surrealism, Suprematism are a prominent few—but in all of these subcategories the principle of expressing essence by means of form remains the same.

All three of these approaches appear in *Sunday Afternoon on the Island of La Grande Jatte* by Georges Seurat. They are more richly developed in the work of Paul Cézanne, who is often called the father of modern painting. *Mont Sainte-Victoire* (Figure 9.16), one of a series of paintings Cézanne made of this mountain near Aix-en-Provence, summarizes his contributions to twentieth-century styles and statement. The pine tree in the center is stripped of all detail: a basic pillar as trunk and a wash of green as leaves present the form of tree in primitive outline. The houses at the lower right are similarly reduced to primitive forms. Tree trunks, houses, aqueduct, mountains, and four-sided fields are transformed into geometric shapes so that a Cubist pattern dominates the visible surface. The painting shuns atmospheric perspective—aqueduct and mountains are as sharp as the trees in the foreground—to convey a sense of inner unity. This sense is heightened by patches of green and reddish tan that recur from foreground to background, linking the uniformly clear elements of the scene into a pattern of relationships with *color as unifying essence.* If we compare this work with a Romantic nature scene like *The Fighting Téméraire* (Figure 8.8), we can see how feeling has given way to objective intellectual analysis.

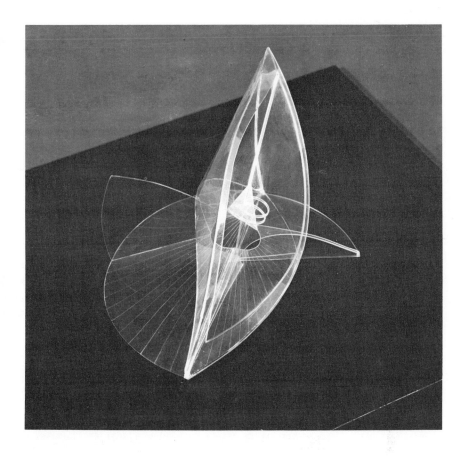

Figure 9.12 (above) Naum Gabo. *Spiral Theme.* (1941). The Museum of Modern Art, New York, Advisory Committee.

Figure 9.13 Le Corbusier. *Villa Savoye.* Poissy-sur-Seine, France. (1929–1931). [Lucien Hervé].

Figure 9.14 Henri Matisse. *The Back III.* (c. 1914). The Tate Gallery, London.

Figure 9.15 Constantin Brancusi. *Bird in Space.* (1919). The Museum of Modern Art, New York.

Figure 9.16 PAUL CÉZANNE. *Mont Sainte-Victoire.* (c. 1887). The Metropolitan Museum of Art, Bequest of Mrs. H. O. Havemeyer, 1929. The H. O. Havemeyer Collection.

One slice from the banquet of Cézanne is *Spirit of the Dead Watching* (Figure 9.22) by Gauguin, where figures pruned of all superfluity convey the inner meaning of death and fear. Another is Braque's *Man with a Guitar* (Figure 9.17), whose muted browns, tans, and blue-grays force attention toward Cubist forms intended to convey inner meaning. Essence became the goal of the Blue Rider school, which flourished in Germany at the start of World War I. Its chief spokesman, Wassily Kandinsky, upheld Expressionism on the basis that "mastery of form is not the end but, instead, the adapting of form to internal significance." His own brand of Expressionism was subtitled Abstractionism, and *Light Form No. 166* (Figure 9.18) typifies Abstractionist aims and achievement. With its clash of bright primary colors, its dark straggling lines and its cloudy shapes the work *suggests* the violence and unconscious drives of the Age of Anxiety. But *Light Form No. 166* states nothing for the visible world to hold on to, and thus directs the viewer toward a world of essence.

An ultimate step into form, parallel with Constructivism in sculpture, was Suprematism, begun by Kasimir Malevich in Russia. In paintings like his celebrated *White on White* he depicted form as essence, a concept taken up by a Dutch group known as *De Stijl.* Its best-known member, Piet Mondrian, converted rectangles and squares into symbols as abstract as those in geometry. Works such as *Composition in White, Black, and Red* (Figure 9.19) defy any personal identification, and become lifeless forays into pure objectivity.

MUSIC.   Music also found ways of subjugating its intrinsic emotion to form. The principal technique devised for this purpose was the atonality, more aptly pantonality, of Arnold Schönberg. In the atonality of Schönberg the twelve notes of a chromatic scale are arranged in any order the composer chooses. But these twelve notes must comprise the entire scale, must all be stated once, and may not be repeated until all the notes of the row have been heard. The initial twelve-note statement is called a tone-row: the tone-row of Schönberg's *Suite,* Op. 29, for example, is E flat, G, F sharp, A sharp, D, B, C, A, G sharp, E, F, C sharp. The tone-row, once announced, may be treated in these four different ways: (1) it may be restated; (2) it may be inverted, that is, restated so that upward intervals in the original row become downward intervals in the inverted row, and vice versa; (3) it may be stated in retrograde form, that is, backward; and (4) the retrograde form may be inverted. These four treatments may use the tone-row as originally stated or else transposed as a whole, so that a great many variant rows are available.

Schönberg completely developed this form by 1923, and compositions in which he made seminal use of it include the aforementioned *Suite;* the *Five Piano Pieces,* Op. 23; the *Third* and *Fourth String Quartets;* the *Quintet for Wind Instruments;* and the *Variations for Orchestra,* Op. 31. These works often make formal use of the tone-row for harmony as well as melody. In the *Waltz* from the *Five Piano Pieces,* for example, the left-hand part consists of chords which begin with the sixth note of the tone-row, and go on with it in order from notes six to twelve and then from one to five; in the *Rondo* of the *Quintet for Wind Instruments* one voice begins with the tone-row while a second voice begins with the tone-row inverted. The *Symphony,* Op. 21, by one of Schönberg's chief disciples, Anton von Webern, opens with a modified tone-row wherein notes seven to twelve are the retrograde of notes one to six. The distilled beauty of Webern's brief compositions plus their preoccupation with form make them the closest parallel in music to Constructivist or nonobjective art. Other composers who made use of the tone-row include Berg, Bartók, Stravinsky, Paul Hindemith, Luigi Dallapiccola, Pierre Boulez, Roger Sessions, Samuel Barber, and Aaron Copland, and while they did not rely upon it exclusively, it served to depersonalize their work in varying degrees.

Figure 9.17 GEORGES BRAQUE. *Man with a Guitar.* (1911). The Museum of
Modern Art, New York. Acquired through the Lillie P. Bliss Bequest.

Figure 9.18 (above right) WASSILY KANDINSKY. *Light Form No. 166.* (1913).
The Solomon R. Guggenheim Museum.

Figure 9.19 PIET MON-
DRIAN. *Composition in
White, Black, and Red.*
(1936). Museum of Modern
Art, New York, Gift of the
Advisory Committee.

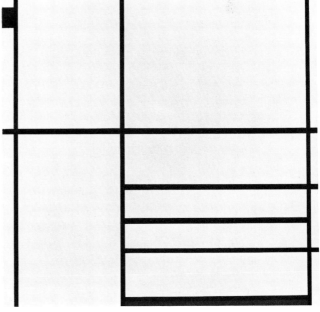

Less rigid a compositional device than atonality is polytonality, music written in two or more keys at the same time, roughly approximating the multiple angles of vision achieved by Cubism. Bartok, Prokofiev, and Darius Milhaud make considerable use of this technique, with the latter carrying it to extremes. In the third of his *Cinq Symphonies pour Petit Orchestra* Milhaud uses six keys at the same time. And while the aural effect is more tonal than otherwise, the music produced, like atonal music, is a slide-rule product whose dominance of form over inspiration is in perfect keeping with the depersonalization of the Age of Anxiety.

The despair, violence, and depersonalization of the Age of Anxiety paint it as a time of unrelieved gloom. Yet men still aspired during that period, and the humor of the 1920s is legendary. In *The Anatomy of Melancholy* Burton classifies excessive laughter as a symptom of melancholy, and perhaps the gusto and yearning of this period are the obverse of anxiety's coin. But the fact remains that a counterthrust begins around the 1920s and builds in slow crescendo through the 1930s. It takes the form of an INDIVIDUALISM that is not the self unbound of Romanticism but a struggle to maintain identity; as such it seeks to infuse form with personality, violence with understanding, despair with hope. It becomes vital to our own time, as Chapter 10 will show, and perhaps only penetrates the topsoil of anxiety. But we are close enough to the 1930s to witness its flourishing emergence there, where its existence can be confirmed by the humanities approach.

The Atlantic Charter, agreed to by America, Britain, and Russia in 1941 is government's contribution to the trend toward identity. It states in part that the signatories "respect the right of all peoples to choose the form of government under which they will live; and they wish to see sovereign rights and self-government restored to those who have been forcibly deprived of them." Both the new humanism which cultivated the rational higher self and the southern agrarian movement to set up an intellectual elite had an impact on the America of the 1930s. And theologians like Karl Barth countered the abandonment and despair of the age with the weapon of emergent individualism. "Man can regard himself and treat himself as the measure of all things," Barth contended, "just as if he were Creator or free or Lord like Him to whom he owes his being. He can therefore think that he dare not abandon himself but must serve and worship himself, and that he can therefore put his hope of salvation in himself." To cap this line of thinking, Camus in 1942 saw the liberation of depersonalized man as the stuff of which myth is made. "Sisyphus, proletarian of the gods, powerless and rebellious," is condemned to push a boulder uphill that forever keeps rolling to the bottom. But, Camus concludes, Sisyphus adjusts to the challenge of his barren existence so that "Each atom of that stone, each mineral flake of that night-filled mountain, in itself forms a world. The struggle itself toward the heights is enough to fill a man's heart. One must imagine Sisyphus happy."

In philosophy Nietzsche, whose Superman concept was recast by the Nazis into the uniform mold of a super race, hurled other challenges at conformity that bore more legitimate fruit. "At bottom," he wrote, "every human being knows very well that he is in this world just once, as something unique." Concepts like this place Nietzsche in the vanguard of Existentialism, which held that each man was endowed with free will and the obligation to work out the course of, and the rationale for, his own existence. Sartre, the spokesman for Existentialism during its surge into prominence at the start of World War II, defined its primary principle as: "Man is nothing else but what he makes of himself." John Dewey anticipated self-determination in 1930 when in *Individualism Old and New* he maintained that man's chief problem was to create a new individualism under the aegis of collectivism. Individuality, he claimed, is unquenchable, and "Since we live in a moving world and change with our interactions in it," a new individualism was needed to replace the "older [Romantic] individualism . . . shrunk now to a pecuniary scale and measure."

LITERATURE.   Joyce's *Ulysses* (1922), one of the pillars of the period, reflects its despair in the alienation of Bloom, Stephen, and Molly from everything around them; its violence in the brothel scene where savage unconscious drives breed a physical need to abase and destroy; its depersonalization in the stream of consciousness technique which makes the protagonists products of forces beyond their own control. Yet Joyce counters despair with gusts of humor—passages of *Ulysses*, read aloud, are as uncontrollably funny as passages in Rabelais. Joyce leavens his violence with compassion: for an impotent modern-day Ulysses, Leopold Bloom who can only explore the streets of Dublin; and for a faithless Penelope, Molly Tweedy Bloom, who confronts her anxious age and her own frailty with a vitality and affirmation that make her in a way the hope of salvation for twentieth-century mankind. Joyce so personalizes the unconscious drives of his characters, of Stephen and Molly in particular, that they transcend the types they represent and endure as individuals.

In *The Magic Mountain* (1924) Thomas Mann probes the limits of depersonalization, his antihero, Hans Castorp, being shaped this way and that by contending philosophies; left to himself at last, Castorp vanishes into the mud of World War I. In his Joseph tetralogy (1933–1943) Mann pits a complex individual against shaping philosophies, and Joseph's ultimate triumph over the traditional and the confining paves the way for Mann's chief contribution to our present age, *Dr. Faustus* (p. 482). Faulkner in *Light in August* creates a Lena Grove as indomitable as Molly Bloom, who survives personal betrayal and the universal betrayal of a modern crucifixion to continue her journey of exploration. In *The Madwoman of Chaillot* (1945) Jean Giraudoux has an inspired dreamer triumph over the leveling forces of technology, and in Sartre's *The Flies* (1943) a modern-day Orestes disperses the guilt and despair that blanket his age by affirming his own freedom as an individual.

ARCHITECTURE.   The work of the masters of the International Style blueprints the emergence, after the 1920s, of individualism in architecture. In his Weekend House at La Celle-St. Cloud, Le Corbusier included ornamented pillars and asymmetrical arches on the front façade. As consultant to a group of architects he designed the Ministry of Education and Health building in Rio de Janeiro (Figure 9.20). Rectangular in outline and with supporting pillars and cylindrical roof towers as in the Villa Savoye, the building breaks with pure geometry by means of its *brises-soleils* (shadow boxes). These disguise the planar surface of the front façade, enrich it with contrasts in texture, and provide a shifting play of light and shadow as the position of the sun changes. Moreover, since the louvers can be raised and lowered manually, the occupants play active, individual parts in the shaping of their building. Gropius experimented with similar varieties of texture in the house he built for himself in Lincoln, Massachusetts, in 1937. Miës van der Rohe brought fresh imagination to his 1933 project for the *Reichsbank* in Berlin. And the rhythmic horizontal brackets of the Philadelphia Saving Fund Society Building (1930–1932) by George Howe and William Lescaze, plus the curve-right-angle relationship of base to shaft, transform the objectivity of Sullivan into a personal mastery of functional form.

The greatest architect of the century strode beyond the dominance of form as early as the Robie House. By the 1930s Wright was manipulating form to serve a kaleidoscope of individualistic experiments. Falling Water (Figure 9.21), his best-known work of this period, is also one of his most successful. It has the same basis in form as the International Style. Vertical stone rectangles intersect with the dominant horizontal rectangles of concrete walls and cantilevers, and long open rooms inside echo the horizontal sweep of the front façade. But beyond this formal ingenuity is the dramatic stillness and solidarity of the cantilever above the flowing waterfall, its daring outward thrust, and the tangle of surrounding trees which, when in leaf, form an arched canopy over the house. The vertical walls, made of rocks native to the region, seem to rise out of the stony ground beneath them while the horizontals reach out and interpenetrate the woods, so that in all its thrusts the house blends with nature in an organic unity. The Finnish architect Alvar Aalto and the American Richard Neutra rank in the forefront of those who, besides Wright, brought a heightened individuality to the architecture of the 1930s. Aalto's superb Villa Mairea is a Villa Savoye in the act of bursting the bonds of form.

Figure 9.20 LE CORBUSIER as consultant architect. Ministry of Education and Health, Rio de Janeiro. (1937–1943). Carl Frank: Photo Researchers.

445

Figure 9.21 Frank Lloyd Wright. "Falling Water" (Kaufman House). Bear Run, Pennsylvania. (1936–1937). [Hedrich-Blessing].

SCULPTURE. In answer to the formalisms of the Cubists, Futurists, and Constructivists, Moore's *Recumbent Figure* conveys an impression of unique identity as well as a tragic sense of life, and the *Standing Woman* of Lachaise (Figure 9.26) is vitally overpowering. *La Montserrat* (1937), a peasant girl constructed out of sheet iron by Julio Gonzalez, touches the same wellsprings of life as Moore's *Reclining Figure*, and the elongated, primitive iron stick statuettes created by Picasso in 1931 are uncannily original and alive.

PAINTING. The work of Picasso has served as a weather vane for the changing styles of Age of Anxiety painting. The geometric form of his Cubist period gave way in the 1920s to a "classical" style, representational drawing based on the forms of classical sculpture. In the 1930s he fused Cubist geometry with representationalism to develop the powerful individual style seen in *Guernica* and *Girl Before a Mirror* (Figure 9.24). In the former work Cubist heads and arms are also living things, and hemispheric lampshade and rectangular doorway take on meanings that carry them beyond mere formal exercise. In a similar vein *The Old King* (1936) by Georges Rouault breathes life into a primitive rectangular design by means of haunting melancholy.

446

The Mexican group spearheaded by Siqueiros, Rivera, and Orozco infused angry life into form to express individualism in the 1930s. *Christ Destroying the Cross* typifies their achievement. Like Braque's *Man with a Guitar* it is built out of geometric forms—cross, pyramid, column, and the stylized body of Christ an exercise in triangles—but the face of Christ, the lines of force, and the intrinsic drama in the work permeate form with searing individual commentary. Like Kandinsky's *Light Form No. 166* the essence of *Christ Destroying the Cross* is tension, but form plus representation make this tension a *personalized* expression.

Music.   Schönberg's finest disciple, Alban Berg, departed in part from atonality to allow room for individual expression. Works like his *Lyric Suite for String Quartet* and *Violin Concerto* are authentic reflections of the Age of Anxiety, yet gain greater permanence by speaking in Berg's own voice as well. The first three movements of the four-movement *Violin Concerto* use a tone-row, but are not straitjacketed by atonality. For one thing the tone-row is chosen for intrinsic beauty as well as form. The row—G, B flat, D, F sharp, A, C, E, G sharp, B, C sharp, E flat, F—is as lovely inverted or in retrograde as in its original form, which is an indication of the personal concern for pleasing lavished on its choice. Moreover the first three movements symbolize personal events. Written to commemorate the death of a young girl Berg knew (she was Manon Gropius, daughter of the architect of the *Bauhaus* and stepdaughter of the composer Gustav Mahler), movements one, two, and three represent her life and death—the solo violin in all cases symbolizes the young girl herself. The final movement, a prayer, makes glancing use of the tone-row but more seminal use of the diatonic hymn, *Es ist genug* (it is enough). Thus form, life, and tradition all interact to produce a work that is of its time but also of itself.

Bartók, whose early *Allegro Barbaro* exploited formal technical uses of rhythm, in his later years evolved a style that synthesized Age of Anxiety dissonance and rhythmic techniques, atonality, folk music, and an undercurrent of powerful feeling. His *Music for String Instruments, Percussion, and Celesta* (1936), *Violin Concerto* (1938), and *Concerto for Orchestra* (1943), all major works, exemplify this synthesis. The opening movement of the first piece, for example, states a dry theme, quietly and with incremental repetitions; then it restates it in retrograde, repetitively, as an exercise in form; but the repetitions gain in power and sonority until the theme throbs with feeling, and an academic gambit becomes an emotionally overwhelming experience.

Like Picasso, Stravinsky put aside iconoclast experiments for a Classical style in the 1920s; his *L'Histoire du Soldat* (soldier's story), *Octet for Wind Instruments,* and *Oedipus Rex* oratorio of the 1920s have a Greek simplicity and coldness about them that suggest a style poised on the threshold of a new modern synthesis. The breakthrough came in 1930 with his *Symphony of Psalms,* whose swirling power ushers in an individual synthesis paralleling that of Bartók. The *Violin Concerto* (1931), *Concerto for Two Pianos* (1935), *Dumbarton Oaks Concerto* (1938) and *Symphony in Three Movements* (1945) develop that synthesis further.

The imperialism of the late nineteenth century opened up a more intimate knowledge of primitive countries, especially in Africa; and a sense of guilt concerning them, plus a growing discontent with the pressures of the machine age, bred a new respect for simplicity untarnished. World War I intensified that attitude, as did the brutality that followed. A famous cartoon of the 1930s showed Ethiopian natives staring up at the bomb-laden planes of Mussolini; its caption read, "Duck, boys, here comes civilization!" Out of such conditions came PRIMITIVISM, the idea that the primitive world held closer to truth and beauty than did the technological, depersonalizing world of the Age of Anxiety. Conrad in *Heart of Darkness* has a civilized European, Kurtz, delve into the ritual mysteries of tribal Africans. What Kurtz discovers is too much for his civilized soul to endure, and after gazing unprepared into the infinite abyss he dies gasping, "The horror! The horror!" Lawrence in *The Plumed Serpent* contends that only the truth in ancient Aztec ceremonies can free twentieth-century man. Faulkner often holds that Negroes, deprived of modern technology, live closer to reality than whites. In "That Evening Sun" an avenging Jesus returns, to the awed terror of the Negroes, while the whites go about their business unaware or else impatient with the whole affair. In *Absalom, Absalom* the Negroes-as-primitives are the only ones who find daily beauty in their lives—Charles *Bon,* the mulatto, symbolizes *good*—and contact with the whites, with industrialism, and with business, contaminates them. O'Neill in *The Emperor Jones* transplants a machine-corrupted Negro to a primitive setting where he is lost and destroyed by truths he can no longer understand.

Kandinsky speaks of "our sympathy and affinity with and our comprehension of the work of primitives. Like ourselves, these pure artists sought to express only inner and essential feelings in their works." In sculpture the figures of Lipchitz often derive from the masks, idols, and shell figures of the Congo, Gabun, Nigeria, New Hebrides, New Guinea, and the Solomon Islands. A touch of these same sources lends mystery to the work of Moore and Matisse. The mobiles of Alexander Calder (Figure 9.25) are primitive machines turned totems that rock imperturbably in time and space. In painting Paul Klee uses childish primitive drawing to comment ironically on the ugly blight of the Age of Anxiety. Maurice Utrillo strips street scenes of all ornament and shows a France, and civilization, as it might be if reduced to primitive truth. Gauguin turned to primitive subject matter to convey the idea implicit in primitivism. *The Spirit of the Dead Watching* (Figure 9.22) depicts a hut in Tahiti where a native girl feels the presence

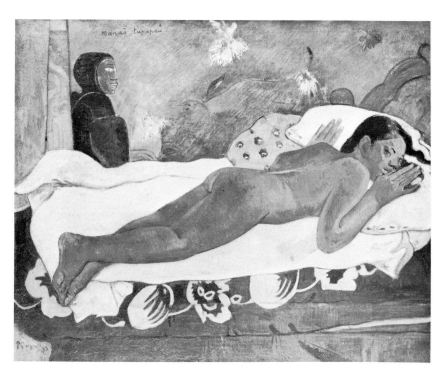

Figure 9.22   PAUL GAUGUIN.   *The Spirit of the Dead Watching.*   (1892).   Albright-Knox Art Gallery, Buffalo, New York. A. Conger Goodyear Collection.

of the Spirit of the Dead. Death is pared of all substance and features except essentials; similarly, the girl's body contradicts anatomy so as to convey a gesture in keeping with the fear which pulls at her features. The work is in the main two dimensional—the body of Death, for example—and flat masses of orange, yellow, blue, and green enhance the primitive effect. Like *Heart of Darkness* it pictures native life as being close to ultimate truth, and like Conrad's novel it does so in terms of carefully wrought symbols, for the concept implied in primitivism is not simple but sophisticated.

Stravinsky's *Petrouchka* and *Le Sacre du Printemps* use primitivism as protest against the constraints of the age, and to judge from its response the first-night audience at *Sacre* must have sensed this. Alois Haba wrote whole compositions in microtones, intervals smaller than half a step, in imitation of primitive music. His opera, *Die Mutter* (the mother), in quarter tones, emerges as intellectual protest against the obtuse, unhearing spirit of his age. Heitor Villa-Lobos combined Brazilian folk music and native percussion instruments with Classical forms to achieve a power and directness akin to *The Spirit of the Dead Watching.* Virgil Thomson tacked intellectual primitivism onto a flamboyant script by Gertrude Stein to create an opera, *Four Saints in Three Acts,* which restates in a novel way the theme of *Heart of Darkness.*

At the turn of the century a new psychology was built up out of the brilliant intuitions of a single theorist. His work made terms like ego, id, libido, neurosis, and free association part of our modern vocabulary, and he himself made them serve a vast range of social, philosophical, and esthetic as well as psychological speculation. As oblique tribute to his achievement, his name came to define a special school of thought which, however, retained very little of his complex edifice and flattened that through popular usage. FREUDIANISM as concept connotes unconscious drives, sex-based for the most part.

In literature Freudianism helped give rise to a special method, christened stream of consciousness by the American psychologist-philosopher William James. By this method the ceaseless flow of the mind—sometimes the conscious part, sometimes the unconscious, sometimes both—is depicted in detail. Joyce in *Ulysses* provides the richest example of the stream of consciousness in English, convoluting the minds of Bloom, Stephen, and Molly with oblique and startling unconscious drives. The Molly Bloom soliloquy that ends the novel has provided a whole new dimension of character analysis. In later life Freud theorized that the censor wall allowed some penetration of the conscious by the unconscious, but earlier he had viewed the mind as a kind of triangle with the censor wall barring the lower part, the unconscious, from the upper part, the conscious. Faulkner in *The Sound and the Fury* uses this earlier theory as the basis for his stream of consciousness technique and even provides italics to show how one part of the mind is cut off from the other; the opening section of *The Sound and the Fury* delineates remarkably the stream of consciousness of an idiot. Virginia Woolf in *To the Lighthouse* makes a practical compromise between pure stream of consciousness and straightforward communication; her novel is a series of interior monologues motivated by unconscious drives. Although not a stream-of-consciousness novel, Kafka's *The Trial* acts out on a literal level the unconscious drives toward despair, violence, guilt, and alienation of its depersonalized hero.

Sculpture and painting explored the unconscious drives which Freudianism defined under the aegis of Surrealism, which in theory meant the free play of the stream of consciousness, but in general practice works became, like *Ulysses*, a guided tour through the interior world. Alberto Giacometti describes his Surrealist *The Palace at 4:00 A.M.* (Figure 9.23) as follows: "It was not important any more to make a figure exteriorly life-like, but to live and to realize what moved me within, or what I desired . . . . Which led during those years (c. 1932–1934) to objects moving in opposite directions . . . construction of a palace with a bird skeleton and a dorsal spine in a cage, and a woman at the other end." While *The Palace at 4:00 A.M.* does not "mean" in the ordinary sense, the nightmare symbols enclosed in symbolic space convey the reality of the unconscious with precise and skeletal clarity.

Several major painters have explored that same reality. Salvador Dali often paints the unconscious as a backdrop as tidy as a Vermeer interior and strews it with symbols of burnt-out sex; his *Persistence of Memory* is a notable Surrealist example. Marc Chagall explores his own unconscious with a roseate romanticism, and the mind-world of his canvases is inhabited by flying lovers, dreaming cows, girls upside down, green-faced boys, giant roosters, and houses that float in the clouds; *I and the Village* is his best-known Surrealist work. Joan Miró makes use of trance-induced shapes and protean blobs to suggest an unconscious shrouded in elemental symbolism; a series of Compositions done by him in the 1930s arrange apparent stream-of-consciousness shapes with ingenious calculation. Picasso tried Surrealism as well as everything else—the shapes in *Guernica* are in part Surrealist—and in *Girl Before a Mirror* (Figure 9.24) he offers the ultimate in Freudian exercise. The face at the left, sharp featured and bright colored, represents the conscious mind; behind and perpendicular to it,

Figure 9.23   ALBERTO GIACOMETTI.   *The Palace at 4:00 A.M.*   (1932–1933).   The Museum of Modern Art, New York, Purchase.

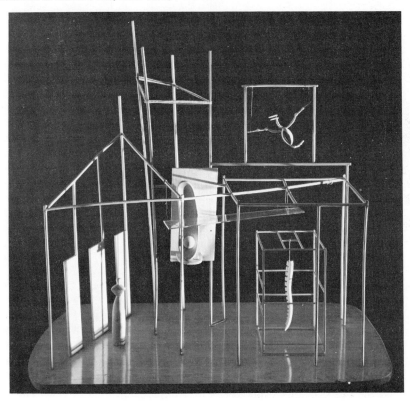

Figure 9.24 PABLO PICASSO. *Girl Before a Mirror.* (1932). The Museum of Modern Art, New York, Gift of Mrs. Simon Guggenheim.

with features less decisive, is a pale yellow face that represents the pre-conscious or superego; to the right, dark, blurred of feature, ugly and remote, is a face that represents the unconscious mind. The transverse arm below represents the trickle of unconscious into conscious, but the walls between the facing pair show that real communication is impossible. A girl before a mirror must see what is not, shielded from truth by a pallid censor whose surface appearance is almost indistinguishable from her own.

While music cannot explicitly express unconscious drives, Freudianism does penetrate the content of some program music during this period, a prime example being the ballet *Parade* with text by Jean Cocteau, decor by Picasso, and music by Eric Satie. Some of its episodes have already been described on p. 427.

Another Age of Anxiety concept in the main the product of a single mind was the SPACE-TIME CONTINUUM first explained by Albert Einstein. Up through the nineteenth century space and time were considered distinct and unchanging; Kant made them the basic transcendental elements of his "esthetic" or sensible world. In 1905 Einstein proposed what came to be known as the Special Theory of Relativity, which rejected the idea of space as a fixed system at rest and acknowledged the subjectivity of time—Einstein's five minutes' kissing a pretty girl versus five minutes' sitting on a hot stove has passed into folklore. Relativity as modified by H. A. Lorenz went on to establish relationships between fluctuating space and subjective time: the faster the passage through space, the slower the passage of time, and vice versa. Thus the world of the Age of Anxiety became a four-dimensional space-time continuum in which an astronomer looks through his telescope backward in time across a warp of space. Bergson restated this concept for philosophy. Intuition, he held, was the only means of arriving at absolutes. Intuition led to an understanding of duration, "the continuous progress of the past which gnaws into the future and which swells as it advances." And "the intuition of our duration . . . brings us into contact with a whole continuity of durations which we must try to follow, whether downwards or upwards"—that is, flexible time, moving forward and backward, merges with flexible space.

In *Remembrance of Things Past* Proust depicts life as a series of selected incidents from the past reexamined in the present in spatial contexts broader or narrower than when first experienced. Memory is reality in these novels, and a morsel of cake soaked in tea can conjure up a whole lifetime, but reshaped so that some incidents are censored out, others capsuled, others extended across broad, sensuous spaces; and these sequences rather than their chronological occurrence become what really happened. Faulkner in *The Sound and the Fury*, following Freud, constructs a conscious present, preconscious near past, and unconscious remote past as a triple edifice occupying multiple space. Mann in his Joseph tetralogy makes pivotal incidents reflect the subjectivity of time.

In architecture Rockefeller Center, composed of fifteen rectangular slabs of various heights, occupies different amounts of space and requires a different viewing time from each subjective angle of vision. In that sense it resembles Cubism in sculpture and painting, whose geometric forms lend themselves to a multitude of different spatial groupings. Futurism attempts an even more explicit interaction between space and time, Boccioni's *Unique Forms of Continuity in Space* expressing in its very title its intended space-time continuum. The mobiles of Alexander Calder represent the ultimate use of this concept in sculpture. His *Lobster Trap and Fish Tail* (Figure 9.25), typical of all of them, consists of shapes, wires, and metal rods which sway back and forth at a touch; as they move through time, the space they occupy alters. In painting the Cubist works of Braque and Picasso and the Futurist works of Giacomo Balla and Gino Severini, as well as Duchamp's *Nude Descending a Staircase,* explore the same spatio-temporal relationships as Rockefeller Center and *Unique Forms of Continuity in Space.* In music the removal of the bar line, as in Charles Ives's *Three-Page Sonata for Piano,* made time and space fluid in a world of sound.

In the Middle Ages woman might participate in a ritual that led man upward to a mystic union with God. In the Renaissance she might through marriage share in a spiritual and physical union that was a worldly fore-taste of eternal joys to come. In the period that followed, Romantic yearning for the unattainable found love, and woman, inadequate. With the Age of Anxiety a new concept of woman developed. The industrial revolution and the emergence of a mass middle class began to challenge the tradition of male superiority. In England at the start of the twentieth century suffragettes demanded equal rights and to obtain them resorted to violence, poured chemicals into mailboxes, chained themselves to the grillwork of the Houses of Parliament, and went on rampages destroying property. In America women achieved suffrage with the passage of the nineteenth amendment in 1920. The Soviet Union proclaimed women equal to men a few years after that. During the Age of Anxiety what perceptive observers had anticipated in the eighteenth century became accomplished fact, and a new concept of woman emerged which held that she was at least equal, perhaps dominant; which often viewed her new power as a released potential for evil; and which in the process of conceding her equal freedom redefined LOVE AS SEX.

Ibsen in *A Doll's House* and *Hedda Gabler* portrays woman's early attempts to break loose and achieve equality. Shaw in *Man and Superman* hails her as having more than succeeded. She is the new superman, cold and objective, who wields her natural weapon, the Life Force, with unerring marksmanship. Virginia Woolf in *To the Lighthouse* describes the feminine essential as aspiring idealism, the masculine essential as logical realism, hovering and dependent. For literature this was a landmark insight, hardly conceivable in the patriarchal society of the past, although Nietzsche had intuited it a generation earlier: woman had more intellect than man, he conceded, but man's will makes him accomplish more than she. Lawrence in *The Rainbow* makes sex the be-all object of worship. His heroine Ursula, the product of a good marriage symbolic of a time past, finds herself

Figure 9.25   ALEXANDER CALDER.   *Lobster Trap and Fish Tail.*   (1939).   The Museum of Modern Art, New York, Gift of the Advisory Committee.

alienated and unfulfilled in the Age of Anxiety because of her superiority. Joyce is more optimistic in *Ulysses:* Molly Bloom in her final soliloquy affirms hope for mankind, but by dint of sex grown rampant and indiscriminate.

In sculpture the giant women of Gaston Lachaise are the unconscious mind of Molly Bloom incarnate. *Standing Woman* (Figure 9.26), one of a series of works on the same theme, stands seven feet four inches tall. Her sexual characteristics attain formidable prominence, and her flat-footed solidity, muscular arms, and masterful expression exude a domineering power. Picasso acknowledged this power in terms of protest in his series of women painted in the 1930s with their flaring nostrils and monstrous eyes and lips, as if to say that when women become dominant they turn love into something as violent and cruel as war. In opera the aggressive Salome of Richard Strauss makes love sadistic, and the same composer's *Rosenkavalier* (cavalier of the rose) comments with regretful accents on the decadent sexuality of modern woman.

The individualism emerging toward the close of the Age of Anxiety supported itself in many cases by the sanction of TRADITION. With form depersonalizing art and society, and with despair enervating them, would-be individualists often turned to the past for meaning and vitality. Tradition for them became something more vigorous than a source to copy or a passive re-enactment of older customs; it became a functioning concept holding that the broadest view of the present rested on a base of past traits and ideas. Official spokesman for this concept was T. S. Eliot, who stated it thus: "No poet, no artist of any art, has his complete meaning alone. His significance, his appreciation is the appreciation of his relation to dead poets and artists . . . . the past should be altered by the present as much as the present is directed by the past." Joyce used the *Odyssey* of Homer as framework for *Ulysses;* Mann in *The Magic Mountain* made Hans Castorp aware of the meaning of life by leading him through all phases of civilization from the Middle Ages to the present; Yeats, feeling that the Age of Anxiety had broken with the past, created an imaginary tradition that meshed with his own time and upon which he based his poetry.

The visual arts upheld this concept of tradition in the name of Neoclassicism, itself a tradition-based term. In architecture Neoclassicism challenged the coldness of the International Style by superadding classical rhythms and proportions to its geometric forms. Otto Wagner in Austria and the Perret brothers in France did much to establish the style, and the Nebraska State Capitol by Bertram G. Goodhue (Figure 9.27) may well be its most successful example. The arched entranceway and circular dome look back toward Rome (Figures 3.3, 3.4), and the square tower capped by

Figure 9.26 GASTON LACHAISE. *Standing Woman.* (1932). The Museum of Modern Art, New York, Mrs. Simon Guggenheim Fund.

Figure 9.27 BERTRAM GOODHUE. Nebraska State Capital, Lincoln, Nebraska. (1922–1926). [Photo Courtesy of the Nebraska Game Commission].

a slimmer one of different shape suggests the church steeples of Wren (Figure 7.19). But the lines of the Capitol are crisply geometric, and the walls and window openings are all functional despite their rhythmic flow. Goodhue has used the structural support of tradition, but as a contributing element to a valid modern work.

Sculpture turned to tradition somewhat later than her sister arts, probably because the impact of nonobjective Constructivism was so potent in the 1930s. In the early 1940s Moore does remote yet wistful Michelangelesque restatements of *The Holy Family* and *Madonna and Child,* and

Henri Laurens, Giacomo Manzù, and José de Creeft blend Hellenism with Age of Anxiety themes and forms. Picasso introduced Neoclassicism into painting in the 1920s, using Greek statues, modified by his own mind and time, as the bases for escape from the formal tyranny of Cubism. His *Guernica* may well be *The Divine Comedy* of the Age of Anxiety, and is at least a violent reinterpretation of the significance of the Virgin and Child. Orozco rests his condemnation of the present on Christian, Eastern, classical, and primitive traditions. Rouault in *The Old King* combines traditional Christianity with twentieth-century despair. Neoclassicism also made an important reentry into music, and many composers employed Classical forms as the framework for twentieth-century techniques. Eminent examples are the *Symphony in Three Movements* of Stravinsky, the *Classical Symphony* of Prokofiev, and Berg's *Wozzeck*, whose despairing and violent scenes are cast in formal molds which include, among others, the fugue, suite, rondo, sonata form, and passacaglia. Bartók, Strauss, Vaughan Williams, Rachmaninoff, Hindemith, Barber, Aaron Copland and even Charles Ives wrote major works in twentieth-century Neoclassical style.

FORMS AND TECHNIQUES

Depersonalization and its ramifications have already treated forms and techniques as aspects of traits and ideas, and some schools—Surrealism, Neoclassicism—have yielded their major possibilities. Others, however, may still offer illuminating technical interrelationships if re-examined from a purely physical standpoint.

CUBISM: This is a reduction of objects to basic geometric forms. Guillaume Apollinaire in *Zone* and Gertrude Stein in "Tender Buttons: Objects, Foods, Rooms" made attempts at Cubist poetry. The International Style in architecture was Cubist in philosophy; this is evident in Gropius' *Bauhaus*, Le Corbusier's Villa Savoye and Ministry of Education and Health, and Goodhue's Nebraska State Capitol. Other examples are Wright's Robie House; Miës van der Rohe's Tugendhat House; Neutra's Lovell House; Mendelsohn's Schocken Department Store; and Oud's Kiefhoek Housing Project. For Cubist sculpture see Matisse, *The Back III;* Picasso, *Head of a Woman;* Archipenko, *Boxing Match;* and Lipchitz, *Man with Mandolin.* A modified Cubism occurs in Brancusi, *Bird in Space* and Giacometti, *The Palace at 4:00 A.M.* For Cubist painting see Braque, *Man with a Guitar;* Picasso, *Henry Kahnweiler, Fernande,* and *Ambroise Vollard;* for Cubism modified see Cézanne, *Mont Saint-Victoire;* Picasso, *Guernica;* and Orozco, *Christ Destroying the Cross.* For Cubist influence in music, see the atonal theory of Schönberg (p. 439).

DADAISM: A technique of adding on irrelevant or shocking materials to an art form, Dadaism is a protest against the smooth functioning of modern machines and the conformist values of the middle class. Examples of Dadaism in literature are the obscenities and the grotesque musical intrusions in Jarry's *Ubu Roi;* in music, the irrelevant sections in Satie's *Parade,* the recorded song of a nightingale in Respighi's *The Pines of Rome,* and the fire sirens used in Varèse's *Ionisation;* in sculpture, the nuts, bolts, and bits of wood tacked onto *Fruit of a Long Experience* by Max Ernst; in painting, the wastebasket clippings of the *Merzbilders* of Kurt Schwitters. For modified examples of Dadaism see Giacometti's *The Palace at 4:00 A.M.* and Calder's *Lobster Trap and Fish Tail.*

FUTURISM: This is a violent, simultaneous movement through space and time. The Bella Cohen brothel scene in Joyce's *Ulysses* is Futurist both in its violence and in its manipulations of space and time. For examples in sculpture, see Boccioni's *Unique Forms of Continuity in Space,* and, nearly as effective, his *Development of a Bottle in Space;* in painting, Severini's *Bal Tabarin* and Balla's *The Dog on Leash;* and for Futurism modified, Duchamp's *Nude Descending a Staircase;* in music, Honegger's *Pacific 231,* which paints the sound of a speeding locomotive and connotes at least the violence and spatial fragmentation of Futurism.

NONOBJECTIVITY: The expression of forms or language devoid of association with identifiable objects or ideas is called nonobjectivity. The free-association babblings of Gertrude Stein and the Dadaist poems of Tristan Tzara bring nonobjectivity into literature. For examples in sculpture, see Gabo's *Spiral Theme* and other Constructivist works by Gabo, Rodchenko, and Pevsner, as well as the Abstractionist concretions of Jean Arp, such as *Landmark;* in painting, see the work of Suprematists Lissitzky and Malevich, such as *White on White,* and the parallel work of the Dutch *De Stijl* school—Mondrian's *Composition in White, Black, and Red* filters all associative meaning out of form and color. For nonobjectivity with the specific purpose of stimulating feeling, see Kandinsky's *Light Form No. 166.* The miniscule concretions of Von Webern (*Orchestral Pieces, Bagatelles for String Quartet*) come as close as possible to nonobjectivity in music.

MECHANISM: The use of techniques modeled after or influenced by the working of machinery is known as mechanism. Henry Adams in his autobiographical *The Education of Henry Adams* hailed the dynamo as a twentieth-century power akin to that of the Virgin over mankind in the Middle Ages. Le Corbusier maintained through the 1920s that a house was a machine for living, and Villa Savoye was designed to serve that function. The moving piston effect of Futurism shapes Boccioni's *Unique Forms of Continuity in Space* and Duchamp's *Nude Descending a Staircase.* Duchamp's *The Bride,* typical of his ready-mades, is a skeletal arrangement of pipes, motor casings, safety guards, and gear wheel. Mossolov in *Iron*

Foundry translates machinery into music, and electronic music, pioneered by Varese, with its mechanical sounds and tape recorder "orchestra," elevates the machine to the role of creator as well as performer.

SYMBOL AND ALLEGORY: Formal techniques akin to the ritual and ceremony of the Middle Ages and the Renaissance, symbol and allegory, revived by twentieth-century emphasis on form, became guiding purposes in the arts of the Age of Anxiety. An excellent example in literature is Joyce's *Ulysses*, an allegory of despair-ridden twentieth-century man's quest for an Odyssean adventure. The characters as symbols show Leopold Bloom representing Odysseus, Christ, and Everyman; Stephen representing the creative artist; and Molly ironically representing the faithful Penelope, the Earth Mother, and Everywoman. Other literary examples of symbol and allegory in the Age of Anxiety are Eliot's "The Waste Land"; Kafka's *The Trial*, with K. symbolizing depersonalized twentieth-century man beset by anxieties and neuroses; and Hemingway's *The Sun Also Rises*, an allegory of despair, violence, and depersonalization whose chief characters symbolize the futility of man. Symbolic sculpture includes *Bird in Space; Seated Youth* and *Recumbent Figure*, symbols of despair, the latter touched with mystery and awe; *The Palace at 4:00 A.M.*, symbols from the unconscious; and *Lobster Trap and Fish Tail*, which expresses the essential worthlessness of modern machinery. Symbols of anxiety in painting are *The Scream* and *La Vie*; allegorical paintings include *Guernica*, depicting modern warfare, and *Christ Destroying the Cross*, expressing man's guilt and impending punishment. See also *The Spirit of the Dead Watching*, which makes use of primitive symbols, and *Girl Before a Mirror*, a model of Freudian symbolism. In music at this time symbol and allegory are best expressed in such tone poems as *Death and Transfiguration* and *A Hero's Life* by Strauss; the operas *Wozzeck* and *Lulu* by Berg; the ballets *Petrouchka* and *Le Sacre du Printemps* by Stravinsky.

SELECTED BIBLIOGRAPHY

History

Allen, Frederick Lewis. *Only Yesterday*. New York: Harper & Row, 1931.

Anderson, Eugene N. *Modern Europe in World Perspective: 1914 to the Present*. New York: Holt, Rinehart and Winston, 1958.

Bruun, Geoffrey, and Victor S. Mamatey. *The World in the Twentieth Century*. Boston: Heath, 1967.

Gooch, G. P. *History of Modern Europe. 1878–1919*. London: Longmans, 1923.

Hall, W. P., and W. S. Davis. *The Course of Europe Since Waterloo*. New York: Appleton, 1941.

Knapton, Ernest J., and Thomas K. Derry. *Europe and the World Since 1914*. New York: Scribner, 1966.

Morison, Samuel Eliot, and H. S. Commager. *The Growth of the American Republic*. Vol. 2. New York: Oxford University Press, 1963.

Social and Intellectual Background

Barzun, Jacques. *Darwin, Marx, and Wagner*. Boston: Little, Brown, 1941.

Burtt, E. A. *The Metaphysical Foundations of Modern Physical Science*. Garden City, N.Y.: Anchor, 1954.

Cassou, Jean, N. Pevsner, and E. Langui. *Gateway to the 20th Century: Art and Culture in a Changing World*. New York: McGraw-Hill, 1962.

Dampier, William C. *A History of Science and Its Relations with Philosophy and Religion*. New York: Macmillan, 1942.

Frank, Philipp. *Modern Science and Its Philosophy*. New York: Collier, 1949.

Glasrud, Clarence. (Ed.) *The Age of Anxiety*. Boston: Houghton Mifflin, 1960.

Horney, Karen. *The Neurotic Personality of Our Time*. New York: Norton, 1937.

Kaufman, Walter. (Ed.) *Existentialism from Dostoevsky to Sartre*. New York: Meridian, 1964.

Krutch, Joseph Wood. *The Modern Temper*. New York: Harcourt, 1929.

Lerner, Max. *America as a Civilization*. New York: Simon and Schuster, 1957.

Morgan, G. A. *What Nietzsche Means*. Cambridge, Mass.: Harvard University Press, 1941.

Mosse, George L. *The Culture of Western Europe: the 19th and 20th Centuries, an Introduction*. London: J. Murray, 1963.

Mumford, Lewis. *Technics and Civilization*. New York: Harcourt, 1948.

Runes, Dagobert. (Ed.) *Twentieth Century Philosophy*. New York: Philosophical Library, 1942.

Sorokin, Pitirim A. *The Crisis of Our Age: the Social and Cultural Outlook*. New York: Dutton, 1942.

Spengler, Oswald. *The Decline of the West*. 2 vols. New York: Knopf, 1928.

Toynbee, Arnold J. *Civilization on Trial*. New York: Oxford University Press, 1948.

White, Morton. (Ed.) *The Age of Analysis*. New York: Mentor, 1955.

Whitehead, Alfred North. *Science and the Modern World*. New York: Mentor, 1948.

Literature

Aldridge, John W. *After the Lost Generation*. New York: McGraw-Hill, 1951.

Bithell, J. *Modern German Literature, 1880–1938*. London: Methuen, 1939.

Brée, Germaine, and Margaret Guiton. *The French Novel from Gide to Camus*. New York: Harcourt, 1962.

Colum, Mary. *From These Roots: The Ideas That Have Made Modern Literature*. New York: Scribner, 1944.

Ellmann, Richard, and Charles Feidelman. (Eds.) *The Modern Tradition: Backgrounds of Modern Literature*. New York: Oxford University Press, 1965.

Hare, Richard. *Russian Literature from Pushkin to the Present Day.* London: Methuen, 1947.
Howarth, Herbert. *Irish Writers 1880–1940.* New York: Hill and Wang, 1959.
Leavis, F. R. *The Great Tradition.* Garden City, N.Y.: Anchor, 1954.
Tindall, William Y. *Forces in Modern British Literature.* New York: Knopf, 1947.
Wilson, Edmund. *Axel's Castle.* New York: Scribner, 1931.

Architecture, Sculpture, Painting

Barr, Alfred H. *Masters of Modern Art.* New York: Doubleday, 1958.
Canaday, J. E. *Mainstreams of Modern Art.* New York: Holt, Rinehart and Winston, 1959.
Cheney, Sheldon. *The Story of Modern Art.* New York: Viking, 1945.
Collins, Peter. *Concrete: The Vision of a New Architecture.* New York: Norton, 1932.
Giedion-Welcker, Carola. *Contemporary Sculpture.* New York: Wittenborn, 1954.
Gutheim, Frederick. (Ed.) *Frank Lloyd Wright on Architecture: Selected Writings, 1894–1940.* New York: Duell, Sloan and Pearce–Meredith Press, 1944.
Hamlin, Talbot F. *Forms and Functions of Twentieth-Century Architecture.* 4 vols. New York: Columbia University Press, 1952.
Hitchcock, Henry-Russell, and Philip Johnson. *The International Style: Architecture Since 1922.* New York: Norton, 1932.
Hunter, Sam. *Modern American Painting and Sculpture.* New York: Dell, 1959.
Klee, Paul. *On Modern Art.* New York: Heineman, 1954.
Motherwell, Robert. *The Dada Painters and Poets.* New York: Wittenborn, 1951.
Newmeyer, Sarah. *Enjoying Modern Art.* New York: Mentor, 1957.
Peter, John. *Masters of Modern Architecture.* New York: Braziller, 1958.
Raynal, Maurice. *Modern Painting.* New York: Skira, 1956.
Read, Herbert. *A Concise History of Modern Painting.* New York: Praeger, 1959.
_____. *A Concise History of Modern Sculpture.* New York: Praeger, 1964.
_____. *The Philosophy of Modern Art.* New York: Meridian, 1955.
Richards, James M. *An Introduction to Modern Architecture.* Baltimore: Penguin, 1956.
Ritchie, Andrew C. *Abstract Painting and Sculpture in America.* New York: Museum of Modern Art, 1951.
_____. *Sculpture of the Twentieth Century.* New York: Museum of Modern Art, 1952.
Seymour, Charles, Jr. *Tradition and Experiment in Modern Sculpture.* Washington, D.C.: American University Press, 1949.
Wight, Frederick S. *Milestones of American Painting in Our Century.* New York: Chanticleer Press, 1949.

Music

Abraham, Gerald. *This Modern Music.* New York: Norton, 1952.
Barzun, Jacques. *Music in American Life.* New York: Doubleday, 1956.
Bauer, Marion. *Twentieth Century Music: How It Developed, How to Listen to It.* New York: Putnam, 1947.

Collaer, Paul. *A History of Modern Music*. New York: Harcourt, 1961.

Copland, Aaron. *Our New Music*. New York: McGraw-Hill, 1941.

Ewen, David. *The Complete Book of Twentieth-Century Music*. Englewood Cliffs, N.J.: Prentice-Hall, 1952.

————. *Modern Music: A History and Appreciation—from Wagner to Webern*. Philadelphia: Chilton, 1962.

Howard, John Tasker, and James Lyons. *Modern Music*. New York: Mentor, 1958.

Mellers, Wilfred. *Studies in Contemporary Music*. New York: British Book Centre, 1950.

Reti, Rudolph. *Tonality, Atonality, Pantonality*. New York: Macmillan, 1958.

Salazar, Adolfo. *Music in Our Time*. New York: Norton, 1946.

Slominsky, Nicolas. *Music Since 1900*. New York: Coleman, 1949.

CHAPTER 10
THE MODERN
PERIOD

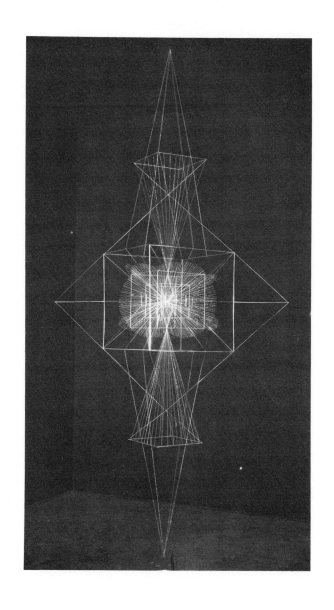

EVENTS

THE AFTERMATH OF WORLD WAR II

Mankind emerged from World War II with two novelties: a global conscience and an ultimate weapon, and each added further complications to the widening political tangle. The shining example of postwar conscience was furnished by the United States, now the major world power—where another power might by straining all its resources compete with America in one area such as science, manufacture, agriculture, or weaponry, the United States continued and maintained full development in all four areas. The Marshall Plan, begun in 1947, provided money and assistance for nations crippled by the last war, regardless of which side they had fought on. Named for General George C. Marshall, then secretary of state, the plan followed these guidelines articulated by him: "It is logical that the United States should do whatever it is able to do to assist in the return of normal economic health in the world without which there can be no political stability and no assured peace. Our policy is directed not against any country or doctrine, but against hunger, poverty, desperation, and chaos." A European Recovery Program funded with $17 billion of Marshall Plan aid enabled France and England to weather postwar slumps and readjustments, and Italy and Germany to regain a measure of prosperity. Italy had fifteen changes in government in four years until in 1948 a Christian Democratic coalition government plus Marshall Plan aid spurred it toward rapid economic recovery. Germany was split into eastern and western sections as agreed upon at the Yalta Conference by Roosevelt, Churchill, and Stalin in 1945. West Germany, aligned after the war with western Europe, benefited spectacularly from Marshall Plan aid. Organized as the Federal Republic of Germany in 1949, it soon erased all evidence of war damage and within a decade doubled its highest previous industrial output. Japan, under American occupation until 1951, was also aided economically, and Japanese recovery matched that of West Germany.

In 1949 President Harry S. Truman announced the Point Four Program which provided technical aid and assistance for all underdeveloped countries. And as further evidence of American world commitment, the Senate ratified the entrance of the United States into the United Nations in 1945 by a vote of eighty-nine to two. Ultimately settled in New York, the United Nations, maintaining a surveillance over world politics, economy, health, education, labor, and narcotics control, has served with varying effectiveness as a global conscience. Its early years were in the main successful. In 1947 it approved the partition of territory around Jerusalem to form a separate state for Israel, thus providing a homeland for survivors of the Nazi holocaust. It intervened in the Indonesian struggle for independence against the Dutch and forced Holland to recognize Indonesia as a sovereign state in 1949. And it oversaw the final liberation of India from England in 1950.

What suited the conscience of the West, however, did not always coincide with that of the East, including the Soviet Union, whose southern and eastern borders face Asia and Japan. Russia rejected the Marshall Plan and deplored the United States' sole possession of the atomic bomb as a threat to world peace. It bound the Balkan states and all of eastern Europe except Greece and Finland to the Soviet Union. It stripped East Germany, Hungary, and Rumania of machinery and food, and embarked on a Five-Year Plan to repair the ravages of war. In 1945 it formed a thirty-year military alliance with China against Japan, and with these new allies in Europe and Asia embarked on an aggressive campaign of hostility toward the West in general and the United States in particular. As Churchill observed in a speech at Fulton, Missouri: "An iron curtain has descended across the European continent." The result was a cold war waged between democracy and communism, a bitter propaganda battle spearheaded by America and Russia with the allegiances of smaller countries at stake. In 1947 America launched the Truman Doctrine which stated that "It must be the policy of the United States to support free peoples who are resisting attempted subjugation by armed minorities or by outside pressure." A gift of $500 million to Greece and Turkey probably kept both countries from becoming Communist nations. The following year Yugoslavia broke free of Russian dominance, but remained Communist, thus reaping the advantages of being wooed by both sides. That same year Russia engineered a Communist takeover of Czechoslovakia wherein the Czechs were required to "vote" for a single list of candidates. In 1949 the West escalated the cold war by forming the North Atlantic Treaty Organization (NATO), composed of the United States and eleven European nations, whose charter stipulated that an armed attack against one or more of them should be considered an attack against them all. Six years later Russia countered NATO with the Warsaw Treaty, in which Russia and seven satellite countries took a similar stand against the West.

On the fringes of the cold war, and in part as carry-over from World War II, localized wars continued to flare up throughout the 1940s. Indonesia fought its war of independence as already mentioned. Greece suffered a large-scale civil war, as did China where a determined and disciplined Communist faction under Mao Tse-tung drove the Nationalists of Chiang Kai-shek off the Chinese mainland and onto the island of Formosa, and in 1949 established a People's Republic with its capital at Peiping. In Indochina a war of independence dragged on until it stirred up international implications. France had controlled the five states of Indochina—Cochin China, Annam, and Tonkin (occupied by Annamese or Viet people) Cambodia, and Laos (inhabited by Siamese)—before World War II and tried to reclaim them from the Japanese after 1945. But Viet desire for independence and Roosevelt's distrust of de Gaulle led to a separation of the Viet territories at the 16th parallel, protected by Nationalist China in the north and Britain in the south. The Viet Minh, League for Independence of Vietnam (land of the south: that is, Tonkin, Annam, and Cochin China) led by Communist trained Ho Chi Minh set up the republic of North Vietnam with its capital in Hanoi. The British ceded control of South Vietnam to France, and in 1946 Ho Chi Minh launched a war of liberation against the French forces there. The early guerrilla warfare grew in size and intensity as help from Russia and then from Communist China began arriving.

In 1950 a more dramatic event focused world attention on another part of Asia. Korea, after thirty-five years of Japanese control, was partitioned at the 38th parallel and occupied by the Soviets in the north, the Americans in the south. North Korea became a People's Republic and South Korea a democratic republic under Syngman Rhee. In 1950 a Russian-trained North Korean army invaded South Korea, and was met by a United Nations' force. After slow and bitter fighting the United Nations' force drove the North Koreans back across the 38th parallel and up toward the northern border; then in 1951 an immense Chinese army advanced into North Korea and drove the United Nations' force back across the 38th parallel. Thus the war ended, in a stalemate, and the truce of 1953 established the 38th parallel as the permanent boundary line between North and South Korea. Although fifteen nations had supplied troops for the United Nations' force, America's casualties totaled nearly 160,000. As the major contributor of troops, the United States became the principal active opponent of Communism. On the other hand, a rift was opened between China and Russia, the two chief Communist countries, because Russia had not furnished troops for North Korea.

THE 1950s

The Korean War ushered in a decade of shifting turmoil and unprecedented change. For the first time since the rise of ancient Greece the centers of control no longer lay in Europe. In England a Labor government in power from 1945–1951 regulated wages and medical care, increased taxes and devalued the pound from $4.03 to $2.80, but in spite of this England never regained its lead in shipping or in export manufacture; a Conservative government, in power until 1964, continued the policies of the Labor government with no better success. The Fourth French Republic, formed after World War II, elected de Gaulle as its first president. He lasted only eighteen months and was followed up to 1958 by a quick succession of presidents none of whom had solid majority support. During this time France surrendered its stronghold of Dien Bien Phu in Vietnam, and in 1954 Vietnam was partitioned at the 17th parallel, between northern Communist and southern pro-Western governments, and France was ousted permanently. In 1956 Tunisia and Morocco declared themselves independent of France, and Algeria began to seek similar independence. In that same year Gamal Abdel Nasser, a militarist strong man who had ousted Egypt's corrupt pro-Western King Farouk, nationalized the Suez Canal and thus controlled sixty percent of Europe's oil supply. Reinforced with Soviet arms, he resisted a coalition attack by Israel, France, and England, and although he was swiftly beaten, American and Russian pressure in the United Nations forced Israel to return her captured territories and France and England to withdraw from Suez.

In its more peaceful endeavors Europe was more successful. In 1951 France, Germany, Luxemburg, Belgium, Italy and the Netherlands launched the European Coal and Steel Community, an organization whereby coal and iron were distributed to all member nations as cheaply and free of tariffs as possible. Industry flourished as a result of this, and in 1957 these nations formed a European Economic Community, dubbed the Common Market, devoted to a similar efficient interchange of all goods. It has done much to restore continental European prosperity.

In 1951 America signed a peace treaty with Japan along with an agreement for mutual defense and withdrew its occupation troops the following year. America thus gained an ally in the cold war, but the Japanese labor unions set up during the American occupation soon succumbed to the *zaibatsu*, the old-time industrial monopolies. The cold war had chilled America's Wilsonian idealism and smoothed the way for compromise and for conservative caution laced with fear, a fit climate for the anti-Communist witch hunts sparked by demagogic Senator Joseph McCarthy. Senate condemnation of McCarthy and popular reaction against him after 1954 returned America to apparent placidity, real prosperity, and a mounting anxiety which bred forces that would explode in the 1960s.

Russia developed its own atomic bomb by 1949 and a hydrogen bomb in 1953, less than a year after the first American H-bomb was devised. With the two nations now on a par in weaponry, Stalin prepared to launch a fresh purge—this time against "cosmopolites," a euphemism for Jews— presumably as a prelude to violence on a wider scale, when he suddenly died. A milder man, Georgi Malenkov, succeeded him, and Russia provided its people with more consumer goods and the world with a thaw in the cold war; although Malenkov resigned in 1955, even the more militant

Nikita Khrushchev who would soon replace him publicly deplored the repressive tyranny of Stalin. The thaw loosed currents in the satellite countries which led to a protest strike in Poland and a surge of revolution in Hungary. Both were put down by force in 1956, and with Khrushchev appointed premier in 1958 the cold war again preoccupied men's thoughts.

In 1956, the year of the Hungarian revolt, the Sudan gained its independence, an act which inflamed all of Africa with a similar desire. In 1957 the Gold Coast freed itself from England and took the ancient name of Ghana. Guinea, Infi, and the Spanish Sahara gained independence the following year, and by 1960 sixteen African states were represented in the United Nations; by 1964 there were thirty-five. Some, like Kenya and the Belgian Congo, gained freedom only after hard and bloody fighting, but for most of them statehood came swiftly, and virtually overnight a new independent continent took its place in world affairs.

Although even the smallest African countries are recognized by the United Nations, Communist China with its population near 700 million is not. The main reason is China's refusal to follow the Russian course of peaceful coexistence with the West and its compensatory increase in hostility as the years go by. Despite its warlike attitude, however, it has also made gains in the arts of peace. In the 1950s Chinese food production tripled; steel and cement production increased twelvefold; and universal education made its first appearance there in 1958—by 1960 the Chinese announced that 100 million children now attended school.

THE 1960s

In 1959 Fidel Castro overthrew dictator Fulgencio Batista and assumed control of Cuba. By 1960 Castro began to communize the island, thus bringing the cold war within ninety miles of America's borders and ushering in the continuing turmoil of the 1960s. Africa, the continent most preoccupied with change, now contributes least to international tension; it is worth noting that the Afro-Asian bloc now controls the voting majority in the United Nations. Asia with its population of close to 2 billion remains a seedbed of controversy. In India the Moslem minority split off and formed the separate state of Pakistan, and in 1965 the two countries engaged in a brief, abortive war. Three years earlier India and China had clashed along the northeast Indian frontier, and the border tension there continues. Red China in the 1960s swings between violence and progress. By 1965 it developed advanced nuclear weapons; in 1966 Chinese scientists discovered a method of synthesizing insulin; that same year Chinese Red Guards, violent and fanatic teen-agers, harassed and purged intellectuals and "Westernized" adults, and rumbles of a party split and civil war continue to reverberate. In Russia a dip in agricultural production, disagreements with China, and diplomatic clashes resulted in the resignation of Khrushchev in 1964. He was replaced by a pair of leaders, Leonid Brezhnev and Alexis Kosygin, whose depersonalized committee methods seem to presage a calmer approach to world affairs. In Russia proper the theories of economist Yevsei Liberman have been adopted; now Soviet industries may keep a part of their profits as inducement to improved and increased production.

In western Europe German economic recovery continues its fantastic growth; its gross national product topped $88 billion in 1962. But Russian-American tension in Berlin, rife in the 1950s, culminated in 1961 in the East German erection of a wall dividing the Communist and western sectors of the city and keeping tensions there near the boiling point. England continues to lose both its imperial possessions and the battle of exports. Its bid to enter the Common Market, vetoed by France in 1963, still remains blocked by that same former ally. In 1964 it restored the Labor party to power, and the attempts of its leader Harold Wilson to bolster the sagging English economy have resulted in higher taxes, increased restrictions, and in 1967 a further devaluation of the pound from $2.80 to $2.40. In 1958 France abandoned its mercurial and unstable Fourth Republic in favor of a Fifth Republic which granted near dictatorial powers to Charles de Gaulle. In 1962 de Gaulle relinquished Algeria, the last significant French imperial territory, to concentrate like Louis XIV on building French prestige on the continent of Europe. Assuming a maverick role, de Gaulle has courted Russia and snubbed the United States, has pulled closer to West Germany and attempted to alienate England, has recognized Red China and yet perversely backs away from anti-American propaganda while in the Soviet Union, and has refused to recognize East Germany. His ambitions for France shine through most clearly in his rejection of the idea, popular among European political theorists, of a United States of Europe.

In the 1960s America has juggled its responsibilities as the world's great power with varying skill. It supported an ill-planned, unsuccessful invasion of Cuba in 1961, but the following year demanded and obtained the withdrawal of Russian missiles from that island. Presidents John F. Kennedy and Lyndon Johnson have both supported the Alliance for Progress which offers aid and technical assistance to Latin America, but American support of anti-Communist dictators Stroessner (Paraguay) and Trujillo (Dominican Republic) has lent impetus to the stirrings of Communist revolution in at least six Latin American countries. In line with the Truman Doctrine, America has intervened in a war between North and South Vietnam, and has also thus become involved in the proliferating civil war between the Viet Cong (South Vietnamese Communists) and the South Vietnamese.

Unlike the Korean War, this one does not have the support of the United Nations, and American troops are now committed in near isolation to this war fought for moral principles—according to the lights of the American conscience. At home a strong civil rights movement has rung in heartening changes for the American Negro, but civil rights issues and poverty have also led to crippling riots in the major American cities. A significant share of the younger generation rushes toward or shies away from American middle-class values with a too sudden intensity. The Peace Corps and the Great Society are gestures of generosity, but industrial wastes and gases poison American lakes and atmosphere, and rising inflation threatens.

Encouraging signs in the sixties are advances in atomic physics and in man's mastery of space; extensive oil discoveries in the Arabian peninsula, which mean new opportunity for that backward area and new resources for the world; increased food production on a global scale; a rise in education on all continents; peaceful settlement of a Communist revolt in Laos by a tribunal representing France, England, China, and Russia; American overtures for peace talks with North Vietnam, and North Vietnamese acceptance; a curb of the gold-buying speculation which threatened the value of the United States dollar by the International Monetary Fund; and prospects of an international banking system based upon world cooperation; a slight Russian shift toward capitalism and thus more congenial coexistence; the Russian, British, and American signing of an Atomic Test-Ban Treaty; and shifting loyalties in the Eastern and Western power blocs—France tending toward the East and Russia toward the West—which blunt the edge of geographical rivalries and reduce the likelihood of global war.

Disturbing signs in the sixties include the population explosion which threatens to outrun the earth's resources; accumulation of enough nuclear bombs by 1964 to wipe out 240 billion people; the rise of the militant *Komeito* (pure government) party in Japan; Western failure to recognize Red China; the decline in effectiveness of the United Nations; increasing American civil and overseas commitments which place a mounting strain on its, and consequently world, economy; and the wanton assassinations of John F. Kennedy, Martin Luther King, Jr., and Robert F. Kennedy. The North Korean seizure of the U.S. ship *Pueblo* in the Sea of Japan on January 23, 1968, added yet another Eastern complication. Powder-keg situations exist in Cyprus, where Greece and Turkey threaten to involve other nations in their own dispute; in the Middle East, where an Arab war of revenge against Israel in 1967 was squelched in six days, but whose tensions continue; in Europe, where Czechoslovakian defiance has posed a serious threat to the Russian-dominated Warsaw Pact; indeed, throughout the globe wherever China, Russia, and the United States jockey for position and influence via maneuvers that court the risk of launching a third world war.

THE HUMANITIES APPROACH

TRAITS AND IDEAS

When the atom bomb made wastelands out of Hiroshima and Nagasaki, the cadence of conflicts begun near the start of the century seemed frozen to a halt. Confronted with the ultimate weapon, mankind had to choose between what historian Arnold Toynbee summarized as "one world or none," between war and peace, between tension and amity. Thus in the shadow of atomic doomsday survival itself became a daily joy, and once the fact of Hiroshima could be set behind, a surge of optimism swept the world. It was a mood made up of many parts: after the ugliest, most total war in history, even comparative peace seemed blessed; and unlike World War I, this war had had a moral issue and freedom had triumphed over slavery; also, the boom period following the war formed exhilarating contrast to the years of depression; and the richest nation in the world cared enough to help its neighbors, victors and vanquished alike, in unprecedented Christian spirit. The new outlook suggested a new period of civilization, and hosts of commentators marked 1946 as the point of origin for what philosopher Huston Smith termed the "Post-modern mind" in an essay unique only insofar as it first appeared in the pages of *The Saturday Evening Post.*

With hardly more than two decades elapsed since World War II, we cannot yet determine with certainty whether these changes will generate a new period or even a different phase of the earlier one, let alone what specific directions its development will take. The sharp decline in optimism since the mid-1950s suggests that even in the speedy twentieth century it is slow time rather than quickly computed evidence that certifies a trait. Thus our humanities approach is hampered in this period by lack of evidence. Nevertheless its breadth of view allows at least a partial insight into modern traits.

The most obvious trait, especially from the vantage point of the visual arts, is the persistence of the stance of the Age of Anxiety: DEPERSONALIZATION. Modern events offer striking examples of this. Totalitarian nations—older ones like Russia and newer ones like China and Yugoslavia—make continual gains in their standard of living and in their influence on the shaping of world affairs. Nations inured to dictatorships before the war—Germany, Italy, Japan—have created the economic miracles of modern times. In Europe dictator-ridden Spain has remained unmolested. France has taken a deliberate step toward totalitarianism by granting de Gaulle autocratic control, and has thereby gained in wealth. And all over the world the major democracies have leaned toward more communal, depersonalizing ways of life. The British Labor government has regulated life from the cradle to the grave. American social reform, inevitable in this modern age, brings with it an inevitable leveling and control: half of American scientific research, for example, is now government sponsored.

Modern sociology sees Western man as prey to a complex of determining forces and in the main "other directed"—the phrase derives from David Riesman (*The Lonely Crowd*). Modern economics adheres to the theories of Maynard Keynes which call for a managed currency and economy with autocratic government control during crisis periods. In philosophy the logical positivism of Russell and the logical analysis of Carnap and Wittgenstein offer detached *summae* of compartmented units of knowledge. For Carnap cold objectivity is the only secure path to understanding. "Metaphysical propositions [on the other hand] are neither knowledge or error; they lie completely outside the field of knowledge, of theory, outside the discussion of truth or falsehood. But they are, like laughing, lyrics, and music, expressive." Wittgenstein delimited logical analysis still farther than Carnap, to analysis of language, by which he meant its use in accordance with customary social practice and nothing more. An outcropping of his philosophy of language is the current emphasis on linguistic science, which seeks among other things to examine literature from the depersonalized standpoint of analysis of its language.

LITERATURE.   Depersonalization, as we saw in Chapter 9, can affect the form as well as the content of art. In modern literature it does both. A prime example of modern literature in which form determines function is the *Alexandria Quartet* of Lawrence Durrell, four novels which survey a central theme from different angles of vision, an approach similar to that of the early Cubist painters. Durrell's preoccupation with scented eloquent cadences makes style as important as substance in these works, further evidence of his concern for form. Other instances in which style determines form and is all dominating include the clichéd irrelevancies of the theater of the absurd—Albee's *The Sandbox*, and Ionesco's *The Music Lesson* and *The Bald Soprano*—and the routinized obscenity in some of the work of Norman Mailer, Le Roi Jones, and William Burroughs. The poet-critic Charles Olson holds that the typewriter, with "its rigidity and its space-precisions," offers the poet "for the first time" the same formal support as the staff and bar measure in music.

The impact of depersonalization on human beings is a frequent modern theme. George Orwell in *Animal Farm* shows how it reshapes citizens of totalitarian states as animals, all of them equal although some are more equal than others. In *1984* he projects a society which carries depersonalization to its ultimate conclusion complete with thought police and the systematic extinction of all expressions of self. Anthony Burgess in *A Clockwork Orange* presents a grotesque vision of Socialist London of the future; its sadistic and near inarticulate citizens, other-directed by violence and by self-indulgence, have all been turned into clockwork oranges, mechanical units similar in shape and function. In *Lord of the Flies* William Golding shows how a group of children, freed from the restraints of civilization, turn inevitably away from innocence and toward a herd brutality which begins to transform them too into clockwork oranges. In *Invisible Man* Ralph Ellison contends that survival depends not merely on conformity but upon total effacement of identity. Once this is achieved, Everyman—in this case Ellison's nameless narrator—can assume and shed a variety of roles until, free of illusions at last, he beholds God as "a robot, an iron man, whose iron legs clanged doomfully as it moved."

Most modern writers view as hopeless attempts to break free of the grip of depersonalization. Jack Kerouac in *On the Road* shows men attempting to flee their straitjacket through sheer movement, but achieving insanity in place of asylum. Mailer in *Barbary Shore* sees modern man, attempting to cut loose from custom, left to grope about emptily in a cell-like rooming house which is the modern world. William Styron in *Lie Down in Darkness* has his heroine, Peyton Loftis, resist conformity with so keen an awareness that at last she has no choice but to commit suicide, finding in death the beauty now lost to modern life. Her final soliloquy verges on poetry: "Perhaps I shall rise at another time, though I lie down in darkness and have my light in ashes" — another time perhaps, but not in the present. Where Peyton Loftis is exceptional, Arthur Miller's protagonist in *Death of a Salesman* is mediocre, and his rage against the slow attrition of depersonalization is inchoate and frantic. His protest too can result only in death, this time mute and inglorious.

ARCHITECTURE.   The impersonal, geometrical International Style has gained greater prestige in this period, as well as popular acceptance. Ludwig Miës van der Rohe, along with Wright and Le Corbusier one of the century's three great architects, brought the International Style to distilled perfection in the early 1950s. His Lake Shore Drive Apartments (Figure 10.1) usher in its epitome. A pair of pure rectangular solids, they achieve as perfect a harmony of proportion as the *Petit Trianon* (Figure 6.11). By facing them differently Miës creates a space-time Cubist effect, and by coating their surfaces with flat panes of glass he underscores their brittle impersonality. Cold, remote, reaching toward the sky, they are in a profound sense modern temples.

Inspired by Miës and the modern temper a majority of modern architects imitate the order and academic regularity of his style. His chief disciple, Philip Johnson, collaborated with him on the Seagram Building in

Figure 10.1 LUDWIG MIËS VAN DER ROHE. Lake Shore Drive Apartments. Chicago.
(1949–1951). Copyright Ezra Stroller (ESTO).

476

New York City; its condensed aspect and massive use of glass make it worthy of Miës at his best. Other older architects have been stirred into action along with Miës by the modern predilection for the International Style. The spare, boxlike Christ Lutheran Church in Minneapolis by Eliel Saarinen has outdone even Miës for stark, crisp geometry in his General Drive Apartments. Breuer and Eric Mendelsohn revived the style in modern domestic housing, and Johnson has brought it to a peak in his Johnson and Hodgson Houses in New Canaan, Connecticut. Most newer architects also adhere in the main to the Miësian style. The firm of Skidmore, Owings, and Merrill has crystallized it into formula in a series of committee-designed buildings. The firm of Harrison and Abramovitz, the principal designers of the solid and striking United Nations building in New York, has done the same. In Brazil Oscar Niemeyer has designed the Capital buildings of Brasilia in cautious imitation of Miës and of the *Bauhaus.* And Eero Saarinen has outdone even Miës for stark, crisp geometry in his General Motors Technical Center in Warren, Michigan.

SCULPTURE.   In a "Sculpture of the 60s" exhibit presented by the Philadelphia Museum of Art the entrance hall contained one mobile, one Cubist work, six Constructivist works, and nothing more; as this breakdown suggests, depersonalized form dominates modern sculpture almost totally. The older Constructivists—Arp, Gabo, and Pevsner—continue to follow their earlier formulas, although in keeping with the modern trend their works are larger and more imposing. Beside them flourishes a new generation of Constructivists, large in numbers and uniformly talented. *Variation No. 7: Full Moon* by Richard Lippold (Figure 10.2) represents them at their best. Composed of wires and brass rods, the work translates a visual image into impersonal yet somehow suggestive geometric terms. Its neat symmetry and use of open space produce a lightness and fluidity that justify its title —this although the work is ten feet tall, its height evoking the same temple effect as the Lake Shore Drive Apartments.

Other prominent modern sculptors preoccupied with form include William Turnbull, who creates primitive patterns with bronze rods; Barbara Hepworth, whose curved, suggestive shapes fall somewhere between the connotation of early Moore (Figure 9.2) and the abstraction of Brancusi (Figure 9.15); Ibram Lassaw, who builds up rectangular jigsaws out of wire segments welded together; and Karl Hartung and Isamu Noguchi, who strip shapes down to primitive, formal essence. Currently popular are various efforts to blend Dadaism with impersonal form, as in the boxes of Joseph Cornell, where real objects are stacked inside a framing box, and in the statues of Marisol, which reform each subject as a pillar constructed out of piled-up boxes.

PAINTING.   A fellow artist complained to Andrew Wyeth that his paintings (Figure 10.8) looked interesting seen from a distance, but seen up close

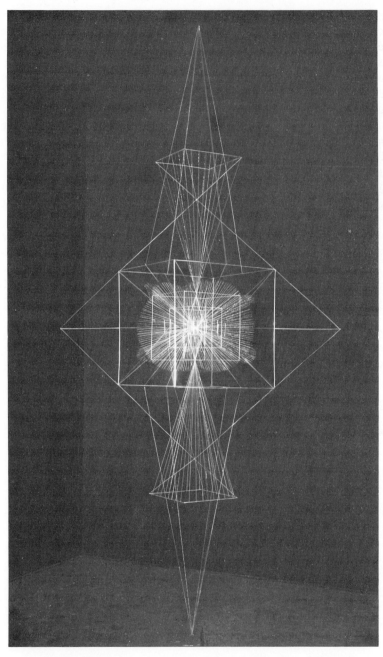

Figure 10.2 RICHARD LIPPOLD. *Variation No. 7: Full Moon.* (1949–1950). The
Museum of Modern Art, New York, Mrs. Simon Guggenheim Fund.

they were found to contain objects. Such an attitude typifies the overriding concern of the modern artist with form, a concern that gives rise to several styles of modern painting. One style relies upon geometric form and functions as a kind of diffuse carry-over from Cubism. Its leading practitioner is Ben Nicholson, whose interlinking planes and cylinders, done for the most part in restful colors, are visually appealing. Other capable adherents to this style include Auguste Herbin, Josef Albers, and Alberto Magnelli.

Another modern style interprets literal themes in terms of nonobjective form, a continuation of, but more regularly patterned than, the abstractions of Kandinsky (Figure 9.18). Jean Bazaine in such works as *Low Tide* and *Child of the Night* creates effective and exciting visual patterns in this style; others who use it well include Renato Birolli, Maria-Elena Vieira da Silva, Robert Motherwell, and Emilio Vedova. In echo of the Suprematists, a school of modern painters uses nonobjective form for purely abstract compositions, notably in a series of works entitled *Painting* by Pierre Soulages and in the work of Serge Poliakoff, Clifford Still, and Hans Hartung.

A further category, of forms put to use, includes the work of Mark Tobey, in which forms run rampant, and that of Mark Rothko, in which blurred geometrical forms are made symbolically expressive. *Earth and Green* (Figure 10.3) consists of a wine-red rough hewn rectangle above a green one, the two of them set against a violet-blue background. The net effect is restful and meditative, as though the rectangles might symbolize a universal tomb. Earth above and green below suggests a reversal of the natural order of things, as if to convey a warning or expression of dismay. And the delicate impreciseness of the forms connotes disintegration, in keeping with the graveyard and topsy-turvy effects conveyed by form, color, and title.

Machine automatism also plays a part in modern art. In the *Lumia* of Thomas Wilfred, for instance, machines project ever-shifting color patterns. Another example is the current popular fashion of "painting" with neon lights: a *succès d'estime* of the 1966 *Biennale* exhibition in Venice was a photograph of a woman on which a pair of orange neon lips had been superimposed.

MUSIC.   Like literature, modern music makes use of form-conscious structure as well as content to achieve depersonalization. Where the modern poet is led by the regular spacing of the typewriter, the composer at times encases his work in rhythms that reflect the influence of Cubism and override all other aspects of the composition: a spectacular example is the *Turangalîla* of Olivier Messiaen, a ten-movement symphony entirely given over to rhythmic effects. And as the *Lumia* of Wilfred substitutes machines for personal expression, electronic music uses them for content as well as for performance. Vladimir Ussachevsky uses echo chambers, resonators,

Figure 10.3 MARK ROTHKO. *Earth and Green.* (1955). Collection, Mr. and Mrs. Heller, Courtesy of the Museum of Modern Art.

filters, and generators to create his compositions. He also uses an RCA Synthesizer, a machine designed to produce a gamut of sounds by means of push buttons, the resultant sequences being a form of automatic writing. Sometimes he blends machine and orchestral techniques, as in *Rhapsodic Variations for Tape Recorders and Orchestra*, but more often he relies solely on the impersonal effects created by machines, as in such works as *Sonic Contours* and *Underwater Waltz*. Electronic music has gained popular acceptance in movie and TV scores, and Ussachevsky's score for the film *No Exit,* for example, combines the recorded hiss of escaping gas with a slowed up rhumba tune.

The American composer John Cage, whose experiments are endless and inquiring, has written compositions for an electric wire coil and for twelve radios to be dialed by twenty-four performers. His compositions for "prepared" piano require that stuffing be packed between the strings so that the piano rather than the performer controls the length and sonority of each note. His *Three Dances for Prepared Piano* has been explicated by critic Lou Harrison in terms that would be baffling if not linked up with Cubistic formalism. "In principle, his [Cage's] idea of form is simple, so simple that it is difficult to grasp. It involves only the prismatic use of temporal schemas."

The modern period at this stage differs most from the Age of Anxiety in its efforts to kick free of the blanket of depersonalization. Worldwide student riots spanning America and Russia, democracy and Communism, and the "revolutions of rising expectations" in Africa, Asia, and Latin America dramatize these efforts in strident and articulate terms. Behind the evidence of events like these is a pair of traits which attack depersonalization on two fronts, and in turning to them we encounter the modern period in broadest perspective. The first develops out of the individual struggle-to-maintain-identity of the Age of Anxiety plus its concept of tradition (pp. 442–448, 456–459). "Our culture," writes André Malraux, one of the universal men of our time, "is not built up of earlier cultures reconciled with each other, but of irreconcilable fragments of the past," and today there are forces and individuals striving to reconcile those fragments. Where successful they give a positive turn to the Age of Anxiety by means of the trait of INDIVIDUALISM AS HEROIC SYNTHESIS—heroic because in our own age, where there is no Ulysses, the effort to integrate in a fragmented and fragmenting culture is at least as noble as a homeward journey to Penelope.

In the world of events the United Nations, the proposed United States of Europe, the Common Market, the Alliance for Progress, and the OECD—Organization for Economic Cooperation and Development, embracing twenty-one nations including much of Europe, America, and Japan —group together political and economic traditions old and new. In the world of culture there is the initial integration, just under way, of Oriental and Western thought and art: Zen Buddhism, for example, now needs no defining on any Western college campus. The church has entered into world affairs in ways undreamed of in the past. The Catholic Church moved in this direction as early as 1931 when the encyclical of Pius XI, *Quadragesimo Anno,* dealt with industry, society, and economics and paved the way for the epoch-making innovations in Catholic ritual and priestly functions of our own time. Less sweeping in their turnabout, other denominations and religions too have responded to the challenge of one world or none.

In philosophy the rich syntheses of Alfred North Whitehead fully articulate this trait. "The useful function of philosophy," he writes, "is to promote the most general systematization of civilized thought. . . . Philosophy is the welding of imagination and common sense into a restraint upon specialists, and also into an enlargement of their imaginations." Synthesis for Whitehead affects not only thought but metaphysical doctrine as well. "It [such doctrine] means that for things to be together involves that they are reasonably together. This means that thought can penetrate into every occasion of fact, so that by comprehending its key conditions, the whole complex of its pattern of conditions lies open before it." Edmund Husserl anticipates this pattern by bracketing each fragment of experience into an *epoché*, a distillation of relevant phenomena, "unshakable because of its conviction of ultimate truth," and then suggests how all fragments fitted together might form a universal *epoché*—in itself a synthesis of the compartmentation of the logical positivists and the universal outlook of Hegel and Kant.

LITERATURE.   In *Brave New World* (1932) Aldous Huxley pictured future mankind as depersonalized by science. But in his preface to the 1946 edition he explained that "If I were now to rewrite the book I would offer the Savage . . . the possibility of sanity," in a community where a synthesis of science, the arts, and the natural life is possible. What Huxley speculates about, Thomas Mann achieves in *Dr. Faustus* (1947), one of the towering achievements of our century. It has two heroes, a composer who creates and a professor-narrator who explains and synthesizes, and their lives from youth to old age re-enact the history of music, the history of thought, and the history of mankind. At the end the modern reader is left on the threshold, impressed by the need for the integration of cultures, and aware of the magnitude of the task. "Creatively dreaming Nature dreamed here and there the same dream," Mann tells us early, but his creative artist, Adrian Leverkühn warns: "Relationship is everything. And if you want to give it a more precise name, it is ambiguity." A pattern of analogies whose purpose shimmers with vagueness represents a formidable ideal. Toward the end of his career Ernest Hemingway encased relationship and ambiguity in a small, simple frame in *The Old Man and the Sea* (1952). His heroic individual is an old fisherman whose adventure encompasses depersonalization, Christianity, primitivism, and technology. The postwar *Pisan Cantos* of Ezra Pound also express the need of the modern individual to synthesize past and present cultures; richer in materials and principle than *The Old Man and the Sea*, they are poorer in accomplishment.

Among the generation of modern writers, Saul Bellow gropes for a large integrating pattern in *The Adventures of Augie March* and misses; in *Henderson the Rain King* he succeeds, at least on an intellectual level, as Henderson absorbs a series of searching experiences, all allegories of past traditions, which teach him pride and humility and the modern meaning of individual freedom. Edward Albee in *Who's Afraid of Virginia Woolf?* places an archetypal couple, Martha and George—after Washington, the father of his country?—in the modern fix of depersonalization and despair and allows them to exorcise one another of all the ills and ailments of the Age of Anxiety. These they ultimately transcend to achieve freedom and identity in terms acceptable to our contemporary syndrome. Allen Ginsberg, despite scorching protests directed at ephemera, is instinctively drawn to heroic synthesis, and almost every line of *Howl* pulls disparate elements and traditions together. Robert Lowell achieves a similar, if neater and less overwhelming, effect in "Falling Asleep Over the *Aeneid.*" In his quiet masterpiece *Franny and Zooey,* J. D. Salinger probably comes closest to the track of Thomas Mann. Set almost entirely in a single house where freaks (Salinger's word) stuffed with knowledge of the past go about their household routines, the novel traces their progress from anxiety to joy. In the homeliest things the deepest traditions lie: A bathroom medicine cabinet foreshadows an altar; and a Fat Lady, Christ himself. And by perceiving the connections between present objects and past traditions and by fitting them together Franny and Zooey at last find contentment and the peace that comes with understanding.

ARCHITECTURE.   Like Mann in *Dr. Faustus,* Frank Lloyd Wright and Le Corbusier turned after World War II to heroic synthesis, and it is difficult to choose between their accomplishments. Wright summed up and moved architecture forward in his Guggenheim Museum, which is not a museum at all but a fresh idea of what a modern building ought to be. The interior (Figure 10.4) with its circular sweep and transparent glass and steel dome suggests the Pantheon (Figure 3.4). The cluttered pillars at the entrance and the wavy lines of the spiral ramp recall the baroque style, while the clean-limbed columns and parallel courses of the ramps reflect a debt to the Age of Reason. The horizontal handrails of the ramps connote the early cantilevered effect of the International Style, as in the *Bauhaus* (Figure 9.11). The winding, stepless spiral of the ramp makes space seem fluid and endless, free to penetrate time. Thus Wright uses, and fuses, Pantheon, relativity, and traditions in between to create a modern synthesis unlike any seen before. The exterior (Figure 10.5) is even more unique, its poured concrete outlines matching the curves of the ramp but its total appearance almost embarrassingly different. It is endowed with the pull of tradition—it suggests the beehive tombs of Mycenae upside down, a Futurist Villa Savoye (Figure 9.13), the tail of an airplane. But in the final analysis its bare, incomprehensible surfaces say nothing explicit, but instead produce nonobjective architecture in keeping with the collection of abstract art the building houses.

Figure 10.4 FRANK LLOYD WRIGHT. Solomon R. Guggenheim Museum (interior).
New York. (1959).

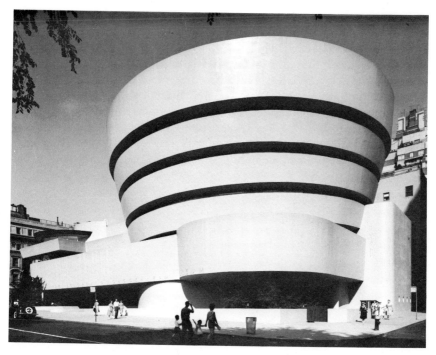

Figure 10.5 FRANK LLOYD WRIGHT.   Solomon R. Guggenheim Museum   New York. (1959). Dick Hanley: Photo Researchers.

An equally marvelous structure is the Cathedral of *Notre-Dame-du-Haut* at Ronchamp by Le Corbusier whose interior and exterior mingle tradition and modernity in a compelling and novel way. His government buildings at Chandigarh, capital of the Punjab, are less rich a synthesis but even more striking with their blending of East and West. Among the newer modern architects Louis Kahn best carries forward the inclusive and original styles of Wright and Le Corbusier. In such works as the Richards Medical Research Building in Philadelphia and the Residence Halls at Bryn Mawr College, Pennsylvania, he creates exteriors whose concern for every organ of structure, including the ducts and pipes, repeats the perfect functionalism of the ancient Greek temple in forms, terms, and materials appropriate to the present.

SCULPTURE.   Since the war several of the older sculptors have richly combined tradition and the individual talent. Picasso anticipates the trend in *Shepherd Holding a Lamb* (1944). The shepherd, a mysterious version of Picasso himself, has the cragged finish and primitive anatomy of Etruscan sculpture and the austere remoteness of the early work of Moore (Figure 9.2).

The lamb, its head in particular, is almost Cubist, so that modern form and Christian symbol, as well as ancient style and the suggestion of Christ as Everyman coexist in this work. Jacques Lipchitz has turned from pure form to figure sculpture as many-layered as Picasso's in works like *Sacrifice* and *Mother and Child*. No sculptor, however, has exploited this trait with the consistent mastery of Henry Moore. His *Glenkiln Cross*, connoting human bones and human body, is similar in complex meaning to *Shepherd Holding a Lamb;* his *King and Queen* adds Celtic primitivism to the mixture. *Family Group* (Figure 10.6) is probably his masterpiece in this manner. It is cast in bronze, in imitation of the ancients, and the flowing

Figure 10.6   HENRY MOORE.   *Family Group.*   (1945–1949).   Museum of Modern Art, A. Conger Goodyear Fund.

rhythms of arms and legs recall the graceful lines of Hellenistic sculpture (Figures 2.18, 2.24). The mother and child resemble a *Madonna and Child* begun by Moore a year earlier, so in a sense this is a holy family. It is also an archetypal modern family, as the simple, depersonalized features suggest. Yet those features are more than merely simple. More explicit than the indentations of *Reclining Figure*, they encourage interpretation yet remain ambiguous enough to suggest a gamut of relationships. *Family Group* looks remote, austere, mysterious, hopeful, overawed, and lost as well as simple—a synthesis of aspects to go with the synthesis of styles.

Like architecture, most newer sculpture is depersonalized, although a few younger sculptors, notably Italians, attempt heroic syntheses. Marino Marini (*Horse and Rider, Stravinsky*) and Pericle Fazzini (*Seated Woman*) offer about the best of the continuing examples of this latter trait.

PAINTING.   At the end of his career Piet Mondrian painted *Broadway Boogie Woogie* (1942) which fused pure form into literal theme and gave fresh impulse to synthesis in modern art. Other older painters who have turned to this trait include Marc Chagall—in the stained glass windows of the Hadassah Synagogue in Jerusalem—and Salvador Dali, surrealists already prone to interrelate unconscious symbols. *The Crucifixion* (Figure 10.7) combines Cubist form, by way of floor pattern, cross, and symbolic nails; literal representation (the bodies of Christ and the Virgin); traditional theme; and ultramodern guise (the beardless, athletic Christ as ideal modern man and a Virgin whose coiffed hair and elegance make her a modern mother thoroughly acceptable to TV audiences).

Among the younger generation Andrew Wyeth comes closest to Dali's achievement, and his popularity attests to the current impact of individualistic synthesis. *Christina's World* (Figure 10.8) like *The Crucifixion* juxtaposes a living being against cold, geometric forms, in this case house and barn. For further contrast and tension, Christina's straining body is blocked by a flat, two-dimensional horizon. Seated in her Edenlike meadow, her carriage is vital and hopeful, an optimism suited to heroic syntheses but irksome to those modern viewers conditioned to the negativism of depersonalization. Other modern artists whose work is as inclusive as Wyeth's are Francis Bacon, who fuses horror and religion; William de Kooning, who twists non-objective forms into sudden life; and Edwin W. Dickenson, who blends classical fragments with geometric exercises that somehow convey the hope as well as the desolation of our postwar world.

MUSIC.   In a recent magazine interview Stravinsky stated: "This desire to return and penetrate with a seeing eye the secrets of the archetypes of our civilization is symbolic of our burning and desperate desire to find a new synthesis, and, in order to find it, to resume a secret and creative dialogue with *all* of our past." All of his postwar music maintains that dialogue, and

Figure 10.7   SALVADOR DALI.   *The Crucifixion.*   (1955).   The Metropolitan Museum of Art, Gift of the Chester Dale Collection, 1955.

Figure 10.8 ANDREW WYETH. *Christina's World.* (1948). The Museum of Modern Art, New York, Purchase.

his opera *The Rake's Progress,* based on Hogarth's series of paintings, articulates it as variously as any of his works. *The Rake's Progress* owes an obvious debt to the *style galant* of Mozart, like Hogarth a product of the Age of Reason. More subtly, but just as cogently, its polyphony harks back to that of Guillaume de Machaut and Josquin Des Prés. Some lyric arias recall Schubert, others Rossini, and, extending the synthesis farther outward, Stravinsky flavors Tom Rakewell's third act ballads with Russian folk songs. All this plus modern dissonance, driving rhythms, and distilled passages that recall Von Webern make *The Rake's Progress* the lodestar to a new synthesis. Stravinsky's *Canticle of Saint Mark,* a masterpiece comparable to *The Rake's Progress,* adds Medieval number symbolism and the Schönbergian tone-row to its gamut of musical styles. Toward the end of his career Paul Hindemith also superadded Medieval symbolism to his kaleidoscope of styles, conspicuously in *Harmonie der Welt* (world harmony), and in the 1948 revision of his song cycle, *Das Marienleben* (the life of the Virgin).

Among the new generation of modern composers the great inheritor of Stravinsky's synthesis is Hans Werner Henze. In operas whose modernity —a blend of Schönberg and Stravinsky—is completely unself-conscious he rings in German mysticism, Italian lyricism, and styles garnered from the total past. *The Stag King* is steeped in allegory and ambiguity expressed in music through a bizarre but never jarring synthesis of modern styles. *The Bassarides* (1966), based on the *Bacchae* of Euripides, rivals *The Rake's Progress* for rich variety of traditional and modern idioms and, since it is constructed as a four-movement symphony played without interruption, it offers a further synthesis of operatic and orchestral music. After *The Bassarides* Henze announced: "I am reading a lot at present, especially philosophy and also on psychiatry, and I am thinking a lot about what these subjects have to do with opera." Other important synthesizing works by newer modern composers include the operas of Benjamin Britten (*Peter Grimes, Billy Budd*) and the songs of Ned Rorem.

The United Nations, *Franny and Zooey*, and *Christina's World* represent ideal reality for our age, and like every ideal require a great and striving effort. Their way of countering depersonalization is a difficult one, which means for many an unappealing one. However, alongside heroic synthesis another form of modern individualism has emerged, equally valid in its effort to maintain identity, yet at the same time an easier way. For heroic synthesis it substitutes nonconformity, expressed as a turning away from or a blunt attack upon society, both forms of INDIVIDUALISM AS PROTEST. Bursting onto the scene in the mid 1950s, this trait has remained an arresting presence ever since. England launched it with *The Outsider* (1956) by Colin Wilson, a study of an insecure youth alienated by the meaningless modern world. In America an essay, "The White Negro," written by Norman Mailer in 1957 registered individual protest in more searing and searching terms. Mailer's White Negro is "the American existentialist—the hipster, the man who [elects] . . . to divorce [him] self from society, to exist without roots, to set out on that uncharted journey into the rebellious imperatives of self." Totalitarian countries also exploded into protest in the 1950s, with active revolts in Czechoslovakia, Poland, and Hungary, and social protests in Russia proper. An allegorical novel by Ilya Ehrenburg, *The Thaw* (1954), with its appeal for greater human freedom, registered the growing swell of protest. Vladimir Dudintsev's novel, *Not by Bread Alone* (1957) lashed out at bureaucrats who stifle a creative inventor.

Modern theology too champions the protesting individual, and Paul Tillich, in accents reminiscent of Norman Mailer, writes: "Man . . . is still man enough to experience his dehumanization as despair. . . . There should be no question of what Christian theology has to do in this situation. It should decide for truth against safety, even if the safety is consecrated and supported by the churches." Even modern motion pictures have turned more and more to protest and to defiant affirmations of nonconformity: *Bonnie and Clyde* has been hailed as "the sleeper of the decade" in large part because it reflects this trait. College students have made protest the means of finding their own identities: in 1967 major student riots swept the

Free University of Berlin, the University of Madrid, The Technical University of Prague, the University of Paris, the University of Rome, and all Dutch universities, where a Students' Trade Union is now setting up its own antiuniversity.

America as modern pacesetter has produced the student riots at Berkeley and Columbia,[1] and a whole syndrome of individual protest. In the 1950s the Beats registered a cold, sometimes apathetic protest against the standardized American way of life. In the 1960s the Hippies (named after Mailer's hipster) have assailed the social mores with passion and intensity —through love, drugs, colorful costumes, and Buddhist mysticism. Some modern youths seeking less bizarre outlets choose a quiet sense of alienation because it is the only consistent attitude in which they can believe in a fragmented world of ephemeral values. Others choose a way explicated by Norman O. Brown in *Life Against Death* as a need to smash present institutions and to return to the spontaneity and genuineness of a simpler way of life. By that way alone, they feel, one can resist the depersonalization of modern society. The philosophy generally followed by protestors is a flattened out existentialism, Sartre modified, which holds that to live one must cultivate one's self regardless of taboos or consequences.

LITERATURE.   Individual protest affects both the technique and the content of modern literature. For technique it turns to Neo-Dadaism, a violent slap at the middle class doubly difficult to achieve because the middle class now embraces almost all members of the Western world, including its would-be Dadaist authors. Extreme methods are necessary, and these are provided by Norman Mailer in his novel *The American Dream*, a search for identity through jarring sexual byways; by such plays as *Dutchman* by Le Roi Jones and *The Blacks* by Jean Genêt, where violence vies with perverse depravity; and by the surrealistic visions of narcotics addiction in William Burroughs' *Naked Lunch*, whose language exhausts the resources of obscenity and makes only repetition possible. There are also the Happenings, or "multidirectional theater," first devised by John Cage, in which the old traditions of drama are swept out in favor of impromptu chaos.

With regard to content, a good deal of modern literature pits an individual against the forces of depersonalization and shows how he loses, his defeat underscoring the protest which motivates his struggle: John Updike's *Rabbit, Run*, Arthur Miller's *Death of a Salesman*, and William Styron's *Lie Down in Darkness* exemplify this struggle. At times the modern author protests in his own voice and attacks society head on, as does Ginsberg in *Howl*, James Baldwin in *Nobody Knows My Name*, and Alex-

---

[1] As testimony to the endemic nature of these riots, shortly after the April 1968 riots at Columbia, the University of Ile-Ife in Nigeria was closed down as a result of riots touched off by students' objecting to carrying their own plates to the kitchen after each meal.

ander Solzhenitsyn in his autobiographical *One Day in the Life of Ivan Denisovich,* an account of life in one of Stalin's concentration camps. Carl Solomon, to whom Ginsberg dedicated *Howl,* achieves the ultimate in protest by retreating from the world into insanity.

ARCHITECTURE.   Although the nature of architecture tends to limit its protest possibilities, significant evidences of the trend appear even here. The New Brutalism, spearheaded by English architects Alison and Peter Smithson, protested the impersonal regularity of Miës by designing "aformal, antigeometric" buildings such as the Sheffield University Extension. Postwar German architects resist prewar German geometric tidiness by designing expressionist buildings more aformal than those of the Smithsons, with undisciplined and tortured silhouettes; prominent examples include the swooping Berlin Philharmonic Hall by Hans Scharoun and the violently asymmetrical *Liederhalle* in Stuttgart by Adolf Abel and Rolf Gutbrod. Edward Stone and Minoru Yamasaki register mild protests against Miesian impassivity, the former by means of titillating perforated screens (the United States Embassy in New Delhi; the United States Pavilion at the Brussels Exposition), the latter by means of gauzy orientalisms (the Reynolds Metals Building). The Hippies defy architectural convention by building geodesic domes (Drop City, near Trinidad, Colorado), colorful mound-shaped patchworks of triangles and squares.

SCULPTURE.   Neo-Dadaism serves modern sculpture as well as literature, painting, and music as a protest technique. Examples in sculpture include *The Patriot* by George Fuller, a pastiche of bits of furniture, hinges, and magazine cutouts; *Monstranz* by Jean Tinguely, composed of a radio speaker, twisted wires, bolts, rods, and a frayed and knotted rope; the "assemblages" of Louise Nevelson, a framed collection of boxes each containing miscellaneous odds and ends; and the squashed bales of automobile parts exhibited by César.

Symptoms of protest affecting the content of modern sculpture appear in *City Square* by Alberto Giacometti, where stick figures stand in isolation, each reflecting some private defeat or despair; in *Spectre of Kitty Hawk* by Theodore Roszak, a spiky, welded monstrosity bristling with violence; in *Girl and Boy* by Reg Butler, a pair of ugly, iron grasshopperlike distortions; and in the useless totemistic machine caricatures of Eduardo Paolozzi.

PAINTING.   Neo-Dadaism occurs in its most challenging modern form in pop art, which interprets the American way of life in terms of the stupidity engendered by its mass media. A few examples will suffice to summarize the methods and purpose of pop art: *Drowning Girl* by Roy Lichtenstein is a blown-up panel from a comic strip whose enormity spotlights the girl's "typical" modern vapidity; *Campbell Soup Can* by Andy Warhol is a silkscreen reproduction of a can of tomato soup—symbolic of the tasteless dullness of modern life; and Robert Rauschenberg flouts the *White on White* of Malevich and public taste, by exhibiting an empty space entitled *Nothing on Nothing*.

A new school of painting, the Abstract Expressionist or Action school, rebels against any and all traditional content by having the artist project himself into the painting in subjective and vigorous ways. Jackson Pollock, who spilled or swung cans of paint over canvases set flat on the ground, is the best-known member of the group. His blobs and intersections form unique patterns that have the merit of pure individuality, devoid of any premeditation: "When I am *in* my painting," Pollock said, "I'm not aware of what I'm doing." Other Action painters whose content and technique reflect revolt against established standards include Xanti Schawinsky, who rides over canvases with a car whose wheels drip paint; Ushio Shinohara, who rubs his paint-spattered head against the canvas; and Yves Klein, who, wearing a tuxedo and white gloves, sits perched on a stepladder as he directs nude paint-smeared models to dive back and forth across his canvas. A more orthodox Abstract Expressionist is Hans Hofmann, whose jerky, upthrusting lines—"push and pull" painting, Hofmann calls it—suggest the violence of Roszak and Butler.

Music.   John Cage, an artist of broad modern sensibility, has produced the most arresting examples of Neo-Dadaism in music. His *Variations IV* is typical. Its "score" consists of a plastic rectangle containing seven dots and two circles, plus the direction that "measurements of time and space are not required." "A performer," Cage continues, "need not confine himself to a performance of this piece. At any time he may do something else." *Variations IV* as recorded includes fragments of Schubert, traffic noises, jazz, telephone bells, Christmas carols, static, a receding train, screams, and the *Blue Danube Waltz*. Cage's disciple, Morton Feldman, has composed silences parallel in Neo-Dadaist purpose to Rauschenberg's *Nothing on Nothing*.

Electronic music (pp. 479–481) offers the best examples of nonconformist content, although the morbid violence of the operas of Gian Carlo Menotti (*The Medium, The Consul*) and the visceral rock of the Hippies contribute their share of protest as well.

One clear-cut paradox, evident right at the very beginning, permeates our discussion of the above trait. Tillich's special viewpoint, the Beats, and modern alienation reaffirm the despair of the Age of Anxiety; modern protest films, student riots and the new Nihilism they represent echo its violence; and Beats, Hippies, Student Unions, and lockstep existentialism are merely new forms of depersonalization. Neo-Dadaism in the modern arts is a fresh expression of violence; the content of protest literature, architecture, sculpture, and painting ranges between violence and despair and is preoccupied (as its technique often reveals) with depersonalization. *In sum, individualism as protest is not individualism at all but rather a revolt against one collective norm by means of another; nor is it a new trait but rather a rehash of key aspects of the Age of Anxiety.* From the vantage point of the humanities approach, then, we may say that the modern period —at least up to now—is a two thirds continuation of the Age of Anxiety with one trait, individualism as heroic synthesis, making some effort to alter the earlier pattern.

EPILOGUE

Although it is not the business of humanities to predict the future or to make moral judgments as to whether any trait is good or bad, its materials tempt one to formulate judgments. As this chapter indicates, we are approaching a crossroads from which one road leads to a depersonalizing civilization saddled with anxiety, the other toward an unknown synthesis. Impelling us toward the first road are the fact of depersonalization and the fact that modern individualism, so vitally desired nowadays, can follow an easy course that soon fades into the formalism and the *Angst* of the recent past. Man can now destroy himself entirely. We do not *think* he will, but events show that he might. In a short time he will reach the moon, but even by traveling hundreds of thousands of miles he cannot escape from himself, and the prospect of violence and depersonalization revisited on other planets offers no solution.

Yet despite a preponderant two thirds probability of the continuation of the Age of Anxiety, there are some stirrings that suggest the possibility of change. The great events of and contributions to modern culture all entail heroic synthesis, and these suggest that instead of living in walled-off, compartmented worlds it is possible to live in complex, integrated ones. The current emphasis on richer and more widespread education reveals the deep need to cope with that complexity—the humanities course, a prime example of a large-scale attempt at synthesis, is uniquely the product of modern times. Finally, there have been ages of synthesis in the past, namely, the Golden Age of Greece and the Renaissance.

Around the dawn of the Renaissance an anonymous poet wrote these lines:

> Western wind, when will thou blow?
> The small rain down can rain.
> Christ, that my love were in my arms,
> And I in my bed again.

wherein he calls upon nature to send down water—small, in keeping with mortality—whose life-giving baptismal force can gather together God, love, and security to produce for him a state of bliss. If an unsung product of one age of synthesis could make so complex a pattern out of such simple elements, perhaps we in another such age can make a simple pattern out of modern complexity.

SELECTED BIBLIOGRAPHY

In large part the bibliography for this period consists of the latter chapters of books recommended for Chapter 9. Some other worthwhile background books are:

Boulding, Kenneth. *The Meaning of the Twentieth Century.* New York: Harper Colophon, 1965.

Bronowski, J. *Science and Human Values.* New York: Messner, 1958.

Brown, Norman O. *Life Against Death.* New York: Random House, 1959.

Burns, Edward M. *Ideas in Conflict.* New York: Norton, 1960.

Clark, Kenneth B. *Dark Ghetto.* New York: Harper & Row, 1965.

Davis, K. *The World's Metropolitan Areas.* Berkeley: University of California Press, 1959.

Feldman, Gene, and Max Gartenberg. (Eds.) *The Beat Generation and the Angry Young Men.* New York: Dell, 1958.

Fowler, J. M. (Ed.) *Fallout: A Study of Superbombs, Strontium 90, and Survival.* New York: Basic Books, 1960.

Goodman, Paul. *Growing Up Absurd.* New York: Random House, 1960.

Heller, Erich. *The Disinherited Mind.* New York: Meridian, 1961.

Kahn, Herman. *On Thermonuclear War.* Princeton, N.J.: Princeton University Press, 1960.

Keniston, Kenneth. *The Uncommitted.* New York: Harcourt, 1965.

McLuhan, H. Marshall. *Understanding Media.* New York: McGraw-Hill, 1964.

Myrdal, Gunnar. *Rich Lands and Poor.* New York: Harper & Row, 1958.

Neill, A. S. *Summerhill.* New York: Hart Publishing Co., 1960.

Riesman, David. *The Lonely Crowd.* New Haven, Conn.: Yale University Press, 1950.

Satin, Joseph. (Ed.) *The 1950's: America's "Placid" Decade.* Boston: Houghton Mifflin, 1960.

Snow, C. P. *Two Cultures and a Second Look.* New York: Mentor, 1964.

Tillich, Paul. *The Courage To Be.* New Haven, Conn.: Yale University Press, 1952.

Valentine, Alan C. *The Age of Conformity.* Chicago: Regnery, 1954.

Vogt, William. *People! Challenge to Survival.* New York: Sloane, 1960.

INDEX

°Page numbers in italics denote illustrations.